Poems: Chiefly Tales

William Hutton

Preface

Perhaps there is no instance upon record of a man like me, upwards of eighty, enlisting among the Poets; and, for the first time, handing to the world a volume of Verse. I may justly be called "A short-lived Poet."

Like my brethren of rhyme, I wish to amuse, but doubt of success. A man may *wish,* but not expect. I am not solicitous after profit; but should be sorry if another suffered by my pen.

I do not attempt those flights of modern Poetry which demand the whole attention to understand, and often oblige the Reader to recede a few lines to recover the meaning. Here sense is lost in sublimity! Nay, I have sometimes doubted whether the matter was understood by any except the writer.

This brings to my mind the remark made upon a school-master— "That he wrote two hands; one of them none could read but himself, and the other was even beyond his *own* ability."

My Poems, like myself, are in the stile of the last generation. They boast no language but the intelligent; neither will the *tale* admit of any other. They are remarks upon real life, character, and incident.

If the modern flowers of rhetoric do not flourish here, I have substituted something preferable—*Truth.* I believe every one of the tales is founded on fact. Many of them fell under my own eye.

The history of my political life is rather singular. Love and Rhyme often start together in the career of youth; I held both in 1747. One half continued till 1752. During that period I composed a volume of Poems, which rested upon the shelf, and were scarcely ever opened, for thirty-nine years. Nor did I write one Poem in the long interval of forty.

'Twill pleasure give to ev'ry eye;
Who sees your face receives a dart,
Who sees your book will lose his heart.

1752

Poems: Chiefly Tales

The Church-and-King Club;

OR

The state of religion in Birmingham at the riots in 1791

The *Catholics* steady, and truly devout,
Are so hemm'd in by Parsons they cannot get out;
They need not be anxious their own eyes to use,
For the Priest will see for them as long as they chuse.

The keen Sons of *Jacob* appear rather low,
Their wealth and their honesty are but so, so;
Perfection, they plead, as from Abraham descended,
So 'tis not worth their notice to try to be mended;
His faith's a soft pillow, without variation,
On which they deposit their future salvation.

The *Quakers* abundant in riches are grown,
And meddle with no man's affairs but their own;
They pay such attention to act as they ought,
We should almost declare, they were men without fault.

Independants and *Baptists,* but let them alone,
They're peaceable people, and quarrel with none.
A Church without blemish is not among men;
Then don't pry too deep, and you'll find none in them.

The *Methodists,* numerous, herd altogether,
And keep their religion quite dry from the weather;
Improving in morals, good order, and plight;
Were the rioters Methodists, all had been right.

The props of *Jerusalem* here a place find,
From *Emanuel Swedenborg's* love to mankind.
May the props never moulder, nor power on them trample,
Till the rest of the Churches pursue their example!

The poor *Presbyterians* to church *can't* resort,
For cruelty left them no church to support;
The children of *Satan,* let loose, did fire bring,
And made a burnt-offering to Church, and to King.
Down tumbled their temples, instructions, and praise,
While Church-and-the-King's-men rejoic'd at the blaze.
The religion of Meekness, which bids us be quiet,
Is the purest religion for—making a riot.

One class of the peoples and hence spring our boasts,
Are so fond of divine things, they drink them in toasts.
Their church's support comes from eating and drinking,
A Church-and-a-King-club prevents her from sinking;
She floats quite secure, on a butt of bright claret,
She'll ne'er find the bottom-they'll find it, ne'er fear it.
The Church-and-King-Club-Men are votaries able,
Their devotions ascend with the smoak of the table;
The more they'll abound, as good eating grows plenty,
And nothing disturbs like a bottle that's empty:
They're models of meekness,—what men can be more
When perfectly tipsy, humbly lie on the floor!
For the good of religion, their appetites cram,
And support Church and King with fervent G—D—.

Nov. 12, 1792

Poems: Chiefly Tales

To the corpulent Counsellor W—

ON HIS BEING COMPARED TO BACCHUS

Comparisons are foolish stuff,
When they are found untrue;
There's no two things are farther off,
Than Bacchus is from you.

Curiously wrought in wood, or stone,
And dress'd in smiles, *his* face,
While *yours,* as ev'ry one must own,
Smiles in eternal brass.

In fable, I'll no verse equip,
But sober truth will tell ye;
In circumf'rence you far outstrip
The God of wond'rous belly.

In that great swell, above your fobs,
A swell outdone by few,
If empty, then a dozen gods
Might dance a jig or two.

His fees pass under him, through the inn-doors,
Yours issue from a flaw,
He kindly casts an eye within doors,
You, to a Court of Law.

One tongue in silence may be laid,
Another talk by fits,
But yours wag by the hour, 'tis said,
White Bacchus silent sits.

He ne'er, in all his days, maintain'd
A thing that was not true;

Though *both* are by the *bar* sustain'd;
Can this be said of you?

Besides his grapes, a wreath divine
His sacred temples bound;
He rides triumphant on a sign,
You waddle on the ground.

Half down, half up, which of the two
In kindnesses surpass;
You hack the Presbyterians through,
He offers them a glass.

His bottle makes *his* clients gay
By dissipating trouble;
But *yours,* their vitals suck'd away,
Perceive their cares are double.

Naked, *he* braves th' inclement skies,
And overlooks the town,
While you, in vain, attempt to rise,
And reach a silken gown.

We'll now conclude, as we begun,
A subject that allures;
His bauble rests upon his tun,
Your *tun* rests upon yours.

Dec. 29, 1792

Poems: Chiefly Tales

Lord Chesterfield and the farmer's wife

The middling, great, and little folk,
Express a fondness for a joke;
And what man can a joke gain-say,
When he, who gives it, means to pay?

My rising Muse shall, now and then,
Record the acts of Noble Men.
Whoe'er on human worth refines,
And glorious in the Senate shines;
I'll never interrupt his course,
He shall rise higher in my verse:
Let *Stanhope* then my verse engage,
A *Stanhope* shall adorn my page;
For he, while I his fame make known,
Will rather tend to swell my own.

An Earl of Chesterfield there were
At *Bretby* Hall, in Derbyshire,
Who ate and drank, who slept and woke,
Soon after Charles had left the oak;
Plain was his person to the scan,
As any farmer, or his man;
While others shone in wig and lace,
He figur'd in a homely case
His manners, too, were like his dress,
A compliment could scarce express,
For what mouth the word *Sir* can spare,
Except it first shall enter there?
He seldom made a courtly bow,
Nay, we much doubt, if he knew how.

The morning fine, sweet sung the lark,
He stroll'd about in Bretby park;
Whoever saw him would not guess
An *Earl* was hid in such a dress

The passenger, from town to town,
Suppos'd he saw a brother clown,
Was neither struck with joy or sorrow,
But gave a nod, or said, "Good morrow."

Along the foot-path, he descry'd
A woman; he attentive ey'd
Her age: we're not exactly told,
But she was far from being old,
Seem'd as belonging to a farm,
A basket hung upon her arm;
A large straw hat her temples bind,
Deck'd with straw ornaments behind;
Her apron, and her stockings too,
With handkerchief, were clean and blue;
What colours might her garters show
My Lord himself did not yet know;
For to a husband should be known
The colours there, and him alone;
Her gown, of house'ife's stuff was trimm'd,
And carefully behind was pinn'd.

"How far away, Dame?" says the Peer.
"To market, with my butter, here."
"How many pounds have you to sell?
And what's the price? I like it well."
"I've thirty, and its very nice;
The weight is large; a groat's the price."
"Give me the basket, as you're willing,
"I'll buy the whole.—So here's ten shilling."

She seem'd surpriz'd, but yet obey'd;
Such customers she seldom had.
But, what was her astonishment,
When to a large oak-tree he went,
And on the root, completely round,
He slamm'd the butter, pound by pound.
So great a tree, all England through,

Had never in May butter grew.
In *silence* she beheld the wrong,
Because amazement tied her tongue;
During seven minutes looking on
The profits of a week were gone.

Her powers within were sorely heated
To see such butter rudely treated;
More waste she saw, in that short strife,
Than she'd committed all her life.
The neat devices on each pound
Were sticking to the bark around,
Which many figures made, no doubt,
But then it blotted all her's out.

The basket, emptied of its ware,
He then return'd, with easy air;
While she the martyr'd butter mourn'd,
He march'd away, quite unconcern'd.
She, too, went back, my Lord could see,
But ey'd the man., and ey'd the tree;
Hurt to see butter in that plight,
She wish'd the *fellow* out of sight;
While he, suspecting her design,
Resolv'd her plot to countermine.

The moment out of view was he,
She hasten'd to the butter'd tree;
Began the work of separating
The clean and foul, for profit-making:
A work she always counted good,
Which she from childhood understood.
"The best would serve for market still,
The rest would serve to greese a wheel."
But ere she could the butter pack,
Lord Chesterfield was at her back.

"What right have you, my Dame," says he,
"To any thing about the tree?
To take that property's a crime,
I bought, and paid you at the time;
The error lies with you alone
For taking what is not your own."
Says she, "'Tis pity to abuse
Whatever we can bring in use;
Some trifling purpose I shall try
To put it to."—" And so shall I,"
Reply'd the Earl, without a frown,
And instantly he threw her down,
Pull'd up her petticoats behind,
Regardless both of wet and wind,
When on her butt-end, slamm'd as free
The butter, as he'd done the tree.

The whole applied, with dext'rous art,
Instantly swell'd her nether part;
She look'd, for all the world, as plump
As if she'd put on a cork rump.
The fashion chang'd of female kind,
Some swell *before,* but she *behind.*

"There, Goody, as you're fond of gains,
Take that large plaister for your pains."
Then, in a moment, turn'd to go,
Regardless whether watch'd or no.
A curious figure you might spy,
A woman, butter'd half-way high.

He's wisdom to a large amount,
Who turns misfortunes to account;
Like bees, who follow nature's law,
Can sweetness from rank poison draw.
This fine accomplishment I name,
Was easy to the farmer's dame;

She long the powers had understood,
From evil of substracting good.

Her fingers did, without delay,
Rake all the, parts where profit lay;
Then knife applied, to *hill* and *gutter,*
With which the buyer tastes the butter;
Moulded it fresh, both neat and round;
Her eye could nearly guess a pound.
Well pleas'd it was but little worse,
To *Burton* market bent her course,
And sold her ware, with profit more
Than ever she had done before.
Of thirty pounds, but five were wasted;
Her pen-knife neither smelt nor tasted;
Nor did the *buyer* once discern
'Twas gather'd from the lower churn.

June 9, 1973

Poems: Chiefly Tales

Lord Chesterfield and the tinker

The lowest class of men may be
Rais'd to state of high degree,
Their blackness gone, such brightness shone,
That self by self is scarcely known.

When we are travelling abroad,
We cannot always chuse our road;
But prudent men will pick the best,
And cautiously avoid the rest;
"But, should a dirty slough appear;
What then?" He never plac'd it there.
All that is ever done by man
Is to tread lightly as he can;
Thus Poets, with a just decorum,
Must take the road which lies before 'em.
My road, but take it not amiss,
Is not so clean I could wish
But rough, or smooth, or dark, or clear,
The Muse resolves to send me there;
And no reluctance must be seen,
I've forty years a rebel been.

Which, Reader, will you most decry,
A dirty truth, or polish'd lie?
Leave it to me, and never fear,
I'll not offend the nicest ear.

The same Lord Chesterfield I sing,
Who dealt in butter in the spring.
He rose, he dress'd, went out of door,
The lark, and morning, as before;
The lawns, the hills, the clumps, were dress'd,
And Summer wore a lovely vest;
Nay, turn his eyes which way he will,
He was the only thing dress'd ill.

Poems: Chiefly Tales

The park most beautifully shone,
'Twas all delight —'twas all his own.

At no great distance, with his load,
A Tinker mov'd along the road;
He bent his back, he dropt a heap,
Which nature would not let him keep.
My Lord approach'd, in angry mood,
Before the Tinker'd made all good;
Or, rather, *seem'd* in wrath to run,
That he might introduce some fun.
"What right have you, you dirty hound,
With your vile filth, to daub the ground?
This instant take it in your hand,
And clean convey it off the land."

Feeling reduc'd by what had pass'd,
The son of Vulcan stood aghast;
He neither seem'd inclin'd to obey,
Nor yet attempted much to say;
For, when surpriz'd in situations,
Rather beneath our usual stations,
The mind feels little, to its cost
Its wonted dignity is lost.
Although his hands no whiteness boasted,
They were not with such stuff accosted;
But, if about that work he set,
They would become more dirty yet.

Much altercation now ensued,
And all that altercation rude.
The Earl grew higher still, and higher,
'Till he blew up the Tinker's fire;
So that, my friend, had you been there,
You would have thought *both* tinkers were.
The colour of each face,'tis true,
Were equally of swarthy hue;
For Stanhopes do, in ev'ry case,

Hold fairer intellects than face;
And tink'rish, to declare I'm loath,
The polish'd manners were of both.
The language us'd on either side
I think myself oblig'd to hide;
For decency won't let me speak,
Nor faithfulness my promise break.

The Tinker made so bold a stand,
He seem'd to have the upper hand;
With doubled fist began to stammer,
A fist as big as Vulcan's hammer,
And just the colour, seem'd to show
The strongest argument we know,
"That if he did not change his note,
He'd ram the bolus down his throat."

My Lord now suffer'd a defeat,
Unus'd, at second-hand, to eat;
For having no auxiliary near,
He was not wholly without fear;
So spoke less loud; parley'd a while;
Stood at a distance; forc'd a smile;
And told the man of black, "that he,
With servants, at the hall, was free;
That if he would attend him there
Was sure to find the best of cheer."
He took the tinker, without cost,
To eat and drink, *full* what he'd lost.
What Tinker would not wish to cease
A war, when offer'd such a peace?
He order'd meat, he order'd drink,
And, to the servants, tipp'd the wink,
Who 'tic'd him to a room behind,
"Where he a charming tap should find."
Yet he no liquor could see there
But what was weaker than small-beer;

For all the vessels he beheld
Was a vast tub, with water fill'd.

The servants told him to untrim
And let them see if he could swim.
The Tinker turn'd a little souer,
But there's no standing against power.
Then, with main strength, they forc'd him in,
Which took him fully to the chin.

He swore, and threaten'd, when he spoke,
But they alone enjoy'd the joke;
To see the Tinker stand in prim,
They all laugh'd heartily, but him.
It seem'd to them a curious matter,
A dark head rising from the water.
He could not bow, I'm pretty clear,
Even had George the Third been there;
Nor bend his back in light or dark,
As he'd just done within the park.

While they enjoy'd the pleasing sight,
Viewing the Tinker bolt upright,
His Lordship enter'd, full of wrath,
And bluster'd like the man of Gath.
With hasty step, with savage eye,
And naked sword, which he rais'd high,
"Where is the wretch, which quarrels foment,
I'll strike his head off in a moment;"
And, while the vengeful spirits flow,
Aim'd a decapitating blow,
Which the poor Tinker, to avoid,
Instantly sunk beneath the tide.

His note was alter'd from before,
For now he rather pray'd than swore.
The Earl he struck, and struck amain,
The Tinker dipt, and dipt again;

Whenever *Stanhope* aim'd a blow,
The frighten'd Tinker sunk below.
Who would not sink as deep to th' full,
When its to save his only skull?
By rising up, and diving down,
Th' afflicted man began to drown.

My Lord's sham wrath began to cool;
A man too long may play the fool.
He gave his folks another nod,
Which was completely understood;
They drew him forth, without a laugh,
For all agreed he'd div'd enough.
The Tinker too, believ'd the same,
As clear as any one of them.

A sight, now curious to be seen,
They stripp'd the Tinker to the skin,
(But all descriptions I shall wave,
That I my former word may save),
And terminating all dispute,
They cloth'd him well from head to foot;
So gaily he appear'd to view,
That now *himself* he hardly knew;

When he'd survey'd his dress awhile,
Could not repress the rising smile;
For, should he meet a stranger now,
He almost merited a bow;
Nay, not one thing could cause the lack,
Except the budget on his back.
He'd thump, in this luxurious case,
A kettle, with a double grace;
And, whether finish'd rough or nice,
Would bring him in a better price.
No soul had seen, for this long while,
So fine a Tinker mount a stile.

His belly fill'd, his budget plac'd,
A gift, in cash, his pocket grac'd.
He now prepar'd to march away,
And shine upon a summer's day.

But now reflection call'd to mind
The dang'rous scene he'd left behind.
He rather wish'd a man would dub him
Knight of the hammer than to tub him.
In casks of water there's no beauty;
He lik'd the pay, but not the duty;
And, as on dry land he'd remain,
Was cautious where he bent again.

Jan. 11, 1793

The sermon

In spite of all the rules you can
On men bestow—he still is man;
For who can, by a human feat,
Divest the sun of light and heat!

Why may n't a Priest, for once, appear,
Better than priests in common are!
A faithful shepherd out I'll trim,
Who lov'd his flock—his flock lov'd him.
By penetration, he could tell
The art of spiritual ruling well,
That mode of ruling ne'er should cease
Which has its origin in peace.

The parts sublime of priesthood knew,
And ev'ry part he brought to view;
Kept up his visits in rotation,
Knew where to find the best potation,
Knew when the jack would turn and rest,
And where the meat was roasted best.
His judgment was exceeding clear,
In strength and quantity of beer;
Could tell what oysters, and what ale,
Were needful for a full regale.

If with the better sort he dine,
He well knew how to praise the wine;
The compliment was sure to pass,
And introduce another glass.

Could praise the girl, and stroke the boy,
Which always gives the parent joy;
For ev'ry mother fancies well
Her child's a perfect nonpareil;

Therefore exerted all his power
In commendations by the hour.

A minister his fate would bless,
In finding all this happiness;
For how can he be reckon'd poor,
Supported by the pantry door;
Nor need he ever fear mishap,
When to assistance comes the tap.

Our philosophic Parson thought
The world might soon be better taught
The reason why men did not mend,
The priest began at the wrong end.
That fowler, who'd success engage,
Decoys the bird into his cage.
If you should want your horse from grass,
You'd think your servant but an ass,
And acted like a silly clown,
Should he attempt to *run* him down.
Through the creation there's a shyness,
Bird, fish, and fair, are caught by finesse.

The first concern of every teacher,
Whether a father, master, preacher,
Should be to find out, if he can,
The greatest enemy to man;
And, when discover'd where he lies,
Then try to conquer by surprize.

He studied men, he studied books,
He canvass'd actions, motives, looks;
He thought, and scratch'd, and thought again,
And many a candle burnt in vain.
At length, with joy, began to own,
He'd found the philosophic stone,
That *lying* was the very devil
Which led to ev'ry other evil.

This enemy was of long standing,
And ev'ry evil had a hand in,
It started up in Adam's time,
And took a part in ev'ry crime.

Cain caught the itch, and down it flew
Through all the sons, and daughters too.
For if a man but steps awry,
He'll try to hide it with a lie;
And yet confession, at the time,
At least expunges half the crime;
But, when we cover with a lie,
'Tis tinctur'd with a deeper dye.

He'd have more joy than at a feast,
Could he reduce this monstrous beast,
Who, for six thousand years, possess'd
A place in ev'ry human breast;
And, to that throne could *truth* restore,
That throne the monster held before.

If telling *fibs* we put an end to,
And simple *truth* alone attend to,
This useful practice brought about
Would drive all other evils out.
"Could I but plant this tree that's true,
Its branches might spread England through."
That this fair scheme he best might thrive in,
Persuasion he preferr'd to driving;
Thought ministers were soul-protectors;
Men were not fond of pulpit Hectors;
Treated his flock with sermons sound,
Taken from Paul—"Let truth abound."

He painted in a horrid view
Whatever should be said untrue:
"That man must always guard his tongue,
And never say the thing that's wrong;

For when he's number'd with the dead,
A vengeance falls upon his head;
Neither must he expect to thrive
For telling fibs while yet alive.
Nor must he only guard his own,
A care must be to others shown;
To let another speak untrue,
A weighty sin will follow you:
For instance; should another say,
"I will do so and so today,"
We never should be so absurd
To suffer him to break his word,
But aid, that he his word maintain,
Although we should a *loss* sustain."

Whene'er a priest has preach'd his best,
Both he, and hearers, ought to rest.

THE SECOND PART

Most sound advice may be ill sped;
A witch's prayer is backward read.

The Sermon ended, people pleas'd,
And Priest, that he'd his conscience eas'd,
When, coming soberly from church,
A person stopp'd him in the porch;
"Accept of what I say as true,
This day, dear Sir, I'll dine with you."
He seem'd a shabby suppliant sinner,
Who very seldom eat a dinner.

Consent was granted with a sigh
His doctrine he could not deny.

The fellow ate and drank at noon,
As if he could not fill up soon,
While the caught Priest, a little low,

Eat his own dinner but so so,
Concluding then, *that* fashion's best
Which lets a man *invite* his guest.

The dinner done; grace after meat
'Twas thought the stranger would retreat,
But, in that moment, he got up,
Cry'd, "Sir, I'll stay with you and sup."

The Parson now was rather vext,
Both at his sermon and his text,
But, by his doctrine must abide,
Therefore his tongue and hands were tied;
He visibly began to fear
His sentiments would cost him dear.

"Your supper, Sir, gives true delight,
I'll take a bed with you tonight."

The Doctor his hard Fate bewail'd,
T'have such a legacy entail'd;
This fatal *truth* produc'd a frown,
A truth that almost knock'd him down;
A truth he no way could deny,
It hurt him more than would a lie;
But to no purpose did he moan,
The argument was still his own;
And though the stranger's bed was worst,
He slept much better than his host.

The Parson, and the morning too,
Both of them rose a little blue;
The stranger, I'd declare on oath,
Shew'd more serenity than both;
Then on the Doctor cast an eye,
"I'll have some breakfast by and by."

The honest Priest began to fear
He'd have the stranger by the year;
For breakfast, dinner, supper, bed,
Were granted just as soon as said;
The moment was one favour o'er,
That very moment claim'd one more.

By some means he must end the strife,
Or he'll demand the Parson's wife,
And then what troubles we begin,
Our doctrine's adding sin to sin!
That weapon we should think the best
To serve the parson, as his guest,
Who careful watch'd the time to hit
When he should swallow the last bit;
For then he thought, without a doubt,
That, as the stranger's glass run out,
He might, by chance, prevent his power,
From being renew'd another hour.
He cry'd, as if 'twas to a foe,
"My friend, you shall this moment go."

The stranger answer'd, with a stare,
"You shall go with me, I declare."

The breakfast ended, they set out,
And walk'd a mile, or thereabout.
"I'll go no further," says the Priest.
"I'll have your purse then," says the guest.
"Then all the money shall be mine,"
Rejoin'd the resolute divine.

The purse and cash now part in peace,
Which, frequently, we find the case;
And, though they strive to meet again,
Their utmost efforts are in vain;
For, like the stranger to the Priest,
Will never more become his guest.

Half of them glad, but *both* obey,
They either take a different way.
The stranger shew'd the utmost wish
To hear a sermon just like this.
The Parson, as to'ards home he came,
Found his reflections not the same;
Review'd his conduct with a sigh,
His sentiments had run too high,
For though in theory they were right,
Yet *practice* gain'd but little by't.

Vile man! to vicious habits tending,
He scarcely thought him worth the mending.
What sermons preach'd! and preach'd in vain!
He's scarcely worth a drop of rain.
Though mighty sums have been expended,
That creature *man's* not one jot mended.

"The human mind is human still,
And must be so, do what he will;
Such doctrine I'll no more advance,
'Twill neither do for here or France;
In future I'll exert less pains,
And bound my utmost view with gains;
Like other priests I'll take the prey,
Like other flocks my own may stray."

July 3, 1793.

Poems: Chiefly Tales

The ant

Perhaps my verse you'll nothing call,
Because, it seems, my title's small.
To ministers I recommend
That they should ne'er their clerks offend.
The smallest animal we know
May soon become a dreadful foe.
Nor ought a priest to speak too loud,
Lest he should wake the sleeping crowd.

Exalted by the Muse, shall shine
A reverend and a fat Divine;
For if in bulk he shall excel
He'll fit a pulpit twice as well;
And if he runs to twenty stone,
I've stuff enough to work upon.

Mild was his temper, you might swear,
As men of belly often are;
Was gently through church trammels led,
He fed his flock—himself he fed;
Though, of the two, it is confess'd,
The reverend Doctor *throve* the best.

His congregation us'd to tell,
His sermons he conducted well;
But this small evil lay on hand—
To preach them, he was forc'd to stand:
This prov'd a double duty straight,
Because he carried double weight;
For two legs *only* was his store,
But twenty stone demanded four.

To remedy this foul defect,
His people, out of pure respect,
As they could hear what he should say,

Whether he stood, or sat, or lay,
('Twas not his posture edify'd,
But what he *said* must be their guide)
A stool they in the pulpit set,
And bass, to raise him higher yet.

This apparatus, all made good,
He seem'd as high as if he stood.
How much it must a parson please,
When people shall contrive his ease!

Thus all went well; from evil freed,
The shepherd and his flock agreed.
Perhaps some little things occurr'd,
Too small to introduce a word;
As heavy bodies, we all know,
Press hard upon the parts below;
So his, which on the bass did rest,
In summer, was with heat oppress'd;
But his own fore-sight could, with ease,
Remove a dozen ills like these.
His breeches loosen'd, down they slid,
And not a soul knew what he did,
That underneath fresh air might go,
To cool the parts which lie below;
Besides, fresh air, he might suppose,
Becomes a sweet'ner where it goes.

And, pray, what is't to you or me
Where any parson's breeches be?
Or, should they hang about his heels,
It is not you, but *he,* who feels;
Nay, e'en to pull them off was naught,
The evil lies in being caught.

Our worthy Priest, as some divine,
Drank deepish of the vestry wine,
And in no moment cast an eye

Upon his clerk, who stood close by;
But, while the wine did merry pass,
Ne'er once said, "Roger, take a glass."
Why did he leave him in the lurch,
For he alone, of all the church,
Was well appriz'd of little arts,
With which he cool'd his nether parts.
Roger must disappointed be,
Who long'd for wine as well as he.

"Such meanness he with rage should spurn,
He'd trick the Doctor in his turn."

A nest of *ants* he took from grass,
And hid them in the parson's bass;
Both old, and eggs, and great, and small,
He found new dwellings for them all.
How much an ant must be elated,
When to a pulpit he's translated!
Nor much expences would he lack;
He was already dress'd in black;
And could a flock instruct at least,
As well as here and there a priest.

The day was hot, the moisture crept,
While half the congregation slept;
The parson preach'd, his breeches down,
And copious sweat, from foot to crown,
As plenteous drew the exhalation,
Arising from the congregation.

The little ants grew tir'd of home,
Like 'prentice lads, on Sunday roam.
What could a bulky parson do;
The liquor stood at eighty two.
He labour'd hard, 'twixt heat and fear,
And felt a tickling, God knows where.
He scratch'd and preach'd, and scratch'd again.

Thy scratching, Doctor, 's adll in vain,
For what man can attempt to stand
Against a *troop* with single hand?

The cruel strife was hard and long;
Employ'd his fingers, check'd his tongue,
He cast a wildish look around,
But still the enemy gain'd ground;
Could not conceive whence rose the pest;
With energy he this express'd;
"Though gospel from my tongue may flow,
"Yet sure the devil lies below."

This wak'd the congregation quite,
No more he said—no more I'll write.

July 12, 1793

The attentive shepherd

Lately was Parson Horseley seen;
Soberly walking to *Hall Green,*
Reluctantly his church to reach,
Where, once a week, was forc'd to preach.
Met by a friend—"Well, how d'ye do,
This Sunday road you still pursue,
Going your nostrums to unlock,
And dress once more your scabby flock."

"Aye, d—n 'em" said the priest again,
But all my dressings are in vain;
For though I dress them e'er so clever,
Next week they want as bad as ever."

Oct. 15, 1794

Poems: Chiefly Tales

King Edgar and the servant girl

Let me again bring on the stage
A monarch of a former age.
Edgar, the peaceable, we'll view,
Whom I'll delineate anew.
Compos'd of good, compos'd of evil,
Medley of man, of saint, of devil;
A little mortal, rather quaint;
A murderer, whore-monger, and saint;
Who understood the practice well
Of keeping fair with heaven and hell;
Who *forty-seven* houses boasted
(That monks and nuns might be accosted),
Built by himself, at various times;
But quite forgot to name the crimes
Which first induc'd him to begin,
Nor mentions he, for each, what sin.

Abbeys, of ev'ry size, he built,
To cover ev'ry size of guilt.
Whatever sin he should commit,
Could make a plaster just to fit.
Should he a trifling oath let go,
He'd patch a stone or two, or so;
And when the crime's not quite so small,
'Twas balanc'd by an abbey wall;
Or, when he chose a girl to ravish,
A nunnery hid a trick so knavish.
The moment he debauch'd a daughter,
Began t'atone with brick and mortar.
If *murder* in his wrath appear'd,
A noble monastery he rear'd.
He sinn'd and built, and sinn'd again;
The building made repentance vain:
This keeps the sinner's balance even,
And quits, exactly, scores with heaven.

He's heir to that divine abode,
For not a spiritual groat he ow'd.
If *Peter* won't unlock the door,
He ought to hold the keys no more.
Whene'er a pretty girl was seen,
He tried to make her wh—e, or queen;
And as the latter were but few,
Left many a lovely lass to rue;
Left many a parent, with wet eye,
And many a worthy nymph to sigh.
For virtue, in those times, was known,
Except we look about the throne.

A noble Earl, respected well,
In Hampshire liv'd, old stories tell;
Among his first possessions, stood
A daughter, beautiful and good;
Who never *did,* as authors say,
Nor shew'd a *wish,* to go astray.
This lady, elevated, fair,
Could not escape the monarch's ear;
His minions, knowing his desire,
Assist in blowing up the fire.
Such minions hover near a crown,
To start the game the King runs down.

The charms of this bright nymph, oft told,
Excite a love of baser mould.
Resolv'd, he'll all delays give over,
And take a journey to Andover.
Happy the monarch, we think still,
Who's power to do whate'er he will.
But then that joy is not full quite,
Except whate'er he does is right.

He saw the noble Earl's abode,
Who view'd him as a demi-god;
He saw the daughter young and fair,

Deported with a modest air.
His passions grew, the fire was fed,
The lady's order'd to his bed!
When both shall enter, *King* and *ruin*;
To houses it portends un-doing.
The state of laws we justly weep,
When what's our own we cannot keep.

The Countess, with distressing fears,
Approach'd her Sovereign Lord with tears;
With words of pity, aspect wild,
She pleaded for her ruin'd child.
But did a Prince, when passion's high,
Ever regard a tear or sigh!
To weakness he'd become a dupe
If e'er he gave a trifle up.
She might as well to winds complain;
Her intercessions were in vain.

The family, in deep dismay,
Knew not to act, nor yet to say.
Through Edgar only they're distress'd,
Who held the power to make them bless'd.
For *self* we've happiness in view
Why don't we give it others too?
For, if we let our neighbours share,
We only give what we can spare;
And while to them we grant the boon,
'Tis an addition to our own.
We may, should desp'rate case appear,
Leave it to WOMAN to get clear.
How many wives have made good shift
To free the husband at *dead lift*!

The Countess call'd the kitchen wench
That she the royal fire might quench.
Nearly the size, at transient view,
Appear'd the figure of the two;

Told her King Edgar lately said,
That she must lead her to his bed.
Her conduct must not be absurd,
And charg'd her not to speak a word:
But should the King a question ask;
To deal in whispers was her task.
"Be steady to mind what I say,
And rise before 'tis break of day.
If you're not up before the sun,
Your morning's work will not be done.
Obey, and you'll be much respected,
If not, you're sure to be neglected."
A small reward was given then,
Which brought a promise back again.
Reward amounting to some cost,
Unequal still to virtue lost.

The King in bed. The night was hush;
The darkness sav'd the damsel's blush.
The lovers pass'd the night with glee;
Edgar was pleas'd—and so was she.

The morning came, serene the skies,
Sol, and the wench, attempt to rise.
The King to let her go was loth,
Although he'd reasons against both:
For love, 'tis said, is oft begun,
Much better by the moon than sun.

She told him plain, "she could not stay,
Because much work before her lay,
Which must be done in haste," she said
"Before her mistress rose from bed;
Or, she was sure to have her hire,
The fat would all be in the fire."

The sovereign view'd her as she lay,
But found her chang'd since yesterday.

Some small vexation it might bring—
A woman over-reach'd a King!

Upon reflection, he thought best
To turn deception to a jest.
The wench had pleasures to bestow;
He'd not consent to let her go.
'Twas only, if he'd his desire,
Raising his abbey three feet higher.

How long they lay, how long caress,
The muse can neither tell nor guess;
But 'twas till so much time was gone,
Her morning's work could not be done.
"She wish'd he'd try her fault to hide,
Or else her lady'd sorely chide.
'Twould foul disgrace upon *him* bring,
If the companion of a King,
Who serv'd him out of pure respect,
Should suffer for a small neglect;
Besides, 'twould have an oddish look,
Should she be beaten by the cook,
Who was with royal favours bless'd,
Whom the first Sovereign had caress'd."

The King, before he left the bed,
Sound reason saw in all she said.

The man who loses his last shilling,
Must bear such jokes as he's unwilling;
But, should he then a *guinea* find
Against the joker turns the wind,
So Edgar, having lost his case,
Resolv'd to treat it with good grace,
To bear the loss without disdain,
As by the kitchen wench he'd gain.

He took her for his concubine,
And she, in splendour, learn'd to shine.
In luxury saw many a day,
In royal sun-shine blaz'd away.
She thought of servitude no more;
Look'd down on those she fear'd before;
While they, their humble suit prefer,
To gain a point look up to her;
Well pleas'd that fate had plac'd her there,
And sav'd their daughter from a snare.

She held the reigns in Edgar's heart
'Till bright Elfrida got the start.

To Miss P—

WHOSE LIP WAS STUNG BY A WASP

Dear Sally, why do you complain
That from the sting you feel a pain,
Forgetting, while you love pursue,
How many pains are caus'd by you
A remedy you want that cures—
Then let my lips be join'd to yours.
Balsamic virtues may be found,
Sufficient for a deeper wound;
But if this should not lay your smart,
'Twill heat the wound that's in my heart.

July 16, 1793.

Poems: Chiefly Tales

The enlightened priest

Our schemes of happiness below
End in disgrace, are mark'd with woe;
If from the hive we'd honey bring,
We may be treated with a sting.

A handsome Priest, but not a lewder,
Lived in the reign of Henry Tudor.
Condemn'd to pass a single life,
Though he'd much rather had a wife;
For prudent wives, in many a case,
Will tend to keep us from disgrace,
And, *vice versá,* we conclude,
There's cases where a *husband's* good.
But if he had none, good or bad,
Could point out many a man who had;
And beauties too. Could he decoy them
His first advances were to eye them.
Nor is it hard for lovely faces
To get into each other's graces.
When youth and charms together mess,
'Tis easy to insure success;
A leer, a bow, a smile, a squeeze,
Are often sent, and often please.
To press the hand, will soon impart
The road directly to the heart;
The heart once conquer'd in the breast,
He eas'ly captur'd all the rest.

A priestly dress is the most sure
To find a way through ev'ry door.
What lock or bolt could ever stand
Against a priest with *cowl* and *band*?
And when he enters with an air,
Becomes the chief commander there;
Knows every dish, is often tasting;

Master of all things, but of—*fasting*.
Possession, if he once obtain,
As easy is to *keep*, as gain.
Then comes confession, absolution,
Advice, and pardons in profusion;
With dinners, suppers, benediction,
Charming barriers against detection.
They'll house him safely, and what's more,
Will keep suspicion out of door.

Our handsome Priest, of fair renown,
Had beauties scatter'd through the town;
In whate'er street he should appear,
A bright seraglio was there.
But what to this would conscience say?
Why, eas'ly argue faults away.
He thought an injury none could tell,
If he drew from another's well;
Because supplies within remain
Which instant fill the well again.

It far'd well with our handsome Priest,
Who, all his life-time, had been bless'd.
The smiles of fortune, and the fair,
Had quite disbanded every care;
And he suppos'd, through life's remain,
They'd never muster force again.

Alas, how shallow are our schemes,
Nay empty, just as idle dreams.
He was, upon a Christmas tide,
Caught in a fact he wish'd to hide;
And, in a posture, I confess,
A posture-I'll leave you to guess.
Yet keen-ey'd servants, at the time,
Accus'd him but of *half* a crime;
The other half, those servants said,
They boldly on their mistress laid.

O, why not on St. Martin call,
To save him from a dreadful fall?
But, close engag'd, the people say,
He'd something else to do than pray.

The matter's blaz'd, the people smile,
He's dragg'd before the court awhile,
Where a stern sentence issued thence is
Of penance for his past offences.

Now to the crowd expos'd to view,
Adorn'd with *sheet,* and candle too,
His face look'd handsome as before,
But modester than 'twas of yore;
For sorrow, with his harsh rebukes,
Will rather tend to spoil our looks.
The rude, among the crowd of folks,
Could not refrain from spouting jokes.
"If punish'd, when he goes astray,
He'll hold a *candle* every day;
At least he should due penance seek,
Be clothed and lighted once a week.
His *powers* have peopled many a street;
He *sins* and *suffers* in a *sheet*:
Is better versed, upon the whole,
In forming *bodies* than the soul.
A candle he takes now and then
To let his light shine before men."

One of the members of the throng
Address'd a priest who march'd along,
And told him plainly, "that the times
Could not excuse such heinous crimes;
And hop'd the priests would keep from wives;
Would live, in future, righteous lives.
The clergy should disdain the sheet,
Nor carry candles in the street.

Their piety should shine agen,
And *lanthorns* be to other men."

The Parson, with a smiling eye,
Instantly made him this reply
"What *priest* or *smith* can work by rules
When you deprive him of his tools?
No *lanthorn* e'er our hand adorns
Because you *laymen* wear the *horns*."

Poems: Chiefly Tales

Justice

When dregs of law corrupt the minds,
It shews that law should be refin'd.

With three grand things will verse look big
A *judge,* an *apple,* and a *pig;*
For, with a mighty pace we trudge,
Though full employ'd, to see a judge:
Nay, it would doubtless give the spleen,
E'en to himself, were he *not* seen.
When power and title on us lie,
Our wish is to attract the eye.

A *tithe-pig*'s what the parson wishes;
It classes with the best of dishes.
And what man in his senses, pray,
His *apples* ever threw away?
These three great points being fix'd upon
You'll bear in mind—so I'll go on.

Justice! a word supremely good,
Which may be eas'ly understood;
It means no more, say all we can,
Than *what is right* 'twixt man and man.
Nor will the word admit a doubt;
The dullest head may find it out;
And yet our practice is so blind,
As if plain sense we could not find.

An inch she'll farther go, therefore,
And *mildness* shew creation o'er;
For Justice cannot smile applause
If we keep partially her laws.
Whate'er has life, insect or beast,
Claims our humanity at least.
No eye could ever Justice see

Wanton in acts of cruelty;
Keeps racks and gibbets out of sight;
To torments she's a stranger quite;
The path of mildness ne'er forsakes,
If life is forfeit, life she takes;
Teaches humanity to man
By soft'ning all the pain she can.
That treasure, *life*, is all his store;
A monster *only* covets more.

Justice! as by the chizzel made,
And is on our Guild-halls display'd,
Appears delightfully, we own,
Modell'd, most curiously, in stone.
Her countenance benign we see,
And grateful flows her drapery:
But by this dress do artists mean
She only must in *stone* be seen?
A pair of scales, just even made,
Declares she a mistress of her trade.
This means, that in temptation's spite
She'll deal to ev'ry man his right;
Or, should a man dispute her cause,
Her sword is to enforce her laws.
Her *robes* and *fire,* her *scales* and *sword,*
Are emblems which her worth record.
Dignity, mildness, right, and *power,*
Are represented by these four.

Treat not this figure with your scorn,
Because I've but an *image* drawn;
Know, this fair nymph is seen no where,
In such perfection as she's here;
For, if we look in common life,
People with Justice are at strife;
For her reception's most unkind;
She rarely can a lodging find;
Attempts the rich, attempts the poor;

Is frequently turn'd out of door;
Treated, while off'ring man relief,
Just like a dog who steals your beef.
People in common speak her fair,
But seldom for her maxims care.

When waves and tempests jointly roar,
And strew with wrecks the British shore,
Keen vultures, in the human form,
Plunder the refuse of the storm,
Justice steps in, with all her might,
And loudly pleads the suff'rer's right;
In vain she pleads—what thief will hear?
She turns her head, and drops a tear,
While savage man, without delay,
Takes what the sea has cast away,
With just that pity in his lip,
As in the rock which dash'd the ship.

She sees another, with dismay,
Contracting debts he'll never pay.
Perhaps his payment is a sneer,
Because a lawyer gets him clear.
The crowd look on with unconcern;
Justice and *creditor* may mourn.

While circumvention money draws,
And men grow rich by bankrupt laws;
Or houses set in flames at night,
That thieves may gain some plunder by't;
While those who judge may often find
An inward bias on the mind;
While many a thousand pounds of debts
Are spung'd off by certificates;
The money spent on bawd or whore,
And creditor may work for more;
While fair recovery's defeated,
And men abuse the men they've cheated;

Can *Justice* all these crimes discern
And still look on with unconcern?

THE SECOND PART

As solid beds of earth we see
Seem to divide the root and tree;
To place this motto, I'll not fail,
Between the preface and the tale.

Two men of wealth, in days of yore,
Quarrell'd, as men had done before;
And when folks quarrel, never stick
T'assign each other to Old Nick;
And if Old Nick cannot be had,
A Lawyer comes, and that's as bad.
But lest a single one won't do
Our bold contenders muster'd two.
By this manœuvre they could see
Each was to fleece the enemy.
But there's a truth, could they rely on't,
Each man, by chance, might fleece his client.

Examinations now begin,
Each party, there's no doubt, will win;
For as one side his case discloses,
The other in proportion loses
Each grows elate, *his case so clear*
That both are right they need not fear.
For, when a cause is fairly tried,
They'll gain it—by the fire-side.
If on the mind some doubts remain,
The lawyer comes—they're gone again.

The 'sizes now approach with speed,
The brief's drawn up, the counsel fee'd;
A crowd attends the Sheriff's coach,
The trumpet sounds my Lord's approach.

As far as our grand suit advances
Each client stands the best of chances;
For all weak sides discover'd there
Were guarded with the utmost care.

Though each had well his part conducted,
Counsel and witnesses instructed,
Yet, on reflection, they could find
A leading person left behind.
Counsel, and evidence, and laws,
Will go great length to win a cause;
Yet these, like hands and feet, 'tis said,
Effect not much without a head.
The *Judge,* they plainly understand,
Holds, like a Prince, the chief command.
His interest, it must be confess'd,
Is twice the worth of all the rest.
His favour then the cause must rest on,
But how to gain it was the question;
To offer him a bare-fac'd bribe
Would hurt the cause, and hurt his pride;
A delicacy must be shewn,
Which to no creature must be known.
For nauseous pills, when gilded nice,
Pass squeamish stomachs in a trice.

One of the suitors got a few
Of the best apples that e'er grew,
And to the learned Judge was sent
His basket, and his compliment.
The valet took the present there,
Who in the Judge's secret were.
"My Lord, a basket here I bring"—
"Open, and let me see the thing."
For curiosity runs wild
From four-score years down to the child.
"Apples! Are these the whole? ad rot 'em,
Does nothing better lie at bottom?"

"Nothing, my Lord," said with a sneer,
"There are no better pleaders here."
"Can such cold language gain applause?
Was trash e'er known to gain a cause?
A single peck of apples sent
To gain a cause of vast extent!—
However, though he'll lose the suit,
I'll taste—they look like finish fruit."

While John a lovely apple par'd,
His knife was stopp'd by something hard.
As knife and John its hardness tried,
A *guinea* seem'd to line th' inside.
"Ho, ho, what's here? I'll cut up more;
An apple with a golden core!
A guinea in each one that's sent!
This is a powerful argument.
Figures in rhetoric are the powers;
These go beyond—they are the flowers.
What opposition can refute
The argument of such rich fruit?"

Thus, while the master and his friend
A fruit so delicate commend,
Or, rather, the rich nest behold,
In which appears an egg of gold,
Was heard a rapping at the door,
And John descends the stairs once more.

"My Lord," with glee the valet cries,
"I'm coming with a second prize.
The other suitor, to prevent
A losing cause, a *pig* has sent,
But can a *pig* a cause restore?
One apple's worth him o'er and o'er.
It shews, howe'er, in point of laws,
That you stand umpire in the cause."

The pig upon the table laid,
The solemn umpire shook his head.
"A sucking pig's a feeble pleader,
He'll neither follow nor be leader."

Now as he lay the board upon,
Nor car'd a pin for Judge or John,
The keen-ey'd umpire soon beheld
His belly more than common swell'd;
For, when the bowels leave the flank,
It ought to look a little lank.

"John," says the judge, "draw out your knife,
And cut the stitches—'pon my life
I never saw a sucking pig
Which shew'd a belly quite so big."
John did the work—the belly thin is,
For out there flew a heap of guineas.
The Judge surpriz'd, and so was t'other,
They eyed the pig, and eyed each other.
Not that they fear'd a tell-tale tongue,
For they'd well known each other long;
But either of them pleas'd to find
The sweet effect upon the mind.
"This," says the master of the law,
"Is the best pig I ever saw;
The owner, we can plainly tell,
Spar'd no expence to feed him well.
Among the miracles of old
We never find guts turn'd to gold;
And sure as liquor's in that cup,
This *pig* will eat those *apples* up."

Nov. 2, 1793.

The pleasures of matrimony

Examine all the weddings round,
See which are rotten, which are sound
You'll find the first, when through you've gone,
Rather resemble two to one.
Then is that state a state of bliss
Where one shall hit and two shall miss?

Why, among laws, was one forgot,
That would *untie* the marriage knot?
Prevent three evils at one view,
As scolding, fighting, killing too?

Of wedlock, let us *say* or *sing*,
For this with man's a weighty thing.
Of all the bargains in his life
The most uncertain is a wife.
The prospect may look fair enough,
But who can judge without a proof?
Shou'd he succeed in this grand test,
Of all good bargains this is best.

When the reverse becomes his state,
Can he be more distress'd by fate?
While other contracts which he'll share,
Compar'd to this but trifles are,
Which if he prudently attend to,
He easily may put an end to;
By marriage only must abide,
Because no law sets it aside.
The chain is fix'd which links them fast,
A chain which must for ever last;
But rests with them what *sort* to chuse,
Whether they'll silk or iron use;
For the chief springs that cause the strife
Arise from either *man* or *wife.*

Their quarrels usually begin
From *nothing, feather, straw,* or *pin;*
While some deplorable I see,
Thank the kind stars that favour'd me.

This life affords, though but a span,
Rattles for every age of man;
Yet constancy he can't engage,
His rattles change in every stage;
For when ten years accomplish'd are,
He'll quit his book to see a fair;
But, turn'd of forty, if you'll look,
He'll quit the fair to read his book.

At *one* year old no dire alarms,
Then every thing we see has charms;
We long for all, for all are new,
And lie within a yard or two.

If we to seven years live by chance,
There opens then a wide expanse;
Delighted now with *taw* and *ball,*
Which three-score could not bear at all,
The scenes which rise all joyous go;
The spirits at that age o'erflow;
For, when we find the spirits high,
What trouble ever can annoy?
Retrench not liberty or food,
Whatever else that comes is good.
To offer your estate's absurd,
For *whip*, for *hobby-horse,* or *bird.*
Nor *bond* of fifty'll purchase quite
His flimzy but his lofty *kite.*
Rather than be depriv'd of play,
He'll throw your bond and deeds away.

Another view may now be had,
To *twelve* years old we'll raise the lad.

Fresh scenes arise from this great ball,
And pleasure issues from them all.
Misfortune has no business there,
Dips into every thing but *care.*
His play-things number by the score,
To twenty's added twenty more;
Which, like your candles, change about,
Some lighted up, while some go out;
And in those games he sought to learn
Now teaches others in his turn.

Two changes in our way are gone,
At *twenty* will a third come on.
He's now enlisted among men;
His fav'rite rattles change again;
And are, though multiplied the more,
Just as important as before.
Tippling and *smoaking* — he's for both —
Gambling, with now and then an oath.
Powder and *dress* now intervene —
Then "All for Love," to change the scene.
"No pleasure's equal to the fair;
Felicity is center'd there;
And, contradict it if you can,
Woman herself was made for man;
And the chief happiness we view
Lies in the union of the two.
Every man, the world throughout,
Holds a degree of bliss, no doubt:
This must be doubled, free from care,
When lovely woman adds her share.
Who then would fool away this life
In solitude, without a wife,
When their united efforts are,
T'increase their joys, and banish care?
For pray what trouble can come nigh,
When, to oppose it, *both* shall try?
If man's philosophy can bear

Against those evils which come near,
United with his heart's delight
They'll quickly put them all to flight."

Such weighty blessings in his eye,
Who can withstand the promis'd joy?
A scene now opens, and most clever,
Fill'd with more happiness than ever;
A wife is added to his store,
And what can mortal wish for more?
But one regret escapes his tongue,
"That he'd delay'd his bliss so long."

Thus, while through life we make a pother,
We quit one bauble for another;
But with this diff'rence from the past,
We've now a bauble that will last.

Through every play-thing that we've gone,
A man may quit them all but one;
Others, like flimzy chattels, fail,
But she's a freehold with entail.

Let me record—Our loving pair
Can scarcely speak without—"My dear!"
Which indicates, it must be granted,
That marriage gives us what we wanted;
And that no state of bliss we try
Can ever raise us quite so high.

But, if a little time we wait,
Some small degree we must abate.
When Hymen's torch shall cease to burn,
Then *Bet* and *Tom* may serve their turn.
Nay, if we sink a peg at all,
Who then can tell how low we'll fall?
For Tom and Bet must now give place
To names which would my page disgrace.

The husband, in his wife, can spy
Faults which scape every other eye;
And, with a vengeance, charges free
Others that he himself can't see.
From bad to worse they quickly fall,
And soon they reach the worst of all.
He knows not how to treat a wife,
But plagues her, and himself, for life.
Detests the very name of *bride*.
"O that the knot could be unty'd!"

THE SECOND PART

A prudent wife is seldom had,
Because the husband makes her bad.
If you'd in happiness rejoice,
Then treasure up this short advice:
With gentle hand her errors cure,
And what you cannot mend, endure.

Where is the loving couple, pray,
Who never sport their bliss away?
When we with ease command a blessing,
It grows insipid by possessing;
This shews, that many a happy hour
We hold compleatly in our power;
But this gay season never lingers,
'Twill, like an *eel,* slip through our fingers,
And darting down the stream of time,
Leave nothing in our hands but slime.

Our former part was meant to say
What happiness we throw away.
A cross-grain'd husband plagues his wife;
They pull two ways, and both in strife
Keep lab'ring on, but without hope;
Yet there's no law to cut the rope,
And turn adrift th' ill-blended pair

To seek for happiness elsewhere.
It shews his gords are stupid still,
Except he change them when he will.
That wives alone, of all the range,
Are rattles which he cannot change.

T'illustrate these, we shall not fail
To bring a *true* and recent tale
Not from Jerusalem, I protest,
But Nottingham, upon the Forest.
Nor shall a Roman date be mine,
'Twas seventeen hundred forty-nine;
And *William Martin*, I'll engage,
The hero who shall tread the stage.

Drawing to'ards manhood, he began
To think himself a tightish man.
Among the passions of the breast,
Love seem'd to dawn among the rest;
Nor is it strange that love he'd got;
Where is the man who has it not!
Love, from his eye, quick sent a dart,
And lodg'd it in Miss *Woolley's* heart.
Yet, strange to tell, and yet 'tis true,
From that one dart another grew.
Cupid knew this, though he'd no eye,
And thought it should not idle lie.
He strung his bow; he took this dart,
And sent it into *Martin's* heart,
Thus assiduity will prove
The faithful minister of love.
For as a looking-glass procures
Another face exact like yours,
So, when fond love a heart shall strike,
'Twill, in another, raise its like.

When two kind folks to love are prone,
They cannot keep asunder long,

The happy moments robb'd from sleep
Our tender lovers often keep;
Nor could they even wish for more,
Much in possession—hope in store,
How enviable is their state,
'Tis only lovers can relate.

There's bounds of honour in our case
Which prudence will not let us pass;
Those bounds poor Martin and his fair
Forgot to keep with decent care;
From toying, loving thus, anon
It chanc'd a pregnancy came on.
Alarm succeeds, and sore dismay;
Martin resolv'd to run away.
A child half-form'd, to life unknown,
Could drive its father out of town.
The father, fearful of his race,
His infant offspring durst not face.
The future mother you might view
Distracted quite betwixt the two.
One half she lost, with her repose;
That which she kept she wish'd to lose.

O cruel world, unlike to heaven,
That *one* false step can't be forgiven!
Repentance pardon can't obtain,
Nor floods of tears wash out the stain;
For weakness no allowance made,
Nor strong temptations which invade.
Ill-fated woman! censur'd long
Through inward bias and a *tongue.*
But should the world abate a tittle,
Relax its scandal but a little,
And take the culprit into grace,
Smile, and give her a smiling face,
Two benefits would thence arise,
One please the good, and one the wise.

The fruits which come from stol'n embrace
Add much to our laborious race—
The *whole* would into life be led,
And not one half be knock'd o' th' head.

A man may run away, I grant
But, if his money should run scant,
He'd find that evil such a bar
As would prevent him running far.
This was *Will Martin's* case, I own
He stopp'd at *Hinckley,* quite broke down.
Then should not *man* some pity find,
When money's gone, and peace of mind?
If these two ills await his door,
We really think he needs no more.

He work'd and play'd with small content,
While many a Sunday came and went.
For who can act, that thinks he feels
A constable about his heels?

Of all the places where there's rest
He thought a Public-house was best
Because, should warrants come about,
There's one door in, another *out.*

While in the ale-house he was got,
Drinking, with company, his pot,
Where, with full freedom, they dispence
With every chat but that of sense,
A woman enter'd to the guests,
And modestly made these requests
"That her dear Man would quit his cup
As soon as he had drunk it up;
Would pay his shot, and with her come
To tend their infant flock at home."

Not touch-wood to the fire applied,
Nor flint and steel to tinder dried;
Not joiner's shavings parch'd in June,
To which you put a candle soon;
Nor gin so fierce a flame will catch,
When you apply a lighted match,
As darted from the husband's eye;
It struck with fear the standers-by.
'Tis wonderful he made demur;
The flame should rather come from her;
For she had cause to be concern'd;
He spent the money which she earn'd.

Unite the thunder of a drum
With words that from a foul mouth come,
With fire above describ'd a little,
You'll see our husband to a tittle.
No reason could his vengeance check;
"He'd break her heart, or break her neck.
To rid his hand he would not fail,
He'd sell her for a quart of ale."

"Your bargain I'll not disappoint,"
Cry'd Martin, "I'll give you a pint."

A contract of such magnitude
Requires some moments to conclude.
For wives, of all the goods we hold,
Ne'er come to market to be sold.
Neither could Martin, I declare,
Examine, as he would a mare;
For, in a market, we suppose
The buyer strips her of her clothes;
But Martin could not then begin
To scrutinize her wind and limb.

Hannah, desponding, sat in fears;
Her only language was—her tears.

Fair decency had mark'd her dress,
Dejected modesty her face;
And every soul alive could see
Some beauty in her face, but he,
Who, of all men, should see it first,
Should prudently that beauty nurs'd;
For if to her he'd acted kind,
He'd found returns to his own mind.
Which proves, to ev'ry one who tries,
That happiness within us lies.
But we want conduct how to use it,
We must destroy it, or abuse it.
It proves too, from the husband's tongue,
He'd kept his rattle much too long.
And what did most his mind derange,
It never could admit a change.

Whether the contract firm will set,
Or not, is most uncertain yet;
The husband, in his price, won't sink,
Nor *Martin* rise one drop of drink.
Hannah's in equilibrio,
Not knowing how the sale will go;
But, like a wife of prudent cast,
Shew'd strict obedience to the last.
She rather would adhere unto
The evils she already knew,
Than venture where the ills are sure,
Uncertain in their size and cure.
For let our state be ne'er so curst,
We always wish to know the worst.

The husband tried to raise the buyer;
Martin declar'd he'd go no higher.

The pint was order'd, bargain struck
And nothing back return'd for luck.
The parties of a halter thought,

But this they found would cost a groat.
The halter scheme was instant lost,
As being twice what *Hannah* cost.
For that same reason *neither* would
Pay four-pence that she might be toll'd.

While they consume the pint in strife,
The purchase of a prudent wife,
'Twas thought a *deed* would best avail,
T'insure the bargain and the sale;
For when a treaty is to last
'Tis needful we should make all fast.

An *article* they jointly draw,
Declaring rights in terms of law.
To all great treaties which are brought on,
There's lesser matters to be thought on:
To these 'tis needful that we look,
Like an appendix to a book,
Two lovely babes our pair had brought;
And lovely babes are worth a thought:
To other fathers they'd have charms;
One us'd its feet, and one in arms.
The first fell to the husband's care;
The last the mother could not spare;
Nay, both so hung about her heart,
As caus'd a bleeding wound to part.

"And will you sell me?" Hannah cries,
While in distress she wip'd her eyes,
"From madness will you ne'er recede?
Has this dear child no power to plead?
But infant cries were never known
To melt, like yours, a heart of stone.
The time will come when this you'll rue;
Repentance I shall leave to you.
My cruel pangs no tongue can tell!
Preserve my infant babe.—Farewell!"

Poems: Chiefly Tales

THE THIRD PART

Why among laws was one forgot,
That would have *tied* the marriage knot;
Uniting in one happy hour
The gentle male and female flower?

What would the antients, think you, said,
To wives being sold two-pence a head?
Why, they'd conclude, as *we* are taught,
"The price being low, the goods are naught,"
Jacob, the Patriarch of old,
Purchas'd at no such price, we're told.
Seven tedious years were forc'd to pass,
Which only brought a blear-eyed lass;
And bound for seven long years again
Before another could obtain;
"And when to him they both were gone,"
Why, then he'd twice the plague of one.
T'asperse the girls I'm very loth,
But I think *Hannah* worth them both.
His treatment to his wives were kind;
To all their failings rather blind;
But our coarse husband, full of terrors,
Saw nothing in his wife but errors.

Of many virtues none could scan;
This is the random creature man!
The liquor drunk, the bargain made,
The wife deliver'd, money paid;
The husband pleas'd that he could part
From her who long had lost his heart;
Or, rather, none could she receive,
Because he ne'er had one to give.

Poor *Hannah* saw the idle tale
To pass through *Hinckley* would not fail
Nay, any town, from Thames to Soar,

Would gladly cuff it o'er and o'er.
It would, of her and child, be told,
They, like a cow and calf, were sold.
This *Martin* saw—they would not stay,
But would for *Loughbro'* shape their way.
Besides, repentance might come on,
And then poor *Martin's* pint was gone.

Celestial folks assemble strait,
And enter into close debate,
"Whether they can, by methods certain,
Assist poor Hannah and Will Martin."
They soon determine on a plan
To serve them every way they can.

The night was dark—the world in bed—
All *Hinckley* in deep silence laid.
The cock brake early forth, and crew,
And sleepy Cinthia rose at two.
She instant quitted her abode,
To light our couple on the road.
But here, alas, as one that mourns,
She shew'd no part except her horns.
Her face was hid, and vex'd, as 't were,
Because she could not serve the pair;
For by the little light she shew'd
Our couple could not find their road.

Cinthia's design might only be
To let the surly husband see
The pattern of what horns to wear;
For he was making up a pair.

The folks celestial still observe them,
And find the moon too faint to serve them.
Aurora issued from her bed,
And grandly streak'd the heavens with red;
To Sol's groom call'd, he being in view,

"To harness quick, and then put to;
That Sol would not a moment stay,
But light our couple on the way:
For, as he'd often seen them both,
Was well acquainted with their worth.
That she, *Aurora,* points their course
Till Phœbus shines with brighter force."

Our couple not a moment waste;
Young travellers set out in haste,
But losing breath, and weary soon,
Are apt to lag before 'tis noon.

Phœbus, to guide our couple, came,
Determin'd to do just the same.
He urg'd his coursers—whipp'd them still—
And gallop'd up the Eastern hill;
When, finding he was far from earth,
Then lagg'd, as they did, to get breath.

Our couple were not incommoded
With chattels, and yet both were loaded.
His right hand, empty, swang most kind
One swing before, and one behind.
Your pendulum the time can tell;
This hand could tell it just as well
And though it might the right leg shun,
Exactly with the left went on.
The centre of a hedge-stake press
On his left shoulder, with some stress;
His left hand pulling at the end on't;
The other end a bundle pendant;
While in his face the features smil'd,
And she trudg'd after with the child.

When two young folks together go,
Fifteen or twenty miles, or so,
And both good-natur'd seem to be,

Much of each other they may see;
And if to love they're both inclin'd,
They'll fathom each the other's mind.
Friendship and love they'll soon impart,
And creep into each other's heart.
This prov'd our happy couple's case,
Who ne'er before could bliss embrace;
As in the sex he never knew
How to select the bad from true;
So, when unsatisfied, the mind
To fix it seldom is inclin'd;
Like running waters, as they fall,
Salute each bank, but quit them all.

But now he found in *Hannah* more
Than all he look'd for long before:
"She, of the fair sex, was the best;
With her alone he'd fix his rest;"
Nor wish'd to change in small degree;
He lov'd the child as well as she.
For innocents, in every case,
Clasp round the heart with close embrace;
Except that heart like marble stands,
Then there's no hold for little hands.

Her state of bliss appear'd much more
Because she'd recently been lower.
She liv'd at ease, which brought surprize,
A new world open'd to her eyes.
For good she look'd, and look'd again,
In her first husband—but in vain.
To all choice fruits he seem'd a foe;
The soil was bad, they could not grow.
In *Martin* virtues found alone,
Which corresponded with her own.
Though man and wife, they act at will,
But find themselves the lovers still;
Nor ever yet appear'd to be

Sick of each other's company.
Then what need they abroad to roam
When both were better pleas'd at home?
Each to the other's failings blind,
They found all which they hop'd to find.
Material errors they avoid;
The lesser they knew how to hide;
Should but a little fault appear,
'Twas quite forgot—for she was there;
Should one with blemish mark a deed,
The other an excuse would plead.

To hear his foot when he'd been gone,
Was harmony of sweetest tone;
It banish'd every gloomy sigh,
And rais'd the joyous spirits high;
A welcome issued from her eyes,
Which he alone knew how to prize;
And should she ever hold forth long,
He never once said, "Hold your tongue!"
For why should he attempt to stint
A tongue with so much music in 't?

Love can do all things with great ease,
Possessing every power to please.
For where the wish is well inclin'd,
The hand will rarely lag behind.
Between them went no jarring sound,
A perfect harmony was found.
Why, when so near to bliss alloy'd
Could not the marriage knot be tied?

THE FOURTH PART

The higher we climb on this hard ball,
The more destructive if we fall.

In our fourth part I end the clue,
But can't poetic justice do;
For married folk who act like these
Justly expect to live at ease.
No fiction in my verse I tell,
But real facts—I knew them well.

A twelvemonth pass'd, or thereabout,
And they from Loughbro' ne'er went out.
Though both were strange to every road,
Happy as those who went abroad.
For happiness, it is confess'd,
Consists in what we love the best.

We'll now to *Hinckley* send the Muse,
To see how *surly husband* does.
Repentance seiz'd him. When alone,
He damn'd himself for what he'd done.
His rattle sold in evil hour,
Because 'twas wholly in his power;
That power departed, he in vain,
Cry'd for his rattle back again.
This random temper verifies
That what we *have* we all despise,
And what we have not, after pant;
"'Tis just the very thing we want."
Now all her charms he saw, and more
Charms which he could not see before.

Himself examines all the streets;
Tells every passenger he meets,
And his egregious folly states
To churchwardens and magistrates.
But all adhering to one rule,
Join, with himself, to call him *fool.*

It happen'd on a luckless day,
When life's sweet stream had no allay,

William and Hannah careless sat,
Amus'd with inoffensive chat,
A sudden voice approach'd the room;
"The overseers of Hinckley come!"

Suppose a catchpole seiz'd a beau,
He could not be reduc'd so low.
No author, when his book's run down;
Nor miser, when he's lost a crown;
Nor you when Chancery suit miscarried;
Nor Betty when her sweet-heart married;
Nor tradesman when his banker broke;
Ever experience'd such a shock.

Two faces pale, but *not* with sorrow,
Were his and her's, but mark'd with *horror*.
"Hannah," they said, "must with them come;
Her husband wanted her at home."

The stile in which these words did flow
Appear'd not to admit of *no*;
Nor in the least afforded rest
To the rough tumults in the breast.

William the art of speech knew well,
In elocution could excell;
And in no period, you'd allow,
Was it so needful as just now;
For who would not, to save a wife,
Speak better than in all his life;
But now his words, through agitation,
All underwent compleat stagnation.
Instead of must'ring up a trope,
They riotted within the throat;
And though he tried to drive them hence,
They still continued in suspence;
Nay, that same power which used to aid them,
Now fast within the gullet made them;

Though sorely wanted, could not use them,
For all internals were confusion.

When wind and words procur'd a vent,
He boldly drew an instrument;
"*Conveyance* fairly sign'd and seal'd,
By which he lovely Hannah held.
And how can this, pray, be undone,
Deliver'd free before the sun?
A bargain that can never fail;
The money paid upon the nail.
This is the title-deed which gives
Me lovely Hannah while she lives;
He, by this writing, did resign
His Hannah, and by this she 's mine.
A man may *sell* his own, 'tis true;
Nor can repentance sales undo.
Were he to have her back once more,
They'd say he'd made his wife a w—.
And who black scandal would abide,
Which is so easy to avoid?
Besides, there's more to think upon,
In pregnancy she's six months gone.
What stupid husband then would groan
Under a burthen not his own?"

These powerful arguments, of course,
With *justice* weigh, but not with *force*;
For he with whom a power shall go
Holds the best arguments we know;
And though sheer reasons flow in fast,
He's sure to win his cause at last.
Nay, should we argue e'er so long,
The hand will always beat the tongue.

They said, "he might the *writings* hold;
They'd shew the price a wife was sold;
But that his title had a flaw;

The purchase was not good in law;
For in that place she should not fix
Though she should prove with child of six!
Might keep the writing for her sake;
But, for the freehold, they would take."
Thus though poor *Will* by far could speak best,
His arguments were far the weakest.

When conquer'd by the tongue or whip,
There's nothing left but to submit;
For William, and his purchas'd bride,
Are doom'd for ever to divide.

The lovers shock'd, with sighs and tears
Pierce every heart but overseers.
For hearts united just like these
Can never separate with ease.

The loss of her he thought was more
Than all he ever *held* before.
And should he e'en to old age live,
'Twas more than all the world could give.
He sorely wept, to be remov'd
From her he most sincerely lov'd;
And while the fair one could be view'd
His eye attentively pursued;
And glanc'd the way, though she's not there,
As well as able through a tear.

Poor *Hannah* wept, being forc'd from one
She'd firmly fix'd her heart upon.
Nor did that one the least degrade
The worthy present which she made.
Now must submit to many an oath
From one who's ign'rant of her worth.
For as in him, if we look round,
Not one good quality was found;

So he no good in her could spy
When view'd by his corrupted eye.

The winning officers were gay,
And in small triumph led the way;
She follow'd, but in anguish cried,
"O that the knot could be untied!"

Nov. 21, 1793.

Poems: Chiefly Tales

The tobacconist

When industry with judgment joins,
And chaste frugality combines,
Dame Fortune is not in the case,
The man is sure to thrive apace.
He'll quickly feather well his nest,
Deposit of his future rest.
But should a *parson* come about,
And slily pluck the feathers out,
The ruin'd family may roam,
And starve for ages yet to come.
We'll first unfold the art of gaining,
Then that develop of retaining.

Whoe'er in trade shall money find,
Acquires a pleasure to his mind;
More joy by far he'll have in heaping,
Than either spending or in keeping.
The saving man never looks duller
Because his bag's a little fuller;
Yet were it always in *one* state
It could not keep the mind elate;
But, when it's lighter by a crown,
It certainly will let him down.
That pleasure which is most endearing,
The florists say consists in *rearing*.

But *Great Moguls* would cause no flame,
Should they continue just the same.
What gardener refrains from sighing,
His *Emperor of Morocco* dying?
What mother can a *smile* refrain,
When *Tommy* shall his feet attain;
But when young master's walk'd awhile,
It never more excites a smile.

Man's a free agent, we think still,
Who must be guided by his will.
If you to drive him have begun,
Just like a pig he'll backwards run.
Should he by chance but step aside,
A silken cord may prove a guide.
This rectifies the milder breast,
And justice comes to drive the rest.
Compulsion us'd in any case
Sits ill upon the human race.

A Christian church for ever itches
After accumulating riches.
And pray what Church could ever rest,
Except with wealth compleatly bless'd?
Her loving sons, of godly mould,
Are vastly full of *power* and *gold;*
For well they know, if gold they find,
Delicious power won't lag behind.
They're watchful early, watchful late,
To lay their thumb on your estate.
They far behind leave in the lurch
The *founders* of the Christian church.
The twelve Apostles seem as naught
For all their wealth was scarce a groat.
Among a dozen men divine
Did not a single *mitre* shine.
They barely could afford to eat,
And in their journeys us'd their feet:
But, though their feet were full in use,
Could not procure a pair of shoes.
If but one shirt to each betide,
Must lie in bed till that was dried;
While their successors smiling pray,
"And fare most sumptuous ev'ry day;"
Appear in mitre, robe, and rocket,
And show a swelling in the pocket.
Adorn'd with purple and fine linen,

Are oft the gilded chariot seen in;
Wear shoes as if they meant to tread,
Though scarce more needful than in bed:
For, being *drawn* along the street,
Have little need for shoes or feet.

What though the *twelve* were poor indeed,
Their Sons have taught the Church to feed.
But modern gratitude appears
To apostolic characters,
For forming a religion that on
The grave Divine can soon grow fat on.
For men who could not spare a vest
Are now in solid silver dress'd;
And further is display'd each saint
In copper plate and costly paint.
For self-denial Parsons hallow them;
But where's the man attempts to follow them?
Thus *industry*.—A thriving *chest*
The cravings of a *hungry priest.*
These three points settled, we shan't fail
To tell you—"thereby hangs a tale,"
Which we'll apply to what's before,
And therefore moralize no more.

While I the faithful tale rehearse,
A *Grocer* shall adorn my verse.
Christopher Stephens now we'll view,
The hero of a tale that's true;
Who sold tobacco; gain'd renown;
Was resident in *Reading* town.
From small beginnings could create,
In length of time, a good estate.
Shew'd in what point the road might lie,
Which other folks might walk and buy.

He daily kept a steady line;
Was never found asleep at nine.

He some commercial maxims chose;
Could well repeat them though in prose:
"'Tis not from *trade* the man is made;
No, 'tis the *man* that makes the *trade*.
Small profits if you once combine,
Compose a mass that soon will shine.
The goods *well* bought are then half sold;
Their profits may be doubly told.
The man who pays upon the nail
Commands the market and the sale.
Exonerate the debts you owe,
Then what you're worth you'll quickly know.
Get money fast, and spend it slow,
Your fortune rapidly will grow.
A growing fortune will impart
A growing pleasure to the heart."

No wonder, by these rules surrounded,
Gold often on his counter sounded;
Would lovely to the eye appear,
And sound delightful in the ear.
And should three pounds the till contain,
He sent back two to buy again.

His mode of living we'll survey;
Milk-porridge usher'd in the day.
'Twas wholesome—to the body kind;
'Twas cheap—which satisfy'd the mind.
And as he eat his breakfast soon,
Like his fore-fathers din'd at noon.
If he weigh'd plums, it was for gain;
He chose to eat his pudding plain,
Because he this conclusion drew—
"The price of *one* would furnish two."

At ev'ning, when at supper sat,
Regal'd upon a frugal treat,
Fragments of dinner—cheese and beer,

With true content brought up the rear.
Of all his food he wasted none,
But scrap'd his crumbs as he went on.

The supper done, he did not fail
T'enjoy another full regale;
A cup of home-brew'd always us'd,
And o'er his pipe and profits mus'd.
Not that he ever seem'd unwilling,
When interest serv'd, to spend a shilling.
But this was rather with a view
That he might probably gain two.

On Sunday he enlarg'd his treat,
'Twas broth and pudding, roots and meat,
Nor was his entertainment spoil'd,
For he eat roast as well as boil'd.

Thus life pass'd on, he watch'd, he slept,
And regular one tenor kept.
He strove to get; he made no waste;
Enjoy'd a station to his taste;
From which he drew that happiness
Which few experience, many guess.

His fortune swell'd on either hand;
His hobby-horse was *buying land*;
Could in that jockyship excel,
For all allow he rode him well.

Old *Time* observ'd him full three score,
And bad *age* rap hard at his door,
And say, "his work was nearly done,
His game was up, his stake was won."

Poems: Chiefly Tales

THE SECOND PART

II you heap wealth upon your back,
Be watchful of a thing in black;
For if that thing once gets command,
'Tis gone, as 'twere by slight of hand.

We're travellers upon the road,
Yet act as if 'twas our abode.
This we find blam'd by our divines,
But here, I think, our conduct shines;
For, if neglected our affairs,
We hurt ourselves, and hurt our heirs.
The farmer, when he sows his wheat,
Is not quite sure he'll live to eat.
Then if into neglect he'll give,
Can the next generation live?
Kind Heaven will this care preserve,
Or we should make the future starve.
And if such evils come apace,
They'll quickly thin the human race.

Our hero now his day had run;
'Twas drawing to'ards the setting sun;
And yet through life no issue made
To heir his fortune and his trade.

One nephew had, he'd often say,
Residing in America.
"This youth he'd back to Reading call,
And constitute him heir of all."
'Tis done—the favour'd youth drew nigh,
To act beneath his uncle's eye.

Schemes are more apt to bring vexation,
Than they to answer expectation.
The youth elate, his fortune made,
And master of a prosperous trade,

His morning rose supremely bright;
He never thought it could be night;
Liv'd gaily; spent his money quick;
And seem'd to *gallop* to Old Nick;
Promis'd the fortune to o'er-whelm:
His uncle could not guide the helm.

The parish priest an opening spies
For parish priests have keenish eyes.
He ponder'd deeply in his mind
Whether he could a profit find?
But he knew well that men grown old
Were rather stubborn stuff to mould;
Yet, not o'er-stock'd with self-denial,
Saw no great loss in making trial;
To *Mr. Stephens* mov'd his hat,
And enter'd into common chat;
Then by-and-by a visit made;
The priest was master of his trade.

The way once found, he fairly seated,
His visit frequently repeated.
The ale was good, tobacco mild,
The story clever, they both smil'd.
Thus the sly priest perform'd his part,
And crept into *Kit Stephens'* heart.

The man who has a point to gain
Attacks in a religious strain.
That antient cloak is hack'd about,
From age to age, yet not worn out.
"Sir," says the priest, with easy air,
"Kind Providence has bless'd your care.
To your affairs you paid regard,
And thousands are your just reward.
He who succeeds in honest ways
Is worthy of the highest praise;
But when by care he's riches won,

He's only half his duty done.
Simply to *gain* is an abuse,
Unless applied to proper use;
For riches, it is understood,
Are granted for promoting good.
But 'tis observ'd by all the town
Your fair-got fortune's melting down.
Your *nephew* will the whole undo,
And ruin soul and body too.
Fair prudence might, ere 'tis too late,
Prevent the waste of your estate;
To distant times record your name,
And save a falling youth from shame.
Your whole estate deposit free
Into the lap of *Charity*.
This, like your bread, on waters cast,
Returns when many days are past;
And the best charity we know
Is to support the church below:
For there the man is taught to rise
And place his hopes beyond the skies.
The *pulpit* plants that heavenly tree,
Which springs up to eternity.
What blessings then on them await
Who aid the Church in this fall'n state!"

Stephens was silent as a door;
His eyes fix'd on the parlour floor;
His elbow on the table rest;
One hand below the cheek-bone press'd;
The other hand, with steady gripe,
Within his mouth retain'd the pipe.

He loos'd it with a closing puff;
His face looked sorrowful enough;
For can a human face look gay,
His lands just wing'd to fly away?

Poems: Chiefly Tales

Lands which had been his dear delight
Two different ways were taking flight.

"Your sentiments I much admire,
They're full of heav'nly desire;
Those sentiments are, to a hair,
True pulpit doctrine, worn thread-bare.
To heaven our thoughts the parson brings,
But sets his own on earthly things.
If to the church we give our lands,
You say for charity it stands;
But can you, Sir, one instance name
Of any priest, when money came,
Becoming better—preaching more
Than ever he had done before?
But I could *some* before you lay
Where priests are idle—people stray.
What minister his flock will heed
When he in luxury can feed?
If they don't preach, nor better live,
Can it be charity to *give*?

Land, too, applied to sacred use,
Becomes a general abuse.
No staple owner—fields grow poor;
Their produce is but half the store.
These may be fairly call'd *dead lands,*
Which ne'er return to private hands.
When a long race of devotees
Have lodg'd in holy hands their fees;
Religion then, at their command,
Wholly consists in *Holy land;*
And property accumulating,
Acquires a power there's no combating.
Man would be taught not to fear God,
But only fear the Church's rod;
'Till an Eighth Henry rise once more,
And rob the Church as heretofore.

Though *Hal,* 'tis said, went to the devil,
Much good we find came out of evil.
Besides, you know, Sir, I presume,
That charity begins at home.
A man's relations, when he's dead,
Have just the right that he once had.
Should I give you what I get rent of,
Then one sin more I have t' repent of.

My *nephew,* I allow, is wild,
By youthful follies nearly spoil'd;
But, should I cut him off by will,
'Twould tend to make him wilder still;
Besides, his money must run scant;
The more he spends, the more he'll want.
But not more pleasure can he find,
In spending what I leave behind,
Than has already been my lot
In getting fairly what I've got.

For pipe and beer I thought you came
Nor were you grudg'd the humble claim;
But when a deep-laid scheme is brewing,
To bring a family to ruin,
Prudence should drag that scheme to light,
And firmness overturn it quite.
I'm not the man to act your farce on,
And so your humble servant, Parson."

Unhappy is that city's lot
When she between two fires has got.
The smoaky tempest hides the land
Distruction lies on either hand:
This was *Kit Stephens'* case, in fact;
Prudence was needful for each act.
The nephew storms, and makes a gap;
The priest approaches him by sap;

But he, by firmness, could oblige
One enemy to raise the siege.

Not many days past in rotation
Before this curious conversation
The nephew fully understood:
It mov'd his ire, it chill'd his blood.
More hard he could not be beset,
If he a surly ghost had met.
He sought his uncle full of fears,
Dissolv'd in penitential tears.
Pure gratitude had fill'd his breast;
"Without a pardon could not rest:
Told him his wish should be *his* choice,
He never more would follow vice."
Drawn by the silken cords of love,
From virtue's paths he did not rove;
But shunn'd the selfish priest with dread,
Who tried to feed upon his bread.
Accus'd the brotherhood of blame;
Thought ev'ry priest would do the same:
And when a man in black he met,
Look'd sour, and never touch'd his hat.

Feb. 26, 1794

The milkman

A husband and wife, when they're both of one mind,
We deem them most happy—read on, and you'll find.

In all concerns a man shall share
He'd better act upon the square;
For then he'll most advantage find;
It shews an open, upright mind.
He'll rise to riches, fame, and worth;
Be courted though he boasts no birth;
While the sly rogue in want may roam,
Who robs another of his own.
For he who rakes in filth for gain
Will at no certain point refrain.
His ill-got property shall end;
The world detest him as a fiend.

What though he's lovely fruit to shew,
Which he hangs out to tempt the view,
And in the road a trap shall lay
To catch th' unwary in his way;
Perhaps his superficial gin
By chance may let the owner in.

While selfish men shall money draw
From the uncertainty of law;
While learned counsel truth despise,
Treat every subject with disguise,
And when he wins rejoices long,
Whether the cause be right or wrong;
While the pursuit of law is worse
Than if a man puts up with loss;
While he, who's right, is often found
To win, yet lose a hundred pound;
Something's amiss, most plain the fact is,
Either in law, or else the practice.

A *barber* led a single life,
'Till tir'd, and then he took a wife;
"But chose to swerve from gen'ral rules,
And thought the bulk of men were fools,
Who labour hard with hand and head
That idle wives may be well fed.
That man appears a silly elf
Who *gives* what he can eat himself.
'Twas *quite the thing,* he thought, through life
To be *supported* by a wife.
For, as to wives, who would not fly them,
Except he gains some profit by them?
A *gentleman* if he was made;
Aye, that must be the nicest trade. "
But here again a man may fall,
Except he's tools to work withal.
Beauty's the finest tool on earth;
His wife claim'd this in right of birth."
Thus was the barber's fortune made;
He'd what he wanted — the best trade.

The *milkman* every morning came,
And with his ware supplied the dame;
For should he ever miss a day
"She'd surely be depriv'd of tea."
And where's the maid or matron who
Would so divine a treat forego?

The time of coming was well known;
He found her usually alone.
He made good measure — stopp'd a minute —
"Her tongue had something pleasing in it."
His pail, he on the table set it,
Apt, for five minutes, to forget it.
He press'd her hand — he glanc'd awhile
And she return'd it with a smile.
Her hand was soft — with love he burn'd;
He thought he felt the squeeze return'd;

But while, in rapture, view'd her face,
Was sure he saw the *smiles* increase.
Thus when on amorous billows tost,
No wonder then the man is lost.

Sometimes he thought, but only guess'd,
A tumult rose within her breast.
His eye could not distinguish well,
But thought his *hand* could better tell;
Yet he was fearful he'd no warrant,
To send it on that dangerous errand.

Prudence was absent, *Love* close press'd;
He clasp'd her round the slender waist,
And, like two harriers, in a tether,
Mov'd gently to'ards the wall together;
When she a dreadful yell begun,
"O help, o help, or I'm undone."

The husband, and a friend in store,
Burst from behind the cellar door,
Where through a chink, convenient made,
They knew whate'er was done or said.
Cursing and blasting he began,
Like any carrier, or his man.

What were the feelings of our lover
Is not quite easy to discover.
All his internal powers were chang'd
His very system was derang'd.
He could not be astonish'd more
If thunderbolt had burst the door;
Nor could he tell, we freely own,
If he was wood, or flesh, or stone.

The husband, terrible to see,
Turn'd out the wife, and turn'd the key;
Seiz'd a large poker in great haste;

The trembling *milkman* stood aghast.
The friend, less wrathful, stopp'd his arms;
Said "it was best to come to terms."
But can a naked person treat
With an opponent arm'd compleat?
Tell me, bright Venus, from above,
Are these the melting joys of Love?

A strict enquiry now was made,
What sum, in cash, the milkman had.
But when they'd search'd his pockets round,
His capital was scarce a pound.
The culprit must, for this was kept,
Make it two guineas ere he slept.
This was a favourable doom,
For sleep was fled three nights to come.

Besides this sum, the husband swore,
"By G—I'll have ten guineas more!"
Then, from a shabby pocket-book,
A dreadful *stamp,* price sixpence, took,
Which, like a catch-pole, took its stand,
The moment wanted was at hand;
And wrote upon it as he sat,
"Ten guineas, two months after date."
The captive now could not resist,
But sign'd it with a trembling fist.

Thus *Frisseur* his new trade began;
Was what he wish'd—*the gentleman:*
And found a charming specimen
How future profits would flow in;
Thought he'd his pinching irons sell,
For he could pinch without them well.

Far other thoughts the milkman seize,
But not a thought was found to please.
"What had he left to live upon?

The profits of his pail were gone.
If Love must play such pranks as these,
Within his bosom it shall freeze."
The dose prov'd, from the barber's dove,
A pill which carried off his Love.

THE SECOND PART

'Twas for decisions such as this
I lost my property and bliss.
Could I have let both parties win,
Then safe most perfectly I'd been.

'Tis easier, in the money way,
To *promise,* than it is to pay.
He, too, who's been in pain awhile,
Or finds himself in durance vile,
To gain relief from cruel ill,
Will sign or promise what you will.
This was exact our hero s case;
Or *milkman* rather, if you please;
From whom all liberty was taken,
Except the art of promise-making.

Full many a night he slept in bed,
And yet the money was unpaid;
For, when fair freedom came in sight,
He view'd things in a diff'rent light.
"He ought, he said, to be reliev'd
From paying, when he ne'er receiv'd."
But to the *barber,* gent. I mean,
The matter as before was seen.
"For if at first it was a debt,
The very same it must be yet,
And a just debt it will be thought,
Or else, how came I by this note?"

Patience will tire, when offer'd wrong;
Nor should a *gentleman* wait long.
"He would not these delays support;"
But sued the milkman in the court.

Now, in the flimzy stile of state,
And solemn form, the court is sat.
The lawyers powder'd, trimm'd, and fee'd,
Muster up all their powers to plead;
For fifty minutes words dispense,
When five would compass all the sense;
Will put the enemy to rout,
But trying, go a mile about;
To win the bench is their chief aim,
For then they're sure to win the game.
The bench, nail'd by long-winded sinners,
Fear only lest they lose their dinners.

By *con* and *pro,* and *pro* and *con,*
Our cause but heavily goes on.
But who can wonder matters stay,
When there's a lawyer in the way?

The fluent pleadings being o'er,
And they the cause left as before;
For howsoever words were priz'd,
Fair *truth* was rather more disguis'd.

The court remark'd—"'Tis now our turn.
At all false colouring we spurn;
To strip the veil must be our care,
And try to see things as they *are.*
No prejudice must we pursue,
But give to every man his due.

If to the note it shall appear
The plaintiff has a title clear,
We'll never wrong him of a doit;

The *money* must go with the *right;*
But should the bold demand be found
To rest upon no solid ground,
We'll quash the action without fear,
And the defendant fully clear.

If this defendant form'd a plan
To trespass on another man;
The fence of virtue trampled down,
And pluck'd the fruit that's not his own;
Then our decision we declare,
Value receiv'd the note must bear.
For every shilling should lie on,
A suit to stifle of *crim. con.*
And in that case we plainly see
The culprit will a gainer be;
But if collusion shall appear
Between an artful husband here,
And a deceiptful wife, to fleece
The man who ne'er design'd amiss,
To bait a trap with female smiles
To catch the innocent in wiles;
Dismission we shall ratify,
And the security destroy.

Though freedom taken with the bride
In *honour* can't be justified;
No prudent thought his love retarded,
'Twas human nature quite unguarded.
Yet if strict justice draws the line,
It merits a *reproof*—not fine.

Value received—the note expresses;
Does that consist in her caresses?
If not, the bargain has a flaw,
No profit could the milkman draw.
If one faint clasp about the waist
Is worth *ten guineas,* snatch'd in haste,

Then full *possession* of the prize
Must to ten thousand guineas rise.
How happy is the plaintiff's lot,
Which so immense a treasure's got!
He'd rather she remain'd alone,
In any arms before his own.

Four things upon the trial shews
The evil from the plaintiff rose;
Shews his aversion to what's right,
And sets him in the blackest light.
Himself, with evidence in store,
Well stow'd behind the cellar door;
And this about the hour of nine
Has all th' appearance of design.

The wife cry'd out, as if for fear,
Although 'twas plain no force was there;
This for a signal was design'd,
A shatter'd character to bind.
In seeming wrath he turn'd her out;
To save appearances, no doubt.
And to complete a scheme, deep laid,
She to a female neighbour said,
'I'll pay a visit to the silkman,
We've had success, and nabb'd the milkman.'

The *time,* the *peep-hole,* and the *man,*
Prove it a pre-concerted plan.
'Tis said, 'the ten pound note he gave
Most freely.'—'Twas his brains to save.
But he, who is the biter bitten,
Should say, 'twas with tile poker written.

How base must be that husband's life,
Who saps the virtue of his wife;
For if he prostitutes her mind,
But one step more he'll leave behind;

This he'll surmount, without dispute,
Which is *herself* to prostitute.
That wife who with her husband leagues,
One to deceive with vile intrigues,
Will, with another league, to leave him,
And, both united, soon deceive him.

To quash the suit we make no stand;
From mischief tie the plaintiff's hand;
Who, from an over-fond desire,
The modes of high-life to acquire,
By any means except the good,
Has nipp'd his profits in the bud.

Now are his future prospects o'er;
Must labour, be despis'd, and poor.
His character so stain'd, no doubt,
That nothing can, but time, wash out."

Mar. 22, 1794

Poems: Chiefly Tales

The wig

Clouds, days, and fashions, rise and wain;
And only set to rise again.
If you some variations view,
'Tis all routine, there's nothing new.
Although the title which I state
Be small, you'll find my subject great

A curious eye is pleas'd to scan
The *fashions* follow'd up by man;
Though 'tis ridiculous to have them,
He thinks it would be more to wave them;
With all their folly he'll pursue,
And all their inconvenience too.

Some writers sing the petticoat;
Some amplify the scarlet coat;
Others on hanging-sleeves insist,
Pendant a yard below the wrist.
The hoop, in Addison's gay lines,
With furbelow and top-knot shines.
Most learned heads in *Stevens* see,
But learned *wigs* shall fall to me.

While *Cromwell* Royalty enthrawl'd,
The *hair* was lank, the head was bald.
When Charles the Second climb'd the throne,
The *crown* conspicuously shone.
This was because the King's thin hair
Made the gay crown more gay appear.
Pray won't a di'mond brighter show
In sable than it will in snow?

But paltry hair was soon discarded,
And nothing but the *wig* regarded:
By ev'ry noble thought a prize,

It quickly grew a monstrous size;
And mantled o'er with wig the King,
What other part to light could bring?
His crown eclips'd, look'd no more gay,
Than thimble on a cock of hay.

Perhaps the reader'll think me wrong
In prefacing my tale so long;
May charge me with poetic sin,
For trifling when I should begin:
Yet pardon me, though not the mode,
I'll introduce an episode.

The noble Duke of Devonshire,
With others, the vast wig would wear;
Its want was sure to give the spleen;
None else in *William's* court was seen.
To order one he did not waver;
Which he could better *wear* than pay for.
A hundred guineas was the price;
A sum not pick'd up in a trice.
For such a sum was then, I vow,
Worth much about three hundred now.

'Twas made, brought home, approv'd, look gay;
But not a syllable of pay.
The wig which was to hide his head
Would well have hidden half his bed.
Without the wig the Peer was goaded,
And with it he was amply loaded.
But every soul throughout the land
Will bear a load at pride's command.

An humble barber's seldom found,
To trust one man three hundred pound.
To trade without this cash's a task;
My Lord is great—he dares not ask.
Through want he visited one day;

My Lord was too polite to pay.
The tortur'd barber ruin saw—
'Tis said, "necessity's no law."

A solemn court-day now was near;
His grace was sure to visit there.
In horrid fright the barber ran,
And pray'd his grace's gentleman
"That he the wig would let him take,
He recollected one mistake:
He'd alter't in an hour or so,
And not a soul should ever know.
For if one part was out of place,
'Twould issue in his own disgrace."

Not a suspicion could he harbour,
But willingly indulg'd the barber.
The wig's detain'd!—the valet mourns;
And mourn he may till it returns.
Frequent enquiries follow'd close.
"The Duke a hundred guineas owes."
The court-day came, the Duke was dress'd,
Call'd for the wig to crown the rest;
But might have call'd it from the skies.
It snugly with the barber lies,
Deposited in ample chest,
Which furnish'd half his shop at least.
The valet, with a dreadful face,
And fearful lest he'd lose his place,
Told the plain truth, as servants ought,
"And on the barber charg'd the fault;
Who wanted money bad, he said,
Must be arrested if not paid."
The Duke, of philosophic turn,
Did not, like some, with fury burn,
Order'd the steward to be found,
And bid him raise a hundred pound;

Treated the matter with some sport,
Redeem'd his wig, and went to court..

When good Queen Anne possess'd the throne,
Then dressing hair was quite unknown.
The gentlemen acquir'd the knack
To load with wig, head, breast, and back.
The stranger would be apt to stare;
Half man and half a Russian bear.
And yet such serious blessings flow,
Who could the powerful bulk forego?
This fine exub'rance when put on
Kept far aloof the scorching sun.
Nor could the winter's cold attack;
It warm'd from noddle down to nack.
No show'r could signify a fig,
A man could only wet his wig.
The barber's art could cure the rain
By buckling up the wig again.

What but the wig could e'er produce
Such wit as then was brought in use?
Congreve, and *Addison,* and *Steele*,
Wore mighty wigs—wrote mighty well;
And half a dozen more that follow
We all allow have beat us hollow.
No other vortex could they shine in;
It was the *wig,* or else the lining.

When George the First, of fair renown,
Acceded to the British Crown,
The bulky wig kept on its pace,
And crept among the vulgar race;
For every male, down to the sprig,
A cypher was without a wig.
Nay, even infants had three things—
A cradle, *scratch,* and leading-strings.

THE SECOND PART

To keep my promise I'll not fail,
Without more preface tell my tale.

A bull appear'd in *Derby* fair
With a most curious head of hair;
'Twas long, 'twas thick, 'twas curl'd, 'twas white;
The eye survey'd it with delight.
This was observ'd by Mr. Bakewell,
Who law and gospel wigs could make well.
He long'd to call that hair his own;
"'Twould cover well a pleading crown
It never should adorn a bull;
'Twould spirit up a head more dull."

The lawyer knows what cause to prize;
And barber where his profit lies.
"Why, *Mr. Lubin,* I declare,
Your bull's an ugly head of hair;
It shades his eyes, and will not fail
To sink his price and damp his sale.
I'll cut it off.—None can cut neater.
"'Twill make him look abundance better."

"Na, but yo shonna sheer, I think,
Unless yole giz a quart o drink.
For aw yo tauke o mending th' lad,
Yole fill yore pocket first egad."

"A quart I'll give you," Bakewell cries,
"Merely to see the creature's eyes."
The scissors find employment full,
To rob the honors of the bull:
And turn those honors into coin,
Which must the barber's pocket line.

From piping, baking, weaving, sheers,
Behold a first-rate wig appears.
Creators should not be elated,
But give joy to the thing created.
But this was not the present mode—
The *wig* was mute—the *maker* crow'd;
And in the height of joyous glee
Threw out this soft soliloquy:
"A face within this wig stuck fast
Certainly never can be dash'd.
This is the cream of eloquence;
'Twill rise triumphant over sense.
No enemy, though e'er so big,
Can stand against this powerful wig.
'Twill oust fair truth, and then supply
Its place with now and then a lie.
A *client* will this wig retain,
Though his last cause he did not gain.
The happy wearer will adore it,
Because 'twill carry all before it.
Give an opponent but a frown,
And right or wrong 'twill fell him down;
Will rise the first and keep it's place,
Beat down all modesty of face;
Will lead the bench, sustain its pride,
And humble every wig beside;
All arguments win at assizes;
From opposition bear all prizes.

In Derby town, if I look round,
Two counsellors are only found.
And yet I need not travel far
Before I find a purchaser;
For that which holds such excellence
Will never long be in suspence.

My fortune's made! The mark I've hit!
'Twill *Goodwin* at the college fit.

He's rather short, and thickish made;
But rather thicker in the head.
For he, of all who follow laws,
Only *attempts* to win a cause;
Nay, that attempt, it has been said,
Has never yet been often made.
And this defect, it may be, lies
In want of wig of proper size:
For, underneath that load profuse
Lie all the talents now in use.
'Tis virtue in the Doctor's pill,
And licenses to save or kill.
But if a man the case can't catch
No wonder if he's not the watch."

THE THIRD PART

Two men deceive themselves, we view,
Without design; each other too.
Then what inducement to believe
The man who will *himself* deceive?

The human mind we'll bring to view;
'Tis ever seeking after new,
And often finds what it has not,
Pleas'd but an hour with what its got.
The change of fashion, we shall find,
Is nothing but a change of mind.
Thus the young *daws,* in twiggen domes,
With open mouth take all that comes;
But ere a single day is o'er
Discharge the whole, and gape for more.

Our wig of rhetoric is buckled,
And in a box, like cradle, truckled;
But not that cradle often seen,
'Twas one without a head I mean;

Nor was it needful for more stuff—
The wig itself was load enough.

The barber shoulder'd it elate,
And rapp'd hard at the college gate;
As men are wont to rap, who rather
Design to *give* than *ask* a favour;
Or one most conscious that he shou'd win,
Could he set eyes on Mr. Goodwin.

Who could be more indulg'd by fate?
The counsellor unlock'd the gate!
"Your servant, Sir," the barber cries,
"Something for your inspection lies
In here."—A smile upon his face,
And finger pointing to the place.

"Oh, Mr. Bakewell, pray walk in;
You're loaded with a magazine."
What counsellor would not rejoice
If he should hear a human voice,
And see a well-dress'd person stand
With *boy* or *bundle* in his hand?
They're deeds of an estate, no doubt,
And he must make the title out.
He kens a fee, or a dispute,
Which may be follow'd by a suit.
His profit flows in just as fast
As one wave rolling o'er the last.

"At dinner we are going to sit,
I hope you'll stop, and take a bit.
We'll dine; and then, you understand,
Enquire into the *matt'r in hand*."

How good the meat, how fine the drink,
How much they say, how little think,
Whether at emptying plates they shone,

Or whether they pick'd clean the bone,
How well the wine look'd through the glasses,
How smoothly through the palate passes,
Shall not a syallable be said;
I'll leave it to a better head.
While not a word was said of finishing,
Poor Goodwin saw his fee diminishing,
And frequently came to a stand.
And now, my friend, " *the matt'r in hand.*"

But this expression, we contend,
The barber might not comprehend;
For where's the fox who will not stay
Who finds a chicken in his way?
And sure that man is void of thought,
Who gives up wine which costs him nought.

Though the great box was long and fast,
The barber open'd it at last.
"I'll shew you, Sir, without a flaw,
The nicest *wig* you ever saw.
For workmanship there's none to vie;
A man need only *see* to buy.
There's eloquence in every hair;
'Twill put to silence all the bar.
This, like a loadstone, profit draws,
Can twist the law to gain a cause."
The lawyer saw he'd miss'd his fee—
"And pray, Sir, what's your wig to me?"
No wonder Goodwin rais'd a frown;
His heart and suit were both let down.
"You spunger! what have I to do
With either your great wig or you?
Go tweak your people by the nose,
And hang your wig to fright the crows."

April 8, 1794.

Poems: Chiefly Tales

John Bolders

Watch well your foot-steps. Should you stray,
Perhaps you'll never find the way.

The man to worthy acts inclin'd
Finds a true pleasure in his mind.
If good alone, not injury does,
What can disturb his sweet repose?
Then all is mild within his breast—
Himself enjoys—enjoys his rest.

Far diff'rent thoughts to him belong,
The tenor of whose acts are wrong;
For going on from sin to sin
Stirs a rude monitor within,
Whose face display'd, such horrors shone,
Enough to make him hide his own.
Himself he hates, nay, all despise;
Without regret a beggar dies.

Bolders shall on the stage be led,
He'll prove exactly what I've said.
A youth discreet; benign his look,
Did well whate'er he undertook;
Mov'd gracefully the *frame*, 'tis said,
In weaving stockings for his bread.
His conduct harmless; bright his thought;
Fluent his words; his friendship sought.
What he perform'd was sure to shine:
Who would not envy such a line?
Or who that had it e'er would break it?
This he might sooner do than make it.

A youth like this, we're apt to guess,
Could scarcely miss of happiness.
The *main* of bliss he'd surely won;

Nay, hold my friend, I've not yet done;
For if by chance he wins the main,
By chance may lose it back again.

If the imprudent builder shou'd
Put bad materials to the good,
These bad will quickly ruin all;
His sumptuous building soon must fall:
This was John Bolders's defeat,
Who rais'd a character compleat,
But mixing actions not the best,
Moulder'd to nothing all the rest.

Love for one sex we count their due,
But Bolders had a love for two;
Hence it appears, without a joke,
He'd twice the love of other folk.
For women he esteem'd: what then?
He equally esteem'd the men.

Passions, like powerful waves, will slow,
And toss the vessel to and fro.
The pilot must *himself* command,
And guide her with a steady hand,
Or else she may, by being tost,
Soon in the surly deep be lost.
John, quite forgetting helm and deck,
His reputation went to wreck.

Amours of every kind, we know,
Behold the sun a deadly foe:
The best will scarcely bear the light,
But some may be as black as night.
Yet though they are in secret done
Are sometimes dragg'd before the sun.
The simple tale may raise offence,
And raise the blush of innocence;

But horrid will the guilty feel,
Except he's made of harden'd steel.

John from his happiness was hurl'd;
His actions blaz'd before the world:
Nay, when alone he did not lack
To view himself, and then start back,
Asham'd to see the face of day,
His fortune dwindled quite away.
Of one resource he could not fail,
Which was, to drown his cares in ale;
But this resource will seldom miss
To change for rags substantial bliss.
A large J.B. led many a score
Of white upon the ale-house door;
And though his creditors he shuns,
Is daily hunted down by duns.
His friends, who with a smile would greet,
Now, to avoid him, cross the street.
His money gone, and fair renown,
He could not stay in *Derby* town.
When character away we chase,
The carcase is not worth a place.

To Ashby-de-la Zouch he came,
In quest of male or female game;
For, as both sexes were his prey,
He could not *easily* lose his way.

Here one among the frisky dames
In Ashby kept a shop of frames;
Bolders stept in, " and took his stand
Upon the widow's jointure land."

Now fortune seem'd to promise fair,
"She'd instantly reduce his care."
Our ills are all on fortune thrown.
We quite forget they are our own.

I think we said, nor is it long,
That *Bolders* had a silver tongue.
But if he had, it is confess'd
'Twas all the silver he possess'd. .
For what he got, or what could borrow,
Were melted down to cure his sorrow.

His person, which appear'd to view,
We must allow, was handsome too.
His carriage met with approbation,
By far more polish'd than his station.

As to his dress, time might derange it;
Nor was he ever prone to change it.
While others Sunday-garments seek,
He wore the same quite round the week.
And *why* he did not change his dress,
He'd reasons good, we shrewdly guess.
If you suppose a filth contracts
By keeping clothes upon our backs,
"Which will offend the nose," you say,
Why then the nose may keep away.

More holes he had, you'd eas'ly scan,
Than suited with a handsome man;
And yet, we argue, on the whole,
That there's some honour in a hole.
For *slits* in garments are no more
Than many of our Princes wore.
And 'twill, you know, an honour bring,
If we can imitate a king.
For this old fashion, we confess,
Was deem'd the grandest stile of dress.
And no great diff'rence appears
If made by *time* or by the shears.

Bolders besieg'd the widow's heart,
And nobly won a *little* part;

But not one half would she let go;
No, 'twas about a third or so.

"'Twould not be long before he married,
For he had all the out-works carried."
Nay, there are folks won't stick to tell
He'd really won the citadel.
But I'll the Muse in silence lay,
Nor female weakness e'er betray;
For, were all secrets brought to light,
'Twould be a most amazing sight.

Of perseverance *he*'d no lack
But madam hung a little back.
He press'd his suit with all his might,
For he alone would profit by 't.
His sentiments went steady on,
But *hers* were rather *pro* and *con*.

The human mind he fully knew;
He'd try what one bold push would do.
Nor was he charg'd in any case
With losing by a bashful face.
This maxim he had always ready,
"Faint heart can never win fair lady."

On Sunday morning, to look big,
He borrow'd a great coat and wig.
A shilling too, as a third boon;
That was, because himself had none.
Furnish'd with dress and motley too,
To Ashby church that instant flew.
His figure in the Clerk's pew roars,
Just while the priest was reading prayers;
And, while the grotesque figure stands,
Offers the shilling and the *banns*.

The Clerk, surpriz'd at such a deed,
Ask'd Bolders "if he must proceed
Because the bride—her daughter too,
Attended in their usual pew;
And 'twas a circumstance uncommon,
For any well-dress'd modest woman
T'assemble among pious souls
And hear herself call'd o'er the coals."

John whisper'd, with a gentle frown,
"Do as you're bid." They both sat down.
The people now withdrew their looks,
And fix'd them on their prayers and books.
Some holy folks the inside minding,
And some eyed Bolders and the binding;
And every soul, as if by chance,
Threw at him now and then a glance.

The Parson read; they did the same;
Th' important moment quickly came:
"The holy banns of wedlock I
Publish before the Church's eye,
Between *John Bolders*"—Parson cries—
I'll place a dash—before your eyes;
For secrecy most dear I hold;
Her name, by me, shall not be told;
For, though the congregation knew,
That's no just ground for telling you.
Because my verses may be read
When the whole congregation's dead.

The widow rose up with a blush,
While Priest and People all were hush;
"*Banns* I forbid," the fair one cried,
"Both in this church and all beside."

Bolders with disappointment burn'd;
He saw the wind against him turn'd;

But was determin'd to pursue
While he'd the smallest chance in view;
For why should he the business close?
He'd nothing of his own to lose.

Rising, the antiquated beau—
"And will you then deny me so?"
"Yes!" cries the dame—all eyes upon her,
While prun'd for flying sat her honor—
"Then, before God, I now declare,
And this whole church, assembled here,
The dread tribunal we're before,
That thou, false woman, art my whore!"

O vile imprudence on his side!
Confusion seiz'd th'intended bride.
What female could refrain from crying,
Her china, or her honour, flying?

The little daughter, in vexation
To hear the mother's accusation,
Started in haste to make reply,
The flashes kindling in her eye:
"You tell a story then, I'm sure,
I know my mamma's not a whore."

The people star'd, like people wild;
The Parson clos'd his book, and smil'd;
For by this love-scene on the spot
All their devotion was forgot.

Bolders sneak'd off, t' avoid a fray;
The place was much too hot to stay.
Then to decamp he did not fail,
And leave me to record the tale.

June 10, 1794

Poems: Chiefly Tales

The coach horses

Man, feeble man, is prone to range;
He changes for the sake of change;
Was well, but would be better thought
He tries, but trying sinks to nought.

How few the people who can tell
The point of time at which they're well!
Give me one instance, if you can,
Then I'll pronounce him—happy man!
But, from the Sov'reign to the Poet,
Not one in fifty thousand know it.
"What! place a *poet* at the bottom;
He humbly thinks he ought to top 'em,
Because he holds a wide dominion"—
But we may differ in opinion.
Your pride, dear bard, I'll never check,
I know all Nature's at your beck.

Some discontent fell to the share
Of him who lately kept the *Bear*;
For how could he have trade to seek
Who drew two hogsheads every week?
But, mighty anxious after more,
Quite happy if he could draw four.
A slender tavern met his view—
"This will the wish'd-for business do."
'Tis done—it sooth'd Ambition's voice;
But broke my landlord in a trice.

The Duke of York in splendor shone
'Till fourteen hundred sixty-one.
But titles, riches, and renown,
Gave no content without a *crown*;
When, trying to secure that gem,
He lost his *all*—the world lost him.

Two suits of clothes were William's fee;
Nay, hold, my master; I'll have three.
These terms, improper, were denied;
In rags he liv'd, in rags he died.

The beasts have spoke in prose and rhime,
From *Master Gay* to *Æsop's* time.
Black fleas and spiders, who could spin,
Masters of rhetoric have been;
With ease then my Coach Horses may
Deliver all I have to say.

A pair of grays, in blethish case,
Would any set of harness grace:
Extreme of friendship you might view,
Firmly subsisting 'twixt the two.
Nor were, for years, which strikes with wonder,
Our couple half an hour asunder.
What a choice lesson they relate
To people in a married state!
Most happy must two folks appear
When they're so loving and so near!

Cobler, obedient to commands,
Was nearly rising seventeen hands;
In manners gentle, always did,
Without the whip, what he was bid;
And never once, in all his days,
Spoke one harsh word against his place.
Whether at home or out he went,
He found his interest in content.

Toby the Sulky was his brother;
In size and colour like the other;
But rather restive was of late,
As if disgusted with his state.
Would stop the carriage in the street,
Nor stir a hand, or move his feet.

Regardless how his master'd look,
Nor paid attention to rebuke.

A table, plentiful and gay,
The master kept, of corn and hay;
But food abounding, and work not,
No wonder he himself forgot.
Ambition fir'd his lofty mind;
He'd work or play, as whim inclin'd.

Cobler sore injur'd was to view
His friend would not his duty do.
As in one cause they were embark'd,
In language of four feet remark'd.

"Dear *Toby,* I'm alarm'd to see
This cross-grain'd management in thee.
Alter thy conduct, and be wise,
Or dreadfal mischiefs will arise.
Shall we, like foolish man, not tell
The point of time at which we're well?
While he attempts to change his trade,
Our fortune can't be better made.
Whether in field or stable seated,
We with the best are always treated;
Morn, noon, and night, *Tom* fills our cribs;
The master hates to see our ribs.
Hence all the pleasures which are known
In choicest eating are our own.
Nor have we reason to lament
The falling under punishment;
For Hutton never knew the hour
To punish us because he'd power.
We seldom feel the biting thong;
Thomas's whip, 'tis said, lasts long.
The saddler tells the coachman too,
'Where he buys one, others buy two.'
Neither do we complain of work,

Or slave like stage-coach-horse, or Turk,
The joyous labours of the day
Are nothing but a change of play:
'Tis exercise, just what is right,
Producing health and appetite.

If of your conduct you've no care,
My master'll send you to the fair:
Then what a dismal life you'll lead!
The very thought creates a dread.
Both you and I, to life's dull end,
Shall daily mourn an absent friend.
Or rather, as a *match* we are,
We both shall ramble to the fair;
Change for the hardest state on earth,
In vile stage-coach be whipp'd to death."

Toby behav'd as man would do,
Knew better than th' adviser knew
He roll'd his eye, he shook his mane
To Cobler thus replied again
"I imitate the human race,
And strive, like them, to mend my place.
There's no complaint of food or play,
I've a full portion every day;
But how can this my conduct bind,
If there's a single want behind?
In friendship I to none resign;
My heart is more your own than mine;
But every soul of every race
Strives to be *master* in his place.
Has not the coachman made a stand,
And clearly got the upper hand?
Over the kitchen, parlour, reigns;
The cellar too are his domains.
And have not I, by art most free,
Brought down the coachman under me?
I treat him, and without disaster,

Just in the stile he treats his master;
Thus I'm establish'd firm and clear;
What then have I, my friend, to fear?"

When prudence won't support our schemes,
They're just as idle as our dreams:
What man, whose head with sense is fill'd,
Would ever on a cobweb build?
Will not a sailor's prospect fail
Who puts to sea without a sail?
Though others judgment he'll despise,
He'll be more apt to sink than rise.

Through want of sight we stumble may:
The coachman was soon turn'd away,
And quickly found himself adrift;
With slender commons made a shift.

Toby might now his fate bewail,
Who in the market found a sale.
His feet sore batter'd 'gainst the stones;
Flogg'd out of flesh, he shew'd his bones.
Both want and slavery attends him
And dreadful usage quickly ends him;
And, gone the road of human kind,
This useful lesson left behind:
"Know when you're well, and there be seated,
Nor by delusive views be cheated.
By climbing up to grasp at all,
You stand the fairest chance to fall.
Let your sound judgment be the test;
Nor change, except 'tis for the best."

July 4, 1794.

Note.—Toby was sold Aug. 29, 1794, to run in the heavy coach; and, in less than a year, whipped to death.—Cobler keeps his place to the present day, Aug. 15, 1804; and enjoys every comfort age will admit.

The parson in pickle

When dire misfortunes on us wait,
Pity, or *ridicule*'s our fate.
Each is bestow'd, and each rejected;
Just as we're *re-* or *dis*-respected.

'Tis striking six—'tis now broad day;
The Muse says, "Rise, compose a lay."

Madam, your orders I receive,
And will a modest poem give.
Please to attend my tale once more
'Twas seventeen hundred ninety-four,
A gentle Parson I shall name
To be the hero of my theme.
Perhaps he'll smile, and smile agen,
The willing subject of my pen;
For if he's by my Muse forgot,
He may in dull oblivion rot.

MUSE. " Nay, if the *parson* you pursue
I'll neither own your verse nor you.
No soul shall my assistance meet
In tales which are not over sweet;
They'll throw your work by in the end"—

POET. "Then, madam, it will not offend.

MUSE. "Or to a greasy use appointed,
Plaister a candle broken jointed."

POET. "Surely no man will vend his spite
On verses that improve his light"—

MUSE. "Or wrap tobacco by the measure."

POET. "Why then, dear Muse, 'twill hold a treasure."

MUSE. "Or light a pipe, as paper waste"—

POET. "'Twill then be grateful to the taste."

MUSE. "May keep the leg of lamb from burning,
While the fierce jack the roast-meat's turning."

POET. "My verse then will not be rebuk'd,
Because the dinner's nicely cook'd."

MUSE. "Or deem'd in thread-papers to share"—

POET. "Then its bright guardians are the fair."

MUSE. "Or line the chest"—POET. "Then 'twill be said
By Chloe's lovely fingers spread.
Nay, farther honours are its lot;
'Twill guard the treasure Chloe's got."

MUSE. "Or prop the pies of some good wife"—

POET. "Then it becomes the prop of life.

MUSE. "No bratt, as god-mother, I'll own"—

POET. "Then I'll stand god-father alone."

Thus my chaste Muse reluctant stands,
Extremely loth to soil her hands;
And leaves me to the powers within,
Like *Swift,* to wade through thick and thin.

A double *Parson* ours was made,
And well acquainted with his trade.
Shall we for talents seek about?
Not *in* the pulpit, his lay *out.*

From Easter dues would ne'er depart;
He'd all the oaths in use by heart;
Knew what would suit in every case;
Could use them with becoming grace;
Could vend them, slow, or pour them faster;
Of this hold rhetoric he was master;
Could size them well, none can deny,
For every place and company—
The soft for parlour and the table;
The rough for kitchen and the stable.

To study sermons were meer jokes,
For he could filch from other folks;
Change paragraphs, and chuse with ease;
Just as we cull in getting pease;
Alter the text, the matter blend,
And *shorten* them at *either* end;
And when they in his livery shone,
They pass'd compleatly for his own.

Then, as to prayers, they're always nigh,
Made to his hand, both cut and dry;
Polish'd and squar'd for each occasion,
To fit a case, or fit a nation.
Nor would he use them o'er and o'er,
But keep them by him as a store.

Domestic savings, 'mong the rest,
Held a firm tenure in his breast;
Could tell when candles burnt too fast;
How long a load of coals should last.
In cupboard history was compleat;
Knew what a servant ought to eat.
Remnants of pies, preserv'd with ease;
For he dealt large in locks and keys.
While some, bemir'd in figures, stick,
He's master of arithmetic.

"A lock of fourteen pence," he'd say,
"In half a year will pay its way.
The little barrel shall hold out
Till June the fifteenth comes about;
And then, if there appears a dreg,
The sixteenth day we'll tap the keg."

If *Molly* broke a farthing pot,
It was not, in a month, forgot.
This a most deadly sin appears,
Was daily ringing in her ears.

He shew'd deep thought when bargains made;
Was rather cautious when he *paid*;
For every piece he deem'd as good
As one of his own drops of blood.
The butcher squeez'd in lean and fat
Then begg'd a dish for dog and cat.

But what can careless *Molly* hope
When she destroys two drams of soap?
Left in the sink while water pours
A text he'd handle full two hours.

This fruitful theme demands his caring,
Besides a first-rate lot of swearing.

Though he'd a thousand pounds a year,
From losses and deductions clear;
Yet he knew well where's the best wine,
And where he could convenient dine.
Why should he eat and drink alone,
When he could easily save his own?
He knew a parson, rich or poor,
Always commands the pantry door.
Assuredly the truth I state,
His knowledge in some things was great;
And yet he might not *chuse* to know

Whether he welcome was or no.
While others hunt, *one* thing pursue,

He 'd hunt a hare and dinner too:
To miss of either he was loth,
But ten to one he'd win them both.
An airing made a hungry sinner;
And how-d'ye-do procured a dinner.

He hated labour like a Turk;
He lov'd the money, not the work.
'Tis said the gods are apt to frown
To see some folks in band and gown;
Because from holy rules they swerve,
And only mean *themselves* to serve.

'Tis nine o'clock—I'll drop the pen;
Breakfast, and take it up again.

THE SECOND PART

At three miles distance liv'd a pair,
Who kept up hospitable cheer.
The pot boil'd free— the jack turn'd round;
The stranger there a welcome found.
Wine, ale, and beer, were freely handed,
Just as the visitant demanded.
Was it e'er known a house like this
A man in black would ever miss?

One windy night, as stories tell,
The back wall of their privy fell.
Ah, what could modest people do?
Their hinder parts expos'd to view.
To shew the world a nether face,
They really thought a foul disgrace;
Nor has the recent fashion been
To let a full-grown beard be seen.

To remedy this vile defect,
A piece of canvas, nail'd erect,
Kept all things private in the rear,
And kept th' inhabitant from fear,
'Till hand and trowel, far more sure,
Could make the tenement secure.

The parson came; he din'd well there
And, for three hours, kept his chair;
'Till eating, drinking free, anon
A motion suddenly came on.
'Tis dinner time—I smell roast meat—
Dame Fortune lets a Poet eat.

THE THIRD PART

The Priest and we our meal have done;
We'll take our hats, and travel on.
His glass set down, he must retreat,
And lose one-third of what he'd eat.
Lose! 'twas a word exciting fears,
And sounded horrid in his ears:
But this idea, to be brief,
Instantly came to his relief;
That what he lost, repeated o'er,
Most certainly no value bore;
Or else he would, without much shame,
The whole into his pocket cram.

To *Cloacina's* altar now
He came to *offer,* not to vow;
And while undoing, to prepare,
This short soliloquy made there:
"Oh, oh, the necessary grac'd!
Madam and Sir, improve in taste.
No vile brick wall above the seat,
'Tis lin'd with canvass quite compleat."

He took his seat— as usual strain'd;
Against th' inviting canvass lean'd.
What could a wretched parson do;
The gods forsook him, canvass too;
He backward tumbled over there,
Prone to the bottom, God knows where.
I'll stop to say no more fine things,
Because the bell for supper rings.

THE FOURTH PART

We left the Priest, where you and I,
In our whole lives, ne'er wish'd to lie.
Ah, why did not St. N—m come
To save him from this cruel doom?
Instant a dreadful noise appear'd,
But unintelligibly heard
For not a soul advanc'd the while,
And all the gods were seen to smile.
For ev'ry one had disapprov'd him;
They *knew* him better than they *lov'd* him.
Besides, it was not understood
Whether a god of land or flood
Should lend assistance to the Priest,
'Till ascertain'd which he possess'd?
Envelop'd in so strange a matter
They could not call it *land* or *water*;
Thus like the child, or bastard rather,
Between two fathers own'd by neither.

The surly fates around him gathering,
'Twas something worse than tar-and-feathering.
While he was sinking lower and lower,
In filth was rolling o'er and o'er.

The gods determine out of hand
"That, as he sunk, it was not land,"

Therefore, in solemn form, declare
Some Water god must have the care.

Neptune was call'd to his assistance.
Damp'd with the smell, he kept his distance.
"The Priest in such a pickle stands,
What god will ever daub his hands?
Should I that labour set about,
Must, with my trident, fork him out.
It's not in Ovid said or sung
That gods e'er ventur'd into dung;
Then what a trident I should have!
To wash it, would cost many a wave.
And while the gods their nectar quaff,
At my expence they'd raise a laugh.
Let B— and Co. extend their aid;
Neptune ne'er follow'd this black trade."
Then made his leg, and turn'd to go,
"Your humble servant, D. I. O.*"

(**Damme I'm off*—The modern polite mode of taking leave)

During delays, we understand,
The parson ate at second hand;
Met such resistance in the way,
He could not well his stomach stay.
He never was in such a hole as
This— nor e'er swallow'd such a bolas;
And thought it hard a parson shou'd,
Just like a savage, chew the cud.
He'd freely give up, with all *his* heart,
The relish of this sav'ry desert.

As help divine appear'd to fail,
The Doctor's cries at length prevail;
Brought forth the servants near at hand,
And set him once again on land:

And yet, when viewing him all o'er,
A human figure scarcely bore.

Like Jewish ladies, must lie by
A month or so, to purify;
And, when no savor shall remain,
Might step into the world again.
"Remain a month in such a plight!
He never more would trust his sight;
By canvass he'd no more be cheated;
He *feel* the wall before he seated;
Nor ever ride again to dine;
They laid a trap to save their wine."

Reflections came while homeward bound;
His head reclin'd, he eyed the ground—
"O vile baptismal operation,
Dreadful prognostic of vexation;
For even *sprinkling* is a curse,
But *dipping* I find ten times worse."
When stinging thought came 'cross his mind
Poor *Dobbin* felt the lash behind.
Thus while he wander'd through the air
Leaves a strong scented atmosphere;
Where an inviting flavour lies,
Which draws a train of hungry flies,
Whose nostrils, at a distance, cou'd,
Just like his own, smell what was good.
The clock strikes ten, I'll march to bed,
Nor shall another word be said.

July 24, 1794.

Poems: Chiefly Tales

The cobbler

'Tis said that wealth has various uses.
It has—we'll see what it produces.

When Prejudice on high is seated,
The soundest judgment may be cheated;
Hood-wink'd, she seldom finds her road,
While prejudice keeps her abode;
Nor on her seat can she appear
While the usurper keeps the chair;
For everlastingly we find
The stronger will the weaker bind.

A powerful influence, we know,
Possesses every soul below.
Not apt to see—to dullness prone,
With *Reason's* eyes, but with our own.

As we can't tell where *bliss* may lie,
In *property* we always try;
But often as wealth meets reception
So we are sure to meet deception.
The higher class have their full share;
The more of wealth, the more of care.

Perhaps true bliss in *ease* may lie,
Then stop a moment, friend, we'll try.
Nature's design we'll not invade,
Man surely was for action made;
If out of use his hands, his head,
His feet, the man's much like the dead.
A breathing something here we view,
Lost to himself and others too:
For how can he enjoy the day
Who stupid slumbers life away;
'Gainst sluggish *time* makes heavy moan,

Whereas the fault is all his own?
If he round four-and-twenty hours
Shall just do nothing, pleasure sours.

If happiness we seek below,
The mind no vacancy must know.
Head, hands, and feet, to action prone
For others good, or else our own;
Studying, reading, conversation;
Variety comes in rotation.
Labour alternately, and rest,
This practice will be found the best;
A practice which we hold most true,
In poverty and riches too.

Have you no hobby-horse to stride?
"I have"—then, Sir, get up and ride.
The prettiest bauble upon earth;
But never ride him out of breath.
Pleasure pursued in haste is vain,
We quickly run it down to pain.
If one hand itches, then the other
Will scratch most eagerly his brother;
This a delightful joy imparts,
But he may scratch it till it smarts.
Keep your best favorite always nice,
Nor let him daub his feet in vice.

These rules attended to, you may
Sleep through the night, sing through the day.
No matter though your wealth runs scant,
Prudence will never let you want.
Suppose no affluence you share,
You're rid at once of all the care;
But if with money you'd be bless'd,
'Twill blot your note, and break your rest.

Poems: Chiefly Tales

John Parks liv'd at—I'll not tell you;
We'll grace his name with E. S. Q.
Because he held, and held them clear,
About six hundred pounds a year.
But, if his house-keeping we view,
It seldom cost much more than two.

Not fond to hoard wealth, nor to waste,
His stile was suited to his taste.
His guinea often you might see
Swelling the score of charity.

Then, as to *love,* he'd long lost sight on't
Or, rather, he ne'er knew a doit on't;
Nor ever made one woman wife,
Nor talk'd of Cupid in his life.
One house-keeper he had, 'tis true,
But she could neither say nor do;
And yet before the setting sun
Did all the work he wanted done;
Not mighty apt to go astray;
Reflection had no room to play.
If you her bed watch'd round the year,
You'd never say—"*two* folks lay there."

An idle boy he'd always use
To polish up the knives and shoes.
If you're inclin'd to keep a spark,
'Tis ten to one he'll hit this mark.

The morning came; he rose at ten;
He ate his breakfast; and—what then?
Quite tir'd with sitting, standing, soon,
A dreadful chasm held 'till noon.

A stable had, where lumber's put;
For he ne'er rode or walk'd on foot.
Nor did he need a horse to chuse,

Who never learnt himself to use.
Supineness through his life attends
He wanted neither foes nor friends.

The dinner came; then at the close
He shut his eyes to court a doze.
And whether bad, or whether good,
He ate as much as e'er he cou'd.
But disappointment wishes sap,
He could not eas'ly take a nap;
Like *tops* some exercise must keep,
Forc'd into action e'er they sleep.
Rising and sitting was his doom;
Trying all chairs within the room;
But, as he could not rest attain,
He tried them o'er and o'er again.

His study, we affirm, consisted
Of the best authors that existed:
Bible and Prayer-book—rather dusty,
Stow'd in a dark room—rather musty;
Because the circulating air
Was seldom suffer'd to come there.
What though their number were but two;
He did not quickly read them through.

His application caus'd no sorrow;
He was not apt to lend or borrow.
Then as the year roll'd round its course,
An Almanack would add its force.

When he must write instead of speak,
Pen, ink, and wafers were to seek;
And though he could not find them soon,
Whene'er he did were out of tune.
His ink was thick, his paper dash'd,
His pen was blunted, wafers smash'd;
Which seem'd to say, through long abuse,

"They could not then come into use."
And he was never so absurd
But would desist, and take their word,
And sealing-wax he would forbear;
'Twas twice the trouble wafers are.

Now, having nothing else to do,
A dish of tea is brought to view.
And where's the female, or the male,
That ever shunn'd the sweet regale?
A pleasure that relieves the cares
By opening ether men's affairs;
Chief entertainment of the nation;
The slaughter-house of reputation,
Which never more to grow is seen
Than heads which pass the guillotine,
The history of a month, we see,
Compriz'd within a dish of tea.
Who would not even love the scent
Of liquor so intelligent?
The solid part, too, of our flutter,
Seems to the eye but bread-and-butter;
But *really* is, when handed round,
A plate of curious knowledge found.

Waiting for *care* to run away,
We've lost three quarters of a day.
Nor could, when supper time came on,
Eat much—his appetite was gone.

The evening came; time hung a load:
He doz'd a bit while Sarah sew'd.
As every *greater* noise was check'd,
The very small would have effect.
While she's the thread through linen pulling,
The sound had something in it lulling;
To which we add, by way of rhime,
Her body, most exact, beat time.

This vacancy of life he led—
He rose, ate, slept, and went to bed;
He'd nought to find, he 'd nought to seek;
Full seven long days made every week.

His body, by sheer sloth oppress'd,
Was unprepar'd for food or rest;
His mind, debilitated grown,
For want of use had lost its tone.

Thus happiness he could not find,
Which quickly brought distress of mind.
Depriv'd of bliss, he envy'd long
The man who ate, slept, laugh'd, or sung.
If humble life had been his lot,
Compell'd to act, he'd pleasure got.
Thus scrutinizing, it appears
Wealth was the cause of all his cares.

THE SECOND PART

Hold up the glass, and you'll confess
The Cobler comes in real dress.

But two doors off, full in the street,
A Cobler held a bulk compleat;
Who food and pleasure copious took,
And rather shew'd a jovial look.
Not only eat, but sometimes drank;
Nor could you see his belly lank.
T'improve his person took some care,
For once a week he comb'd his hair;
His white shirt sleeves his arms adorning,
The whitest were on Monday morning;
His waistcoat, Phœnix like, we note,
Ascended from his last old coat;
And fit so well you scarce could match it:
The sleeves and skirts laid by to patch it.

His leather apron hid with ease
The holes upon his breeches knees,
Fasten'd behind as firm as any,
With a large buckle, price a penny.
Button and loop-hole, near his heart,
Clubb'd to support the upper part:
These partners held a great contest,
Which longest should possess the breast;
Agreed like husband and like wife,
Who gall each other during life.
But let the Muse in sorrow tell;
The button, in the contest, fell:
The loop, triumphant, kept the field—
Beheld the conquer'd button yield!
But, when she found her help-mate dead,
The mournful flap hung down its head.

Great wits are seldom at a loss;
The Cobler cut a shred across
His apron; hung it, without clatter,
About his neck like knight o' th' Garter;
But wanting George to grace the end on't,
He let the leather flap hang pendant.

Sure as the sun went down and brought night,
He chang'd his stockings once a fortnight.
The Muse professes not to know
Whether he garters wore or no;
Only observes a curious eye
Might see his hose in wrinkles lie
Except till Sunday he should wait,
Then they were tolerably strait.

Turning two ways the observer sees
Two buckles grace his breeches knees;
But here we modestly declare
The two did not exactly pair:
But this by no means signifies,

As none could two ways turn his eyes.
We'll not say which is worst or best,
But only say they're East and West.

The Cobler we've describ'd compleat,
'Till we've descended to his feet.
Where his two shoes compleatly shewn
He others soled before his own.

Our hero thus describ'd, you know,
Could not appear a perfect beau.
For all gay colours he must lack;
We'll only say—a beau in black:
For when a bulk abounds with wax
All neighbouring objects it attacks;
And then, Camelion like, is known
To change their colours to its own.

To tempt fresh customers that way
Would all his splendid powers display:
New-mended shoes, arrang'd most nice
On his bulk top, mark'd with the price.
Who would not then be of opinion
He sov'reign was of this dominion.
What bulky care could enter free
Into his shop, six feet by three.
His powers most ably could, no doubt,
With ease keep all intruders out.
Fix'd on his throne, with pride compleat,
Whoever spoke stood in the street;
And, though the weather made resistance,
Were forc'd to keep an awful distance.

He kept true time as any cock;
Enter'd his bulk at five o'clock;
And like a cock whose spirits flow,
As soon as up began to crow.

With various notes his voice adorning,
His treble usher'd in the morning.

The neighbours knew the time to rise,
Though perfect darkness veil'd the skies.
His shining candle had the power
Through the broad chinks to tell the hour;
And though no day-break spread the skies,
Told drowsy people when to rise.

"Wake, husband, let not sleep o'erpower,
The Cobler's been at work this hour."
"Pho, dame, don't make so much ado,
I know he's up as well as you."

A master was of self and song;
He dealt in music all day long;
And entertain'd the world with glee;
" I love my Billy, Billy me.
Ye gentle gales that fan the air,
Then who can with my love compare?
We never will for riches quarrel,
We'll find the bottom of the barrel."

You'd see the last new song of all
Nail'd with four tacks against the wall.
Nay, the whole length of Chevy Chase
Found in his little bulk a place.

In joyous temper all the day
Smil'd, work'd, and sung his cares away;
And never, as we understand,
Did once complain time hung on hand;
But, as with hasty wing he flew,
With hasty step he would pursue.
Nay, at the Crown was heard to say,
"Sol and his ale went fast away."

They'll make an evidence with ease;
Say, or unsay, whate'er you please;
Have ample power t'explain the laws,
And let e'en falsehood gain a cause.
Nay, make a conscientious jew
Say any thing except the true.
The meek divines well understand them;
They cramp the conscience or expand them.
The Priest that doctrine will defend
Which all religions comprehend.
They'll make the tend'rest lovers part,
And give a hand without a heart:
Or in a twinkling disappear,
And change to any form that's near.
Become a bonnet lac'd, for Phil,
For which she'll grant you what you will.
They'll give a sprucer gait; what's more
Will swell the carcase just before;
Give self-importance too, and tend
To make a man o'er-look a friend;
When rhetoricians powers are spent,
They're the concluding argument.

A canvas bag the Squire procures
To hold these hundred bright allures,
In paper wrapt to swell the size,
That sooner it might catch the eyes;
And while the Cobler did not fail
To leave his bulk in quest of ale,
The squire, in careless mood, passed by,
Threw in the whole as none could spy.

That man, you'd think, the worst of ninnies,
Who thus disposes of his guineas.
Yet well that money may be spent
Which buys the very thing we meant.
Who would not send it to the deep,
If it could bring up *ease* and *sleep*?

The Cobler soon return'd again
To his diminutive domain.
"Hey day!" he whisper'd in surprize,
"Fresh work I see before me lies.
What simpleton these shoes could bring,
Not worth the paper or the string?
I warrant he who brought them here
Durst not, through pride, let them appear."
But, when the flimsy covering's rent
Himself was all astonishment,
His jovial spirits instant fled,
And left him with a thoughtful head,

He rac'd his brains in pond'ring o'er.
From whence could come this golden store.
His mental powers were all on fire;
Could no more sleep than could the Squire.
His mind kept changing every hour,
And soon became a little sour.
Corroding cares came on apace;
The wrinkles deepen'd in his face.
His eyes upon the pavement pore;
Was seven years older than before;
His mouth was rather narrow'd in,
And sunk almost an inch his chin;
His peace was gone, his trouble not;
His joy, and all his songs forgot.
And Chevy Chace, which grac'd his shed,
Was never after sung or said.

Aug. 24, 1794.

A.B.C.

A poem is not more absurd
Because its title is no word:
And yet that title, although small,
Is the great fountain whence spring all.
From this most copious source we'll draw
Youth, beauty, wedlock, love, and law.

The two extremes we'll surely find.
Which *please* and which *torment* the mind
For if we love and law can trace
'Twill be sufficient for our case.
A parson's work it nicely fits,
Who often join two opposites.

Nothing on earth the heart can move
To pleasure, like that passion love.
It reigns triumphant in the breast;
Supports and governs all the rest.

But *Law*'s a monster that devours
The choicest comfort of your hours.
All other mischiefs may keep off;
Involv'd in law, you've plague enough,
This maxim then admits no doubt,
He who is *in* would fain be out.

Long dissertations are absurd—
We'll close without another word.

THE SECOND PART

As much of love shall now be told
As ever A. B. C. can hold.

That urchin Cupid knows his duty;
He'll always shoot a heart for *beauty*;
This he more eagerly will deign,
Because he seldom shoots in vain.

If *Plutus* too should give a nod,
He's willing to obey the god;
For wealth and charms in any state
Most certainly will captivate.

But if *Miss Prudence* claims his care,
"He seldom has a dart to spare."
Thus what should merit most respect
Is apt to meet with most neglect.

Of all the pictures earth can boast,
A handsome woman pleases most;
And the most powerful she appears
Over fourteen or fourscore years.
The moment you a sight can have,
That moment you become her slave.
The looker-on is all on fire
Either with wonder or desire;
Supremely then is beauty bless'd;
No creature is like her caress'd.

But view the fair in her last stage,
Struggling with long decays of age,
When kind assistance is most needed,
There's not a soul so little heeded.
The picture's dash'd, no pity's nigh,
The looker-on turns off his eye:
In solitude she may abide;
Her sov'reign powers are laid aside.
That which was most of all high-priz'd.
Is now the most of all dispis'd.

Only three persons we'll engage,
By summons to adorn our page;
And all their names must secret be
Close shelter'd under A. B. C.

Miss A. was tall, and mov'd with grace;
Strait, and most beautiful of face;
To much good-nature was inclin'd;
It play'd both in her face and mind:
No wonder then, in deep surprize,
B fell a victim to her eyes;
For when those eyes but gave a glance,
A lover fell-you'd think, by chance.
But, should you *doubt,* then take a view,
You'd *see* her powers—and *feel* them too:
For, like a power that's magical,
Spite of yourself you're sure to fall.

In lover's eyes are plainly seen
The language that is held within.
With bowing, smiling, on his part,
He found the road that reach'd her heart;
While she, a stranger to disdain,
Would never let him sue in vain;
But, form'd for love, she, without guile,
Sweetly return'd him smile for smile.
Should, by her eyes, a lover drop,
She well knew how to raise him up.
Or, if he should a wound endure,
She'd perfectly perform a cure.

That state of bliss is half divine
When two bright flames in one shall join.
Can greater happiness remain
Than love, and be belov'd again?

When two folks are to union prone,
Then Hymen's cause moves gently on.

To grasp his torch he will not faulter,
That he may light them to the altar.
Examine whether 'tis in case right,
Give it a rap to make it blaze bright.

The *banns* put up, the ring was there,
The bride in satin would appear.
Now all the joyous blessings flow,
Except that time mov'd rather slow.

When most delicious fruit is nigh
It strongly tempts the stander-by;
And if no obstacle is near,
It is not easy to forbear.
What motive was there to have staid
Until the parson grace had said:
Our happy B those joys possess'd
Design'd to make a husband bless'd.

When a stale lover nothing wants,
Because he's all the sex e'er grants,
Would he call *his* a happier lot
After the priest had tied the knot?
For all that ever law has made
Only a licence is to trade.

No further pleasure B could know;
She no more pleasure could bestow:
A secret coldness was th' effect,
Succeeded by a small neglect.
His eyes, which met her eyes with glee,
Now rang'd a foot below her knee.
A conduct slighting he shew'd to her
More like a *husband* than a wooer.

The day pass'd by, indiff'rence planted,
Ring, gown, and parson, were not wanted.

"And, as the bell for supper rings,
I'll stop to say no more fine things."

THE THIRD PART

Both law and love compose the past;
Poetic justice comes at last.

Love, like a blooming rose, is press'd
Within the precincts of the breast.
The owner often casts an eye,
Delighted with the pleasing toy.
Perhaps an hour it may not rest
Till planted in a second breast.
So on, from breast to breast it flies;
Wanting a *prudent* root it dies.

A young and handsome man was C;
The friend and intimate of B:
They oft converse, and notes compare,
Of laurels gather'd from the fair.
Between these two it was agreed
"That B should be compleatly freed
Of beauteous A; and C should take her
While B for ever should forsake her.
That as the *banns* 'twixt A and B
Stood in the church, they'd serve for C;
By which they'd save expence and time,"
And I procure a word to rhime.

Whether Miss A ponder'd a while on't
We cannot say; history is silent:
Yet no more grief appear'd to view
Than changing an old gown for new.

But now to church went A and C,
And married in the name of B.
The joyous day gave great delight;

Perhaps more joyous was the night;
But, like his predecessor, he
Cropp'd the ripe fruit, and left the tree:
For soon with matrimony cloy'd
He turn'd his tail upon the bride.
What though his conduct was absurd,
It left her ready for a third.
Nor can we think much hard *her* case
Who still commanded half the race.
Her beauty'd such a powerful sway
'Twould pick a man up ev'ry day.

Now while Miss A'd no husband near
She liv'd a life of "as it were."
Her person to support in state
Was much inclin'd to run in debt;
And when we debts contract, they say,
The time will come when we should pay.
But if neglect be on our side
Compulsive methods must be tried.
For common justice holds this tone,
"That ev'ry man should have his own."

In vain for cash Miss A being sought
Was to the *Court of Conscience* brought.
The plaintiff thus the fair pursued,
In C's surname Miss A was sued.

The crowd, surpriz'd, began to stare
That so much beauty enter'd there.
Nay, cold Commissioners, 'tis true,
Would lick their lips and steal a view.
Thaw'd from the ice by warm desire,
A frozen stick will catch the fire;
Disguise the passion how you will,
'Tis nature, and 'tis nature still.
But seniors are not apt to fall;
To look and lick their lips is all.

A lawyer made appearance there,
And loudly pleaded for the fair;
Arrang'd his tropes, his figures dress'd,
In lofty stile himself express'd:
And pray what lawyer would dispute
To plead his best in beauty's suit?
But what was his *retaining* fee
Is no concern to you or me.

He pleaded with decisive air;
Resolv'd to win the cause—and fair:
"That none an action can support
Against a *wife* in any court.
That though her marriage had a flaw
It perfectly was good in law;
For as the ritual she'd gone through,
A wife must be to *one* of *two*;
And that's her real husband still
With whom she said at church *I will*.
Then if the plaintiff will pursue,
The husband is the mark in view."

The bench was then my sole delight;
My care was parting wrong from right.
As I sat president of three,
Decision was referr'd to me.

"Was perfect beauty ever made
To hawk its charms for want of trade?
We hope no great defect comes forth
To quash the sale of so much worth.

That she ne'er chang'd a marriage vow
With the first man, we all allow;
So far from marrying the dame,
He never to the altar came;
Nor once commission'd any one
By proxy, to make *her* his own.

Nor could she be by right fix'd there,
No, not if *Madan* held the chair;
For he'd suppose, without reflection,
This might not be her first connexion.

Survey the second husband's claim;
His title will be found the same:
He left both parties in the lurch,
And put a trick upon the church.
A name that's stolen appears to view;
Also a borrow'd person too.
No *banns* put up 'twixt C and A,
Which must to wedlock lead the way;
For this is what the law demands;
On this a union falls or stands;
Therefore, if marriage has a flaw,
It can't be ratified by law.
Then this assertion springs from all;
No man can *this* a wedding call:
Or, if it should that phrase invite,
'Tis but the wedding of a night;
Or like one that is hatch'd up quick
By dancing round a candlestick;
Or one of military stamp,
That's solemniz'd within a camp:
The loving couple's plighted word
Is only jumping o'er a sword;
That sword, intended to divide,
Will there unite, and make a bride.

Besides, when there appears demur,
We must consult the register;
And though there should B's name appear,
Yet B himself was never there;
and if for C you chuse to look,
His name was never in the book.

This wedding's founded on no laws;
We must, of course, dismiss the cause;
For as a husband A ne'er knew,
No husband can the plaintiff sue;
But if he will pursue his claim,
May still sue A in her own name.

There's one delightful word we see
Compos'd of our A B and C.
To girls, whose flimzy virtue lies
Quite dormant, and whose passions rise,
That dear word *husband* stands the first
Of all the alphabet can boast:
In that cornpriz'd is every thing
That either Heaven or Earth can bring;
But, when that blessing *husband*'s granted,
Then ev'ry other blessing's wanted."

A, rather out of credit grown,
Display'd her charms upon the town.
"But why in *Birmingham* appear
Among the dirty bunters there?
Whose manners are a foul disgrace;
A satire on the female race.
She might a constellation rise,
And figure in the London skies;
Could charms display as bright as any,
In evenings when it was not rainy."
'Tis done—and she acquir'd renown,
As the first beauty on the town.
Dress'd in the pink, she took her stand
Among the ladies of the Strand.
Thus beauty, by imprudent steps,
To sure destruction slowly creeps.
For she, when to that bevy's got in,
Takes much about three years to rot in.

Sept. 24, 1794.

Poems: Chiefly Tales

The silent priest

We'll tell simple truth, and our story comes pat,
No matter if acted in this age or that.

Dear Friend, let us saunter to Baxterly church,
Where good Mr. D—left himself in the lurch;
For there the gay hearer will, sure as a gun,
Meet with a sweet morsal of high-season'd fun.

The pray'rs being ended, and no blunder made,
The Clerk his desk mounted—he well knew his trade;
Two staves out of Sternhold he struck up compleat,
While climbing the pulpit the Priest took his seat.
Now heav'nly music, a Clerk's highest boast,
Calm'd every breast, but the Vicar's the most.

The psalm being over, deep silence came next;
Not a single breath sounded, expecting the text;
But, to the surprize of the serious and gay,
The Vicar himself was as silent as they;
For he'd dropt to sleep, being drench'd with mild ale,
And dream'd of full bumpers, the last night's regale;
Or, rather, till five in the morning had hanker'd,
Before he could find the last drop in the tankard.

Now the congregation became rather wild,
They look'd at the Priest, at each other, and smil'd.
If a shepherd should fall fast asleep in the day,
No wonder his flock goes a little astray.
Then Moses look'd up—"Sir, we've done," cried Amen;
The Priest, half awake, replied, "Fill it agen."

Nov. 15, 1794

Poems: Chiefly Tales

A sermon

ON THE ENORMOUS HEAD-DRESS OF THE LADIES IN 1777

Of all the gay fashions the Ladies pursue,
We hold that the worst which keeps beauty from view;
For how can those charms strike the heart with surprize
Which ever continue eclips'd from the eyes:
Then surely the hat must be out of its place
Which skips from the crown, and which creeps down the face;
While the top, like a sun-dial, points to the star,
The bottom's descending twelve inches too far.

If a lover should find himself smitten within,
It *can* be from no other part but her chin.
She gives up a beautiful face, it is said,
That she may deck out the back part of her head;
And hides all the charms of her eyes and her face
To shew fifteen ribbons, with flounces and lace.
'Tis Nature inverted, for ne'er was the back,
Instead of the fore-part, design'd to attack.
Bright guineas, bright eyes, and bright di'monds, we own,
Are useless in darkness, but sterling when shewn.

With pads and with rollers, and cushions plac'd o'er,
Her head becomes just twice as tall as before.
Like two-headed Monsters shall ladies appear!
And baldly attack us with tier over tier.
Whene'er we attempt the fair charmers to view,
We're pleas'd with one head, but disgusted with two.

At *Melbourn,* a Methodist preacher, we find,
Held forth, quite regardless of North or East wind;
For when we've determin'd a scheme to compleat,
We seldom resign it for cold or for heat.

Our intrepid champion, elate with success,
Made this bold remark on the ladies head-dress:

"The pride of our females all bound'ry exceeds;
'Tis now quite the fashion to wear double heads.
Approaching this town to disburse heav'nly treasure,
I pass'd by a head that would fill a strike measure.
If I'd had that measure but close by my side,
I certainly should the experiment tried.

By sins a man's said to be cover'd all o'er,
With bruises, and many a putrefied sore;
From the sole of his foot to his crown they aspire,
But the sins of a woman rise half a yard higher."

Nov. 16, 1794

Poems: Chiefly Tales

The jack daw

When gardens with foul weeds are planted,
The cultivating hand is wanted.

A numerous troop I lead along
Of actors, to adorn my song.
Renown'd for wisdom, yet they fall;
A Jack Daw holds the most of all.

'Tis needful we should understand
That infant minds come pure to hand:
Elastic too, for they'll receive
Impressions which you chuse to give;
Then to the tutor must belong
To lead them right or lead them wrong.
If errors should be planted there,
In spite of reason they'll appear.
The seeds once sown will come about;
Philosophy can't root them out.
Like the pock-marks upon your face,
Old Time can mend, but not erase.

Let nurses then but guide your son,
And from that moment he's undone;
For then the child a bias takes
In error, which he ne'er forsakes.
Nor must we only nurses note
Who wear the cap and petticoat.
But there are nurses, we declare,
Who empty heads and breeches wear.
Nay, there are nurses of renown
Exalted in a band and gown.

Whate'er untruth the tutor speaks
The harmless child for *real* takes.
Hence similies and metaphors

Are quite unfit for childish ears.
Fable and figure, though they shine,
The child should never read a line;
But quite through infancy to youth
Be treated with the simplest truth;
And then you'll certainly discern
He'll have but little to unlearn.

But when the tutor, or his charge,
Not one idea can enlarge,
His thoughts lie dormant in the rough;
His words are common senseless stuff,
Conveying sayings o'er and o'er
Repeated many an age before.
His utmost erudition lies
Among Poor Robin's Prophecies.
Believes all myst'ries to a tittle;
Thinks they, ten thousand, are too little.
For numbers give, when large they're grown,
More food for faith to feed upon.
When first he's with a new moon struck,
Makes a large mark to mend his luck—
"Some mighty trouble sure is nigh
Armies are fighting in the sky.
To kill our pig's exceeding vain,
Just while the moon is in her wane.
Hark! sure I hear the ravens sound!
I'll cross my fortune on the ground,
A pimple on my tongue descry,
My mother thinks I told a lie."

When heads with such like trash abound,
Tutor and pupil are unsound.
If reason from the man be chac'd,
No wonder that his mind's debas'd;
And, like a butcher's swilling tub,
Holds offals well, but nothing good;

But makes, if we to Burke allude,
Part of his "Swinish Multitude."

Ere you attempt a task so mild,
To lead the judgment of a child,
And place it in the truest light,
Take special care your own is right;
You'll then be to the race a friend,
And lead them to a noble end.

A genius brighter than a dunce
May follow up two trades at once;
For mending shoes, and teaching school,
Are seldom follow'd by a fool:
Two occupations here we find,
One props the body—one, the mind.

A Cobler liv'd—to tell I'm loth,
Who, with some credit, follow'd both.
He bent his back, he bent his leather,
To keep folks dry-shod in wet weather.

Nor were these two professions all;
He knew the science medical.
By application, from his youth,
Could, with his pincers, draw a tooth.
With his broad awl could breathe a vein;
Nor coat nor character would stain;
The blueish channel swell with ease,
And turn the tide which way you please:
Thus he *three* trades could carry on,
And only use the tools of one.

Of truth we shall observe strict rule,
And give a list of all his school.
The scholars did not much abound;
In his whole school but *one* was found—
A plient *Jack Daw,* large and able,

Rear'd up to manhood from the cradle,
Were all the pupils you'd discern,
And all the Cobler had to learn.
Jack danc'd about him all day long;
And from him learn'd the English tongue.
Though read he could not, nor indite,
Yet this we hold exactly right.
'Tis like our petticoats, who teach
To petticoats, three halfpence each.
Importance swells a little bit
When people as *directors* sit;
Though 'tis not easy to discern
Which ought to *teach,* but which to learn.

In one great point they both succeed;
Master and scholar well agreed:
The only instance, take my word,
You'll ever find upon record:
For half our modern education
Consists of quarrels and vexation.
The Cobler never, which is odd,
Infus'd his knowledge with a rod.
He knew at which end to begin
To plant the sprig of learning in;
Which, if you through our schools should go,
Is more than half the tutors know.

Our Daw pronounc'd, without a stammer,
Or either dictionary or grammar.
He learn'd to swear, with all the flow
And graces of a modern beau;
But o'er this reprobating band
He had, by far, the upper hand.
As he for sins could not atone,
His oaths were not worth setting down:
'Tis needless to throw time away
After the man who'll never pay.
But beauish oaths are all concenter'd,

And fairly in Fate's ledger enter'd,
Balance brought, divines will say,
And reckon'd for another day.

From monosyllables he rose
'Till he pronounc'd in verse and prose.
Some thought he'd up to Pindus climb,
For he was known to deal in rhime.
Nor should they wonder if he took
His pen in hand to write a book;
Which probably the world would please
As much as that great bard J. T's.

They don't pretend he would surpass
The merits of our Hudibras;
Whose beauties he could ne'er attain,
But from his faults he might abstain.
Nor do they mean our *Daw* to lift
So high in honour as Dean Swift;
Who, as a humourist, will reach
In Fame's fair temple the first nich.
Let me, illustrious shade! abide
A willing vot'ry by thy side!
Enjoy the singular renown
Of binding laurels on thy crown.

What man can call that boy a fool,
Who holds the highest place in school?
This was the case with our Jack Daw,
Who not a soul above him saw.
An orator! and so compleat,
Might hold a senatorial seat!
Would represent, you'd eas'ly tell,
A Jack Daw borough pretty well;
For *I* and *no,* from day to day,
Is all his honour has to say.
He need not act, nor even think,
But vote just as he's tipt the wink.

What minister would not make trial
Of one so supple and so loyal?
Besides, he'd be, it may be noted,
The cheapest vote that ever voted.
He'd follow what his leader said,
Just for a little milk and bread;
Nor had he, like the selfish tribe,
A pocket that would hold a bribe.
What minister need fear disaster,
When hand and glove are he and master?'
Then Fox's, Sheridans, and Greys,
May take their hats and go their ways,
For fear the Jack Daw nest shall rout them;
The minister can do without them.

Jack now a single word threw out,
And then whole sentences would spout
For if the child would not lie still,
"I'll take the Joe, by G—I will."
If an old woman chanc'd t'appear,
He'd call her bawd with easy air;
And if a young one came, what's more,
Then issued forth two words—"Thou whore."
'Twas taken for a merry joke
By all but her to whom 'twas spoke.

If we his conversation view,
His greatest fault was telling true;
For from his beak more truths would fall
Than you'd find in Westminster Hall.

Most serious things he turn'd to jokes;
A power beyond us two-legg'd folks.
A reputation he'd cut up
With all the ease you'd sit and sup.
Destroy the honour of a lass,
As soon as you could drink a glass.

What profit could a Proctor draw?
Our hero was above the law.

THE SECOND PART

Be not o'erwhelm'd with deep surprize,
Though you should see the Jack Daw rise.
Assail'd by Heaven and Earth around,
He keeps his throne, he spurns the ground.

The Cobler chanc'd to take his work in;
The Jack Daw after him was lurking;
Where, sorely frighten'd, as a stranger,
Hopp'd in the parlour, out of danger;
Though odd it seems, yet strictly true it be,
Mounted the chimney for security.
The Cobler sees not this, nor feels;
He minded neither soles nor heels;
For, cash receiving, home he went:
Receiving gives the mind content.

The Jack Daw mourn'd, he'd lost his master;
The Cobler mourn'd the same disaster.
'Tis far more easy, we pretend,
To *lose,* than 'tis to *gain* a friend.
Yet the first case, we still maintain,
Gives, of the two, the greatest pain.
Nor is life worth a pebble-stone,
If we live 'till our friends are gone.

The chimney now produc'd a noise,
Which gave the family surprize;
Gave every hair compleat erection,
And every spirit much dejection.
All struck with fear, both man and woman,
"They heard a voice which was not human!"

A serious consultation's held
"Good lack! what has the chimney fill'd?"
But no decision e'er belongs
When judgments various are as tongues.
Like other long disputes, it therefore
Ended at last in why and wherefore;
'Till one important point came on—
"For really something must be done."
The chimney-sweeper, all agree,
Shall climb the dismal road, and see.

We now behold the man in black
Determin'd on the bold attack;
Who stoutly told the people there,
That he himself was void of fear.
If others won't our powers make known,
'Tis needful we should praise our own.
While they express'd joy unexpected,
And smil'd at being well protected.

The brave defender now unbound,
And threw his garments on the ground.
Half garments, we should fancy, rather
Which just half screen'd him from the weather,

His knees began to quake all o'er;
His hands and fingers rather more;
With some few signs of fear beside,
Which he did all he could to hide.
Yet, howe'er for the task unfit,
He'd gone too far t'admit retreat.

While all were anxious, and all fear'd,
A horrid voice within was heard—
"Thou dismal varlet, most impure,
I tell thee I'll have thee for sure."

A frighten'd aspect you might trace
In every line of every face;
But the bold chimney-sweeper stood
Like man of stone, or block of wood.
Perhaps you'll disbelieve my tale,
If I should say his face look'd pale.
No, all the ghosts that walk'd by night
Could not convey one jot of white;
But you might see with some surprize,
Astonishment in his two eyes.
One solemn wish he had to spare—
"That he had never enter'd there;
But left the spirit, and the rout,
With kicks and cuffs to deal it out.
Some imp was lodg'd in evil hour
Beyond the chimney-sweeper's power."

THE THIRD PART

When one tool we can't work withall,
We boldly for another call.
For *one* a preference may lack
Although they both appear in black.

Like travellers we've rov'd about,
But find ourselves where we set out;
Nay, some may think, since we begun,
We've lost a little more than won;
Yet, like a gamester, ere we go,
Court Fortune in another throw.

What family can eat or sleep
When Satan shall the chimney keep,
An inlet, open to the air,
Which they can neither bolt or bar?
Deplorable must be their case;
He'd got the upper porter's place.
What house would not be full of fear,

When he shall act the overseer?
He'll hear and see what's said and done;
A score of sins will be chalk'd on.
Much rather they'd a robber see
Who lock'd them in and took the key.

A second consultation's held—
"O dear, what has the chimney fill'd!"
And *how* it emptied may become—
But the grand question was—by whom.

"The Parson is, they all agree,
The only one to set them free.
Let spirit or let devil come,
He holds them fast beneath his thumb;
For when the Priest a prayer has said,
A spirit dares not lift its head.
He is the man who keeps the key
To lock them up in the Red Sea;
For long or short can hold them there
To starve on salt-fish round the year.
With *leave* may Pharaoh's host pursue,
And see the king his trops review.

Now dress'd, as on a Sunday dress'd,
The Master visited the Priest;
With heaving sighs made this confession—
"My chimney Satan's got possession;
And now my house, by such a foe,
Will grow as hot as his below.
Pray, Sir, the hostile spirit lay;
Or, rather, send him off to sea."

The Priest look'd dull, but did not speak;
He'd rather heard a tithe-pig squeak.
For where's the parson, tell me, pray,
Who'd Satan meet before his day?
He rather would the work forsake;

But saw his credit was at stake;
And told the Master, with a sigh,
"He'd wait upon him by and by."

As he ne'er laid, in all his life,
A *sprite,* not even of his wife,
He might, if he a wrong step made,
Be thought defective in his trade;
He ought, ere he began to rout it,
See what great authors said about it;
For, in divinity, are folks
Much like our *Blackstones, Hales,* and *Cokes.*
If he a president could find,
'Twould guide his tongue and ease his mind.
This plan, when he came to review it,
Gave him a spirit to go through it.

He turn'd a dozen volumes o'er;
Consulted *Lilly, Glanville, More.*
Among the authors on the spot,
Sands, the great *Sands,* was not forgot.
Then *Demonology* produced,
The sov'reign work of James the First;
Who, perfectly, from genius known,
Knew every world—except his own.
Deep *Culpepper* now left his station,
To add his mite of information.
Not one astrologer was idle;
All were less dusty than his Bible.

Howe'er, he took the Bible next;
He'd not renounce the sacred text;
For, if the scriptures he seem'd wise in,
He might facilitate his rising;
And, as he'd be their staunch defender,
Consulted Saul and Witch of Endor,
To learn what power old madam had
To raise a spirit from the dead.

For that same power his hopes would crown,
What rais'd one up would lay one down.

That he the surer might divine
He drew an astrologic sign.
While working up the figures clear,
His mind was toss'd by hope and fear;
Finding the aspects rather mild,
The planets and the parson smil'd;
Then clos'd the book, put on his gown,
And march'd to pull Old Satan down.

When you are sick, and keep your room,
You're glad to see the Doctor come;
Or, if your coat be stol'n, you'll grant
The taylor is the man you want—
So far'd it with the people frighted;
To see the Doctor were delighted:
And this appear'd the only sight
In which he ever gave delight.

How much he drank, and relish'd well,
The Muse will not presume to tell;
For Parsons have peculiar skill
To make the corks fly when they will:
Besides, 'twas thought another sup
Would tend to keep his spirits up;
For, if the devil would destroy him,
He should have every prop that's nigh him.

The Priest, with solemn words, prepare
To send Old Nick into the air;
For, upon second thoughts, 'twas found
The air was safer than the ground;
But when he bent his knee to stoop,
And his first course of prayers send up,
A voice was utter'd which seem'd odd—
"Vile sinner, I'll have thee by G—."

Horror the parson did not lack,
Which made him instantly start back;
But left him master of one word,
Which he repeated once—"O Lord;"
With a deep sigh fix'd at the end on't
Blasting the word to which't hung pendant;
You'd think him, he so hugg'd his tripes,
Sorely afflicted with the gripes.
No thief, who in the fact was took;
Nor school-boy when he blotch'd his book;
Nor Molly when she sing'd her cap;
Nor Tom when he perceiv'd the clap;
Nor sailor when his hands are tied,
Stripp'd buff, and feels the cat applied;
Nor Lucy when she daub'd her stocking,
Did ever shew a look more shocking.
Saving a whiteness in the face,
He'd ta'en the chimney-sweeper's face.
"Save and except" one trifle more—
The smell was stronger than before.

THE FOURTH PART

Of moral life we'll take a view;
A scene of tender love pursue;
And as there variations be,
Perhaps we may a quarrel see.

Can man pursue a proper way
When those who lead him go astray?
And yet the fault's not solely his,
Who was in childhood led amiss.
Teachers themselves have been deceiv'd;
They can but pay what they receiv'd;
For sterling knowledge through the nation
Is charg'd with base adulteration.
So on for generations long
Our education has been wrong.

Such learning that's not worth a groat
For many ages has been taught.
With idle falshoods men run wild;
With idle falshoods fill the child.

Before three suns were rose and set,
Our Jack Daw crept in the Gazette.
O! not a bankrupt was he found
To pay three shillings in the pound,
Nor one of modern fashion seen
To spend or pocket seventeen.
Then tell the world, with drooping chin,
"A down-right honest man he's been."
Then urge his friends both soon and late
Till he gets his certificate.
Then utter forth this genteel speech—
"My creditors may kiss my—.
By law I take another's store;
I'll tread the steps I trod before.
To humble his, and raise my pride,
He'll walk on foot, while I shall ride."

Neither like one, whose filthy face,
Is white-wash'd with an Act of Grace.
The creditor is basely trick'd,
His hands are tied, his pocket pick'd.
Which is the worst, can it be said,
The white-washer or white-washed?

No, Jack appearing far more right
Was treated in a fairer light.
A greater honour far he shar'd;
For he with Satan was compar'd;
Who, from the time the world began,
Was never known to rob a man;
Nor turn the spit, nor boil'd the pot,
With property another'd got;
Nor, as a spunge, determin'd yet

A statute should rub out the debt.
Then ar'n't I, Sir, if I grow fat on
Another's labour, worse than Satan?

It there was said, and not in jest,
"The devil such a house possess'd;
And that the people made a rout;
Nor could the *Parson* drive him out."

The Cobler saw the news retain it;
Was silent, though he could explain it.
He issued forth in utmost haste
To have his dearest friend releas'd.

"Sir, I'm inform'd your house is haunted;
This devil I attack undaunted.
Let me, Sir, but the chimney see,
I'll lay the spirit, or he me."

The master stood with features down,
And heard him rather with a frown,
The door was open'd, in he fled;
The master car'd not what he said;
Was there shut up by way of ending;
They never thought him worth attending.

"Jack, Jack," he cried. That well-known sound
Brought Jack that moment to the ground.
Who can describe the joys compleat
When two lost friends together meet?
Of all the social pleasures given,
This surely comes the nearest heaven.
They met, but not like love and lover,
Who, for whole evenings, bill and slaver.
The Cobler, which is all you'd seen,
His pocket open'd, Jack hopp'd in;
Welcom'd that cupboard where he'd fed,
Full many a time, on crumbs of bread.

The door set wide then out he run,
Smiling just like a man that's won
"The spirit, Sir, which used to vex you,
"I've laid—It will no more perplex you."

The husband sullen, you might view,
Firmly believing all untrue,
Wrinkled his nose, and look'd ascance;
The Cobler was not worth a glance.
The wife then gave her head a flirt;
For wives, sometimes, are rather pert—
"I tell you, Cobler, we've had two
Already, better men than you."

The Cobler, much amus'd to meet
For favours granted such a treat,
Directly mov'd his hand an inch,
And gave the Jack Daw's foot a pinch;
When instantly was heard to roar
A voice the spirit used before,

"Thou impudent whore,
Thou shalt have a rod;
I'll have thee for sure;
I'll take thee by G—."

Their faces of a whitish hue
Directly turn'd a little blue.
They now began to raise a riot
"The Cobler's treatment gave no quiet:
For their accumulate vexations
Proceeded from his machinations."
She us'd a tongue which never fails,
And was prepar'd to use her nails.
"He was th' offender, all decide—
The voice came forth from *his* inside.
His conjurations should not save him;
Before the justice they would have him.

As evidence against him there
The injur'd Parson should appear.
Though *one* he 'd conquer'd, yet, at last,
They'd found a third would set him fast."
And coinciding with our plan,
Young Misses lisp'd out "naughty man!"
Nay, were a *parrot* in the case,
He'd meet the Jack Daw face to face.
But here it may with truth be said,
He'd but a paltry figure made;
For how would ign'rant *Poll* come off
With Jack as learn'd as College Soph?

THE FIFTH PART

We've tried one black, we've tried his brother;
Have patience, Friend, we'll try another:
Though not so dark, he holds, 'tis true,
Just as much wisdom as the two.

O glorious laws! in which abound
Blessings which no where else are found.
In thy great vortex we can see
More *grace* than in divinity;
Faith, Hope, and Charity in store;
With half a dozen graces more.
Repentance and Humility,
Among the rest, belong to thee:
But, as to Love, which sweetly sounds,
We cannot say it much abounds.

If you should chance to have dispute
The next thing is, commence a suit.
You'll be delighted to begin;
For, being right, are sure to win.
And who can tell the joys which rest,
Except the winner, in his breast?

Now lively Faith takes her firm stand,
And Hope and she go hand in hand.
Sir, if you're worth ten thousand pound,
Your Charity will much abound:
To feed the hungry is one grace;
And lawyers are a hungry race.
Whether attack'd, or you attack,
You'll feel a mind upon the rack;
Whether you throw, or are o'erthrown,
Perhaps you'll find yourself undone.
Your pocket you may turn at will,
And find that pocket empty still.
You'll shun your lawyer's frowning looks
Because he had not cross'd his books.
And here again; what blessings wait
Upon the poor in their fall'n state.
An empty pocket, you may see,
Quickly draw forth Humility.
Thus law, before we've had a full-bit,
Brings more Repentance than the pulpit.

Two ships, by grappling-irons tied,
Fight on, till vict'ry decide;
So our contenders fight most true,
Grappled till Law divides the two.

The Cobler now, by high commands,
Before an awful Justice stands,
Who fill'd a chair quite full, you'd see,
With just as many arms as he.
His eye-sight *he* thought clear enough
To see a cause through, four yards off.
But some most wickedly suppose
He could not see beyond his nose;
And yet his sight might not be near,
Because his nose projected far:
That noble out-guard held its place
The grandest feature in his face,

Which hover'd over many a feast,
And was—two handfuls say, at least.

His deep-sunk eyes were rather blearish,
Which caus'd a look a little quearish;
And yet when eyes a fluid's urging,
It only shews "the drink is spurging."

In hills and dales his face was parted,
For here and there a ruby started.
His cheeks were puff'd beneath his cap
Like the four winds in your old map.

Whate'er his body was denied
In height, in thickness was supplied.
The servant girl, 'twas shrewsdly said,
Thought on him when she dumplings made;
Nor could she find, she'd often tell,
A pattern that would suit as well.
Nature and she, 'twas plain enough,
Compleatly rounded up their stuff;
And though his worship was the lofty'st,
They both were rather with the softest.

The chair's two arms his sides press sore
Swelling the promnence before;
So that an Irishman might say
"He'd stand the highest when he lay."

The moisture, snuff, and mucus rather,
Perfectly harmoniz'd together,
The swellings of his breast expose
The treasures falling from his nose;
So that whate'er the nose might cost
The breast resolv'd should not be lost;
Which made appearance rather drollish,
And, like a breast-plate, bore a polish

He took no nap, but after dining;
From many a tankard drew the lining;
And by a slight, to him long known,
With dextrous hand improv'd his own.

Plac'd in his magisterial chair,
Though short, the greatest personage there,
And rolling round his eyes to see—
"Where is the culprit? Bring him me.
A drunken Cobler I'm to view.
Which is this powerful conjurer? You—
Eh—
There's not a day in which you fail
To try the potentcy of ale."

"Your worship I may follow up,
Provided I don't touch your cup."

"Of all the tankard, the last drop
You chiefly long for."—"No, the top,"

"I'd told a Cobler you appear."

"I'm not the only Cobler here."

"Make your confession full and free,
Then you'll much goodness find in me."

"Your worship I allow as much,
If multitude of flesh be such."

"Anan!
From what place, Cobler, do you come?
I'll have an instant answer,"—"Home."

"And when abroad, what business then
Do you pursue?"—"Go home agen."

"You with the devil deal, I'm told."
"I never heard he leather sold."

"Well, but you've some connection though."

"We deal in soles, but not in Co."

"You must, like him, bemuch to blame,
If your pursuits are found the same."

"His trade is mischief, when he can;
But mine's the great support of man."

"You're charg'd with acting much amiss.
Are you concern'd with spirits?"—"Yes."

"What place in chimneys do you lot 'em;
The top or middle?"—"No, the bottom."

"Where do they rest when they don't pass
In seas or church-yards?"—"No, in glass,
In a dark cave, with fasten'd door,
I keep them safe 'till supper's o'er;
And when all's still, at my desire,
They issue forth in smoke and fire."

"Then, I suppose, you force them out,
Whenever they appear?"—"No doubt."

"But they, before they take their flight,
Remain some time within you?"—"Right."

"And, when they leave you, do they fall?"

"They fiercely fly against a wall."

"Will they return, as heretofore,
To serve you?"—"No, I order more."

"Which haunt your neighbours when in bed,
In houses, chimneys, eh?" — "Your head."

"Ha, ha, ha!
Well, Cobler, you may travel hence;
You've made a pretty good defence."
The Cobler bow'd, but did not speak;
Then gave the Jack Daw's foot a tweak.
The same voice spoke which spoke before—
"Vile sinner, I'll have thee for sure."

Now sides were chang'd; the prisoner eas'd,
The justice was with horror seiz'd.
His head and shoulders would have reel'd,
Only the chair before was fill'd.
The scarlet hue declin'd apace;
A few old sins flash'd in his face;
And *some* of an enormous kind
Made bold to step into his mind.
A stander-by might eas'ly scan
A fluid from his breeches ran;
But this he did not wish were known
Because it *tallied* with his own.

The Cobler smil'd at Justice Quorum—

"I'll raise the spirit now before 'em;"
And instantly, full in their view,
The Jack Daw from his pocket drew.

Jack and the Justice both were pleas'd,
Because they found themselves released.
Jack, perching on his master's hand,
The Cobler, at full length, harangued—

"Can reasoning man be so absurd
To tremble at a harmless bird?
Nature inverted here we view;

'Tis he, should run away from *you*.
Man musters eager, and maintains
A troop of horrors in his brains;
And, not contented with the store,
Is ever gaping after more.
His spungy faith, replete with fear,
Imbibes the dirty moisture near.
In *cards, palm-lines* and *coffee-ground,*
His future destiny is found.
To tell, and then explain the dream,
Becomes, at tea, the morning theme.
In omens spends the day, and then
At night begins to dream agen.
Can we, with all this faith, engage
To call our own 'a faithless age.'

In prophecies believes of men
Whose utmost skill is counting ten!
A prophecy is seldom found
To rear its head on barren ground:
Let ignorance then in silence pass;
True prophets are a higher class.
The man with a judicious eye,
Who *times* observes, can prophecy;
Eas'ly the future can divine,
And hit the mark eight times in nine.

Man, reasoning man has lost his place;
The only dupe o every race.
This learned bird I left behind
Has shewn the follies of mankind:
Bold follies, which the mind debase,
And practis'd by o other race.
Yet he claims reason for his guide,
Which he denies to all beside.
Te fairy, trance, the witch, the gobbling,
Those hads, ill-taught, are sure to hobble in.
Creatures which creep beneath his view

Believe exactly what is true.
The only animal he is
Who exercises prejudice.
His faith, luxuriantly, will thrive,
And well bear pruning four in five.

To miracles he gives applause,
Without consid'ring Nature's laws;
Who her own steady work observes,
A course from which she never swerves;
But always with herself agrees,
Nor tries impossibilities.
Did ever *Sol* neglect the day,
Or *whale* trot on a turnpike way?
Did e'er stand still the heav'nly host?
Or the North Star desert his post?
Did water e'er run up the hill?
Or ever lamb the mastiff kill?
When these shall happen, Nature's gone,
And days of miracle come on.

Yet some few instances we quote,
Wherein we must relax our note.
Though miracles do not abound,
We know, by chance, one may be found;
Such as a Courtier so absurd
As now and then to keep his word;
Or Priest who humble would remain,
And loves his people more than gain;
Or honesty in Law appears;
Or a recruit who never swears;
Or tradesman who'd not tell a lie
Although it throws his profit by;
Or fair one twenty months a bride
Who never wish'd the knot untied;
Or heir at law who yet abhors
To wrong his father's creditors;
Thinks it unjust himself to serve,

And sells th' estate without reserve;
Or priest, from holy resolution,
Firmly detests all persecution.

Such are the miracles, we know,
Which private and which seldom grow.
Mighty enormities appear
From love of min'stry, and from fear.
If we look back we find two things,
An error, and from whence it springs;
And these are wont to gain admission
Through an erroneous tuition.

The evil's pointed out most sure;
My Jack Daw will point out the cure;
Perhaps improve by ardent study
Some heads which are a little muddy;
And if he can the fountain cure,
The running stream will then be pure.

Who should correct, attempt at least,
To guide, so ably, as the priest?
If his bright beam upon us pours,
It instantly will kindle ours.
But he's as dark as is the other—
Can one dark lanthorn light another?

When sheep shall rove, the shepherd may
A shepherd want, as much as they;
As he who preaches still appears
As foul within as he who hears,
How can a stream be better made
By mixing with a stream as bad?
Or if the blind shall lead the blind—
You know what follows close behind.

My learned Daw, with his advice,
Shall mount the pulpit in a trice

On Sunday next; he thinks it best,
Before the scabby flock are dress'd,
Whisper the Priest who hunts for pelf—
Hark ye, physician—heal thyself."

Feb. 11, 1795

The jealous head

That man is daily prick'd with thorns
Who makes imaginary horns.

If you follow Reason's sway,
You'll be happy while you may;
But you will, if her you spurn,
Want her when she'll not return.

Most happy is that husband's life
Who sees no errors in his wife.
The social hours glide gently on
When all is right that's said and done;
A spring of bliss; and 'tis confess'd
The fountain lies within his breast;
And this we hold the happiest state
That ever is indulg'd by Fate.
What husband would not wish to find
The benefits of being blind?

Not quite so happy is his share
Who sees her errors as they are;
Sometimes a silken chain he finds;
Delightful seems, and gently binds:
'Tis iron now, and heavy found;
Can hardly raise it from the ground:
'Tis roughly form'd, and, what is more,
The galling jags have made him sore.
Have patience, friend, it won't remain,
'Twill by and by be silk again.

The great majority must pass
Of married people in this class.
A state too bad to be respected;
A state too good to be rejected.

Another class to view we'll call,
The most deplorable of all;
The husband, with malicious eye,
Can ev'ry trifling error spy;
Nay, that same eye, involv'd in mist,
Sees faults which never did exist;
Feels on his brow the antlers start,
Which grow from his corrupted heart;
And every horror round him haults
Attendant upon real faults;
To make him most compleatly curst
Ideas fix'd upon the worst.
No bliss his jealous thoughts retain;
The best of wives becomes a bane.

We'll now begin our short harangue
On this last case our tale shall hang.
Your pardon, should a slip be found;
We'll lightly tread, 'tis dangerous ground.
We'd rather not offend the ear
Of vulgar, or the chastest fair.

George Baggarly shall now be shewn;
We'll give this name, for 'twas his own.
A village taylor he'll appear,
Who drove the thread in Leicestershire:
At *Groby* he might be found out;
Or in the villages about.
From one town to another wander'd,
Just as he found his business squander'd;
On Monday morning left his bed
Soon as *Aurora* put on red.

His tackle muster'd, out he set;
Good-morrow bid to all he met.
You'd know, the moment he appears,
His errand, by his goose and sheers.

In jovial mood he cross'd the stile:
His whistle sounded half a mile.

His work began with so much glee
His needle travell'd more than he.
With making, mending many a robe,
Us'd thread enough to band a globe.

Needle and thread laid by at night;
Three meals and sixpence were his right.
Lab'ring to Saturday from Monday,
He dress'd the village spruce for Sunday.

No other job could now remain,
Only to whistle home again.
But whistling *solus* would not do,
For now the song was added too.
You'd think he might for silence seek,
After the toil of one whole week.
But he'd, if I the truth must say,
Three cogent reasons to be gay.
On roast and boil'd he supp'd and din'd—
Three shillings bright his pocket lin'd.
Lastly, he's on the eve of text-day,
Sure of a holyday the next day.

What man would not rejoice to see
Himself in such prosperity?
Could he one little play-thing meet,
'Twould make his happiness compleat.
If bless'd but with a lovely bride,
He'd set at nought the world beside.

THE SECOND PART

But if love shou'd seize your breast,
Jealousy may break your rest.

Dear friend, by the first part you'll know,
We're not contented here below;
For, let the Fates give what they will,
There's always something wanting still.

George eyed the girls; he dress'd up prim;
Nay, even the girls would smile at him.
The man who o'er twelve towns can trample
Is sure to have a choice most ample.

The giddy tribe he much avoided,
But fix'd his heart as prudence guided:
Nay, in his choice, we freely own,
His judgment most conspicuous shone.

Much beauty did his bride inherit;
Which was her smallest part of merit.
Her virtuous heart surpass'd her face,
Just as the jewel does the case;
Full in her aspect you'd discry
Good-nature, chiefly in her eye.
Her conduct was as chaste as day;
Scandal had not a word to say;
And her deportment all along
I think an honour to my song.

But gloomy thoughts attack'd him soon—
Oh! not till chang'd the honey-moon.
That will the gayest season prove
The very harvest-moon of love.

No more he whistled o'er the leas,
But cherish'd thoughts which only teaze;
No more he view'd the objects round,
But kept his eye upon the ground;
And if by chance a man he met,
He started up as if beset;

But still kept poring on his way,
Without good-morrow or good-day.

"How shall I *Dolly* leave?" he thought,
"In many a trap she may be caught!
Though round her all the virtues throng,
Those virtues can't continue long;
For human nature tempts to sin
A tempter always lurks *within.*
Then, *man,* survey the world about;
Ten thousand tempters lie without.
Beauty's unguarded when alone:
Business demands I must be gone.
When golden apples strike the eye,
They 'tice the man who passes by;
And if no guardian hand is shewn,
He'll quickly make the prize his own."

Had George, ye Sophs, committed sin?
No! yet he found a hell within;
The flames of which attack'd his wife,
And sing'd her happiness for life.

"An ample cure must be divin'd,
To save his wife, and ease his mind.
He told his Dolly, with a groan,
Her case was bad, but worse his own.
She stood upon a dreadful brink;
Without a remedy would sink;
And must a little pain endure,
To make her perfectly secure.
One gentle operation o'er,
Your honour's safe—*I'm* plagued no more.
His needle, well applied, would cure
Those pangs which he could not endure.
He could, and not a stich would miss,
Close up the avenue of bliss."

She heard the sentence with surprize;
The tears descending from her eyes.
Her injur'd cause she durst not plead;
'Twould raise suspicion from the dead;
And if once rais'd she was afraid
It never after would be laid.
For jealousy's a foul inmate
When once it gets into the pate.
She, half submissive, hung her head,
And half reluctantly obey'd.

He quickly brought a part to light
Which never should appear in sight;
And made a dozen wounds or more
Where not a wound was made before;
So firmly did his business there,
That water-proof he left the fair.

His gloom now fled, his peace restor'd,
Resum'd again his goose and board;
And, with a smile, to'ards work he bent;
Could almost whistle as he went;
View'd the gay fields as he were us'd,
And this soliloquy produc'd.

"It has been said, in days of yore,
When steed is stol'n, we shut the door;
But I, with ease, in lucky minute,
Secure the door and all within it.
A taylor, ninth of man, good Lord!
Himself despis'd, his goose, and board;
Yet he's the only man, we see,
Able to guard his property.
Others complain, but must endure it;
None but a taylor could secure it.
Taylors will shine in fame and sway,
And I'm the man who leads the way."

His joyous spirits rising soon,
He instantly struck up a tune:
But here we are oblig'd to tell,
As his notes rose, her spirits fell.

THE THIRD PART

When one Taylor must engage
Forces of united rage,
Justice, clerk, and Females all,
Wonder not if he should fall.

A running stream demands its course;
For if you stop it up by force,
The rising waters soon o'er-flow,
And danger bring where-e'er they go.
This happen'd to our injur'd fair,
Whose health was lost, and pleasing air.

The neighbouring wives around her press,
To bring assistance in distress,
Glad when they've nothing else to do;
For gossiping is always new.
Mighty inquisitive to know
How matters with their neighbour go.
But how could she explain her case;
And not divulge her own disgrace?
The less the injur'd fair confess'd,
The more to know the good wives press'd.

Our great divines, perhaps, are right—
"Whatever *must, will* come to light."
Nor could a sight surprize them more,
Than seam, where seam ne'er was before.
Their exclamations rose apace—

"His insults reach to all our race!"
Their voices rose till out of wind;
Nor did their threat'nings lag behind

"If he were here," they boldly said,
"With ladles they'd have broke his head.
He'd not trod this place, nor another,
If thus his father'd serv'd his mother.
A precedent we can't produce
Since fig-leaf aprons were in use.
No remedy at all we know;
Instantly fetch the doctor, go."

What surgeon, like a knight of old,
Would not rejoice when he was told,
He must his trusty lance prepare,
With hasty steps relieve the fair.

Advancing to the afflicted dame,
He found the dextrous taylor's seam;
Sew'd neater than a surgeon cou'd;
Sew'd firmer than a surgeon wou'd.

He cut one stitch, and then cut more—
The women threaten'd, grinn'd, and swore.
A picture of these female faces
Would far surpass great *Hogarth's* cases.
Susanna was as much provok'd
As when her puppy dog was choak'd;
Fair *Mrs. Trim* as boldly swore
As when the *Tinker* call'd her whore;
Bess look'd as black, for all the world
As when her teapot down was hurl'd;
And *Kitty* made just such a grin
As when she water drank for *gin*.

The wife reliev'd, the lancet shut,
The husband curs'd from head to foot.

The females sallied out to look him;
When caught, before the Justice took him.
His visage fall'n, his whistle broke,
Their clam'rous tongues against him spoke;
The fact was prov'd by numbers by;
Nor did the husband once deny.

His worship old, and nearly blind,
Had left the paths of love behind.
The tools which he could use no more
Might lie and rust upon the floor—
Told them "to fill a friendly cup,
And o'er it hush the matter up.
Assur'd them there'd be no applause
Even to those who won the cause;
For, if they drove at such a rate,
'Twould set the vilest tongues agate:
And when a dreadful flame runs high,
'Twill ruin bring before 'twill die;
Besides, this crime, though great it looks,
Is no where found in Statute Books:
How can it then so black appear,
If not describ'd or sentenc'd there?
I think we'd better let him go"—
Sukey, Bess, Mrs. Trim, "No, No!"

His clerk was neither quite so old,
Nor yet to love so very cold.
He understood, as he pass'd by,
The glances of an amorous eye;
Not only able to discern them,
But just to what extent return them;
And if he met a smiling dame,
Could well with her unite his flame.
He judg'd, should this a fashion prove,
There'd soon a famine be in love;
For, had we food, we must eschew it,
If we have never a mouth to chew it.

"A crime, Sir, of so deep a die
We should, on no account, pass by
But, if with this we now begin,
It will discourage men from sin.
The case, I think, but you best know,
Must under 'sault and batt'ry go."

"What, 'sault and batt'ry with a needle!
Your mittimus will be too feeble."

"Perhaps your worship will consent
To call it anti-ravishment."

"The law for *crimes* will punish sore,
But not for that which goes *before*."

"Your worship then, without more naming,
Under this word commits him—*maiming*."

"I think we'd better let him go."
The ladies cried out—"No, no, no!"

And now the altercation ceas'd;
O'er-power'd, his worship acquiesc'd.
Thus servants, with a growing pride,
Seem to submit, but *really* guide.
Justice is, as some men have Kings,
Held, by his clerk, in leading strings.

THE FOURTH PART

All his efforts are in vain;
Ruin follows with her train.

His mittimus was quickly made;
And George to Leicester gaol convey'd:
Secur'd within this black retreat
By jealousy, a clerk's deceit;

To which we add, by way of make-weight,
Some female rage, which carries great weight.
From this abode he can't recede
'Till Judge approach, and Counsel plead.
He'll know this by the trumpet's blast;
Nearly as dreadful as the *last*.

To that great hall he's summon'd now
Where Justice sits with awful brow;
And elevated in his place
Meets no face but a roguish face;
Where every soul who comes in view
Is seiz'd with fear and trembling too.
While one for pocket-picking's tried
Another picks one by his side;
Where lawyers golden showers discern;
Where clients hang the head and mourn;
Who pay that money as a fee
Often another's property.
Too deeply sunk the storm to weather
Must call their creditors together.
Where jurymen, not worth a groat,
Assume a rank—are great in thought;
And the spruce clerk, not apt to lag,
Struts forward with his gay green bag;
Seems to the bar-keeper to say
"This moment open; Sir, make way:"
Where crowds crush crowds, and never fail
To listen to a luscious tale;
Where sheriff, counsel, and their suit,
Know how to relish mellow fruit;
Where George must now a culprit stand,
Commanded to hold his hand.

Th' indictment wrought up without a flaw,
Held all the rhetoric of law;
And though the meaning was but blind,
We think you *words* enough might find;

For when they'd gallop'd on a while
Sense found herself behind a mile.
A waggon load of dross they hurl in,
But not an ounce of real sterling.
When over fifty lines you've gone,
You may comprize the sense in one:
Thus ships may travel on the sea,
And zig-zag make but little way.

"He, instigated by the Devil,
Malice aforethought—wrought an evil.
The culprit did this wicked thing
Against our Sov'reign Lord the King;
Against the Crown he set his face;
Against the statute in that case;
No fear of God—but when, and where,
With force and arms, did then and there,
A certain needle—in his wroth—Did—violently"—and so forth.

Our much immodest trial then
Only attended was by men;
For not a female came in view
Excepting Bess, Kate, Nell, and Sue;
Who, by authority, came nigh since,
Supœna'd, they possess'd a licence:
All other ladies absent were,
Who had not then a blush to spare.

While all to listen did not fail,
Th' unfolding of a curious tale;
And strong desire was on the itch,
Was strung up to the highest pitch.
George thought the scene should not enlarge,
Then pleaded guilty to the charge.

This prov'd to all a sore vexation,
In disappointing expectation.
They wish'd him punish'd at the time,

More for his *pleading* than his crime:
For who'd rejoice to take a seat
At a rich feast, yet must not eat.

This pleading made his Lordship silent;
Who seem'd to ponder there a while on't;
But this he thought was rather wrong,
For if a judge should ponder long,
If, when the sentence he should speak,
That very sentence was to seek,
He knew his credit would be falling,
As not being master of his calling;
For not a *case* in print or out
Could e'er be found to solve his doubt.

While fluctuating *pro* and *con*
Something must instantly be done—

"That twenty shillings George should pay-down;"
'Twas nineteen more than he could lay-down;
"And back to prison should be sent,
Sustain two years imprisonment."

Now female vengeance at him flies—
"Their nails shall tear out both his eyes.
In future shall in darkness dream,
Nor see to sew another seam."

What greater evil could attack;
A troop of females on his back!
He'd better all the laws engage
Than fall a prey to female rage.

We've told our tale; we've told it true;
Except an inference or two.
Much happiness the man betides
Who knows he's well, and there abides.

If he attempts to climb a wall,
His foot may slip, and cause a fall.

Let *Husbands* ne'er, for George's sake,
Wear horns but those of female make:
They fit best which your loving spouse
Silently places on your brows.
When she conducts them you'll look big;
She'll regulate them like your wig.

Nor *Taylors* boast superior skill
In driving needles where they will;
For if a living seam they sew,
In dreadful anguish lurks a foe,
Will punish all their errors past,
And cause that seam to be their last.

Let *Justices,* 'mong our remarks,
Use their own brains, and not their clerks:
For if the laws you can't dispense,
Then take your weak heads off the bench
Humbly submit to this disgrace,
To put your clerk's head in its place.

The lovely *Fair* come next in view;
They are the game I must pursue.
No—at a distance I shall stand;
I own they've far the upper hand.
No character my Muse assails;
I'd rather have their lips than nails.

If you the *laws* will take in hand,
You'll read the *most*—least understand.
Your journey's long, you may depend on't;
Never expect to reach the end on't.
You'll blunder, hurry, reel about,
And, after all, must give it out.

Lastly, to *Judges* we shall turn;
They're not so learn'd but they may learn.
Choice sentences they should lay by
For all occasions, cut and dry;
Then, if a cause come strait or cross;
You'll never find them at a loss.
Tell me, ye Sages of the nation,
Who bind by your determination,
How George, when he's to prison gone,
Could twenty shillings pay with one.

April 19, 1795.

Poems: Chiefly Tales

The happy family

If you, my Friend, should want an heir,
Your cellar search—you'll find one there.

A love sincere is, we confess,
The only source of happiness:
When man and wife attain this bliss,
Affairs will seldom go amiss.
But if fond love should take a flight,
How much goes wrong! how little right
Full often is the husband said
To cast an eye upon the maid;
Full often, when his passion burns,
He finds, from Betty, sweet returns;
Can wives excuse a case like this?
I'll give an answer for them—"Yes."
They surely will a pardon shew:
Don't take my word—read on, and know;

Bob Handford pass'd a single life
Three times seven years—then took a wife.
They liv'd, they lov'd, they slept, they woke,
Much in the stile of other folk.
Sometimes, indeed, she'd pat his cheek,
As if some favour she would seek:
Then he 'd look on her face awhile;
And, peradventure, raise a smile.
Perhaps a smile was all his store,
Because he seldom could raise more.

But pats and smiles with time declin'd,
And left some little frowns behind:
Cross words attended; sometimes jeers
Muster'd their force, 'gainst loves and dears
But frowns and jeers, we understand,
Had of the two the upper hand.

One disappointment more was said—
"No issue grac'd the marriage bed."
This sore defect will often prove
Attendant upon languid love;
Some altercation it procures—

"You know, my dear, the fault is yours."
"I beg your pardon, think agen;
You don't behave like other men."

"Nay, you must think, for 'pon my life,
Who'd bear with a defective wife?"

" No such defect can me betide—
Examine well the other side."
Thus, while they eloquence display,
Affection's argued quite away;
And in most cases, we may learn,
It never after will return.

The mind possesses, like a fashion,
A certain portion of each passion;
And, corresponding with our case,
Love, amongst others, holds a place;
This each signs over to their mate
When they commence the married state;
Then doubly happy, night and noon,
The pair who ne'er recall the boon;
The only case, our Muse maintains,
In which a man by *giving* gains.

But Robin's heart and tender care
Began to wander from the fair;
And as that soft abode resign'd
Must soon another lodging find;
For love and money, Sophists say,
Are rather apt to fly away;

And, like the waves upon the deep,
But seldom one position keep.

Our husband had a heart to let
It left the *mistress* — fix'd on Bet.
A small transition, it was said,
Only from Madam to her maid.

The girl that's slender, tall, and neat,
Completely turn'd from head to feet,
With features smiling to your view,
Tending to draw a smile from you;
Where red and white distinctly part,
Is rather apt to win the heart.
This was exactly Betty's case,
Whose manner pleas'd as well as face.
Nor did she ever *go* a wooing;
Her looks did all she wanted doing.

Now ev'ry art of Courtship's brought on;
Our loving wife is no more thought on;
Except it was in open day,
When she was rather in the way;
For lovers are in highest glee
In darkness, when no eye can see.

The whole artillery of a lover
Our turn-coat husband now play'd over;
As ogling, smiling, glancing, stand;
And, when he could, to squeeze the hand.
With circling arms above her hips,
His lips, with joy, assail'd her lips.
His busy hand, which could not rest,
By *accident* fell on her breast:
For lovers make a rapid way
When nothing does their progress stay.

Yet, from the moment he begun,
She was not easy to be won.
Some sparks of virtue took their rest
Within the precincts of her breast.

But if a house stands e'er so fast,
Assail'd by *time* must fall at last.
What *fort,* though guarded e'er so clever,
Can well sustain a siege for ever?
Bess seem'd to promise with her eyes
"She'd at discretion yield the prize."
Thus assiduity, no doubt,
Will win whate'er it sets about.

'Tis needful, in so nice a case,
To regulate both time and place;
To disappoint the watchful spies;
For jealous wives have keenish eyes—
"On Monday night's the time, no doubt,
For Mrs. Handford will be out;
When to the cellar we'll both flee,
Where none can come, and none can see."

Though daylight, as we said above,
May be no enemy to love,
Yet will, in that expos'd condition,
Exclude the lovers from fruition;
With joy they contemplate the theme,
And both applaud the well-laid scheme.

Bess all the pleasure now relinquish'd;
The virtuous sparks were not extinguish'd;
She told her mistress out of hand
What she and master just had plann'd.
They both determine, in short space,
The mistress shall supply her place.

The time was come which both had set;
The lovers in the cellar met;
Where all was safe and all was free;
Where all was love, and all was glee.

Though in the cellar raptures were,
Before the sun they shan't appear.
The bashful Muse shall draw the veil,
And not a syllable shall tell;
Only one circumstance remark,
Fairly extracted from the dark—
The joys effective center'd there,
Quickly produc'd a son and heir.

To haunt a cellar's thought a sin,
But Robert found the *best* within;
Perform'd a wonder on the floor,
A wonder he ne'er wrought before.
Though cellars are the place of bliss,
Yet none produc'd so much as this.

The parties ruminate a while,
Then treat th'adventure with a smile.
Of joy the husband had his share;
The proper person brought an heir:
The mistress found herself o'er-paid;
Excus'd the husband, bless'd the maid;
And Bess enjoy'd supreme delight,
She'd set a wand'ring husband right.

Let man and wife forbear to chide
'Till they've, like *Bob,* the cellar try'd.

May 29, 1795

The wager

PREFACE

This master preface, I indite,
Suits all I've written, or shall write.

When work is great, and powers are small
A verse-man may assistance call;
For every bard, from *Pope* to *Vickars,*
The Muses teaze whene'er he litters—

"What Muse, thinks he, will not make haste,
Her poet struggling, yet set fast?"

Let all Parnassus understand,
If rhyme should prove above my hand,
Like other bards who know their trade,
I then would ask the Muse's aid.
A boon I might for once implore;
She knows I never ask'd before.
Nay, should I try my powers in vain,
'Tis ten to one ne'er ask again:
However, as I'm not fast set,
Assistance is not wanted yet.

If thought should frozen up appear,
I might prefer the following prayer—

"Now, chaste Urania, heavenly muse,
Put on your buskins, or your shoes;
Adjust your handkerchief and gown
Tie fast your apron, and come down;
Lend me assistance to indite,
And be attentive while I write.
Let me perform my work so nice
That Johnny Smart may read it twice.

If I should scratch my head an hour,
Because no thought is in my power;
Culture the barren soil, and sow,
That here and there a rhyme may grow;
Or, which is valued rather more,
Supply me from your ample store:
For in your lap, Bards understand,
Are bundles ready made to hand;
Of measure, rhyme, and thought that wise is,
Like bakers tallies of all sizes.

If in a falshood I should trudge,
My elbow give a gentle nudge;
If that won't answer, give a frown,
And knock pen, ink, and paper down."

Now should I find th' ill-natur'd Muse
Her kind assistance shall refuse;
And 'tis most probable she will,
As follows, I would guide the quill.

Let me ne'er make a reader weep;
Nor ever let him fall asleep;
For human life brings *real* woe,
Which blasts our comforts here below;
And leaves no room, most sure we are,
For making artificial care;
And if he sleeps, 'tis my desire,
The book should tumble in the fire;
Then whatsoe'er I brood in rhyme
Will not offend a second time

The chearful tale, I do engage,
Wards off the spleen, disease, old age;
Bids blooming health keep on its way,
And bids the doctors go to play.

THE WAGER

When you're in danger, never doubt
A golden wager'll bring you out;
Nor entertain the smallest fear,
For Madam Fortune will be there.
Then, if you win, there's joy in store;
But, if you lose, there's ten times more.

The curtain's up-we'll *four* engage;
Ambrose and *Joe* first tread the stage;
Two batchelors—two seniors rather,
Who liv'd in harmony together
Agreed like brother and like brother,
Though one was plumper than the other.

For much good sense was *Ambrose* fam'd;
And much good-nature *Joseph* claim'd:
Whatever secrets of the heart
One had, the other took a part.
Neither commanded nor submitted,
But, like a pair of scales, were fitted.

They each possess'd, from mortgage clear,
About one hundred pounds a year;
And rather kept a frugal store;
No want appear'd, or wish for more;
And thus they held an even state,
Like gentlemen of second rate:
They walk'd on foot; they kept their word;
And well on Sunday serv'd the Lord.

Then on shrewd politics would sit
Under Lord Bute, Lord North, and Pitt;
While they one steady line maintain,
The year march'd round and round again.

Their family we've plac'd in view,
Consisting, in the whole, of two;
Except a servant maid, we'll say,
Who faithful serv'd them night and day.
There was indeed a handsome dog
Which answer'd to the name of Pug,
But, not being of the present train,
We'll never mention him again.

Most frequently they bought their meat
Of *John,* the butcher in Moore Street;
Who ne'er knew love, nor e'er knew spouse,
But kept a maiden and a house;
Could sleep himself alone; nay more—
Could leave his maid alone—to snore.
His back curv'd out, as might be seen;
His belly follow'd, and curv'd in
Was tall, though bent, but yet not old;
Was moulded in a coarseish mould.
With bulk his garments were not fill'd;
Was boney as the ox he kill'd.
His fat ware on the bench was laid;
His *hands* were all the parts that fed.
Wielded with grace his steel and knife;
His thoughts ne'er compass'd that word—*wife.*
One of the shortest words in speech,
And yet a word above his reach.

The knife laid by, the market o'er,
Counted his shillings by the score;
By which he knew whether or not
His profits bore another pot.

"I wonder, *John,* upon my life,"
Says *Ambrose,* "you don't take a wife!
To keep a house and follow trade,
Assisted by a servant maid,
Is thought by some not worth pursuing;

Or, rather, deem'd the road to ruin.
Besides, two interests it brings on;
Whereas a wife's and yours is one.
A butcher can't be worth a groat,
Except assisted as he ought.
Besides, there's peace of mind, no doubt,
To think all's well when you are out."

These weighty reasons John thought good;
Return'd a smile as if he wou'd.
Told Mr. Ambrose, " That the road
To courtship he had never trod;
Nor knew a woman, he confess'd,
Of all the race, who'd make him bless'd.
But, Sir, if you'll point out one fair
That suits, I'll try to bring her here."

"I'm happy," Ambrose said, "to lend
Assistance to a worthy friend.
One of the best I have in view,
Adapted perfectly for you,
If you've address enough to win her,
Our *Sally*—you have often seen her;
As to her beauty, you can see
Her stock in hand as well as me.
She's prudence, carefulness, and honour:
She'll prove a fortune to her owner.
Then I some service too can render;
To fetch the meat I buy will send her:
Besides, if you've this scheme in view,
Our door is on the latch for you."

John bow'd and blush'd, and bow'd again—
"A sense of favours should retain."

Now Joseph, with his walking stick,
Approach'd.—One half began to speak.
"Why, *John,* it secretly is said,

You've ta'en a fancy to our maid.
Whate'er may be the public voice,
I much commend your prudent choice:
In her the virtues grow like plants;
Which every wife should have, but wants.
Domestic bliss to you'll be kind,
Which all can seek but few can find
If you place there a heart that's true,
And she can fix her heart on you,
You'll be pronounc'd, I dare engage,
The happiest couple of the age."

John bow'd and blush'd, and bow'd again—
"A sense of favours should retain."
He often to their house resorted
To court her who was dully courted.
He'd half a mind to join in one;
The other half to let't alone.
He ponder'd well, both *con* and *pro*;
His courtship mov'd on rather slow.
The Loves took time to prosecute,
As lawyers do a Chancery suit.
Yet cases will occur, which may
Be injur'd by a long delay.

The gentlemen at length discover
That John is but a sluggish lover.
Like a dull beast to slaughter gone,
'Twas needful they should goad him on.
Told him, "while he, with sleepy eyes,
Survey'd, another'd *take* the prize.
That such a prize, they needs must say,
Cannot be met with every day.
That two or three, upon my honour,
Already fix an eye upon her.
You'll find it difficult to carry her;
I'll lay ten guineas you can't marry her."

John thought he could no hazard run,
And, in a moment, cried out "Done!"

What mighty wonders crowd in view,
That *wagers* of all sizes do:
They bring you joy, they bring vexation;
They prop a falling reputation;
They make a wife, they make an heir;
They bring a husband to despair.
The *wager* argument refutes;
Instantly finishes disputes;
For, when one side begins to lay,
The other's but one word to say;
And if that word should not be, *done!*
The first has most compleatly won.

In rhetoric its powers are shewn;
The boldest figure ever known.
'Twill your antagonist o'erthrow;
It fells him with a single blow;
Is the most cogent we insist,
Except a blow with double fist.

In altercations held by man,
The *wager* never leads the *van*;
But, when disputes assail the ear,
We find it bringing up the rear.
Should reasons offer, great or small,
The wager overcomes them all.
Can eas'ly turn friends into foes,
And give to each a bloody nose:
Makes the nabb'd squire cry out for bail;
The bell-man—"houshold goods for sale."
Repenting eyes produce a flood;
And *pam* at once cut down a wood,
The *horse* the squire did once bestride,
And kept a groom to rub each side,

Now master has been sore humbugg'd,
Is by a pair of panniers rubb'd.

The pair of scales we'll use once more,
Which we produc'd some lines before:
If even perfectly they stand,
Ten guineas plac'd on either hand
Will make that scale drop down in haste,
And make the other rise as fast.
This was our lover's case, in fact,
Who now resembled scales exact.
His sentiments quite even seem,
'Till ten bright guineas turn'd the beam.

Three days were scarcely turned about
Before the Parson was sought out,
To tye a knot 'twixt man and wife,
Which very often galls for life,
Though he's a fee to *make* the noose,
They'd double it to set them loose.

Before six weeks were fully gone,
Sally brought forth a lusty son.
For *once* the gossips did not trace
Its likeness in the father's face;
For *once* were sparing of those jokes
Which flourish among child-bed folks,
For recent wounds may hurt so much
As not to bear the slightest touch.
John was amaz'd, and deemed it rude,
A stranger should so soon intrude;
Thought, if they follow'd this career,
Might half a dozen have a year.
The pasture, with this rising flock,
Would be too scanty for the stock.

With anger, that created heat,
Upbraided *Sally* with deceit;

Poems: Chiefly Tales

The double wedding

Two Ladies and a Gent, I sing,
As by the Muse invited,
Bound in the matrimonial string,
All bitten, or else bited.

Ere you take Beauty for a prop,
Be certain that 'twill bear you up;
Or, if a fortune you'd obtain,
The road is pointed out most plain.

Some Bards shine forth with depth of thought;
Some are with pleasing humour fraught;
Others, a mongrel species making,
Worship a calf of their creating:
This maxim of the last we hold;
The calf has neither brains nor gold.
But let fair truth with me abide;
Be thou my patron and my guide:
For falshood we must deem a crime,
Whether held up in prose or rhime.

Miss Flora was that lovely lass
You'd wish to meet—be loth to pass.
The piece that charms and gives surprize
You'd rather have *before* your eyes;
Was tall and strait—a pleasing face;
And mov'd with a becoming grace.
Whenever so much beauty starts
It draws a train of eyes and hearts.
What Stoic can refuse an eye
Whene'er Miss Flora passes by?
Her captivating power she knows;
Returns side-glances as she goes;
Draws in the incense of the street,
And finds a flood of homage sweet.

If one sex mounts her beauty high,
'Twill in another raise a sigh.
Nay, some would even take an oath
That she excites a sigh in both.

The stranger is surpriz'd to meet
So fine a girl in Coleshill street;
Will turn, before three steps are took,
His head, to gain a second look;
Keep walking, turning left and right
So long as she appears in sight:
His eyes behind, his toes before,
Hoping to see her find her door—

"Look forward, Friend, or you'll be lost,
Her charms will run ye 'gainst a post!"

Slipshod a fine young man appears;
Would class with first-rate grenadiers;
Was strait, was handsome, and well made,
And was a master in his trade;
Yet one defect we must allow
His face possess'd—a clouded brow;
But this a match can never spoil;
While *lovers* we assume a smile:
'Tis time enough for clouds to rise
When marriage tempests veil the skies.

He look'd—he lov'd her—and what then?
She look'd, and she lov'd him agen.
Two distant flames keep a dull course;
United, act with double force.

Then, as to wealth, by what appears,
His fortune was the same as hers.
What's that, pray? Why, Sir, can't you guess?
'Twas nothing—neither more nor less.

But now, before the Parson draws
The marriage noose, they stop and pause—
"Two nothings in a man and wife"
They saw would cause an irksome life.
While single, we can dine, at least
On beauty, as a first-rate feast;
But when the marriage state commences,
That eye-sight treat quite banish'd hence is;
And something solid in that case
Must lovers find to take its place.
Beauty's a treasure, or 'tis not,
According to what market brought;
And bears a price for high or low
Exactly as the markets go.
When single it is worth the saving;
When married it's not worth a shaving;
Neglected quite from day to day,
And quickly after thrown away.
Its end is answer'd; and pray why
A useless tool mayn't be thrown by?
Dame T—n's beauty, we aver,
Is seen by all—but John and her.
Nature design'd the transient guest
But as a stimulus at best.
Then why should *Slipshod* and his fair
Depend on such deceitful ware.

THE SECOND PART

As ev'ry excellence, we know,
Can never in one female grow,
And as they all are worth your heed,
Take this advice, and you'll succeed—
If in *one* fair *all* can't be reckon'd,
Add to your first wife, wife the second;
And, further, if there still wants more,
Augment them into number four:

Thus you'll have *all*, without a let,
Of virtues in the alphabet.

Now Mistress *Dorcas* we'll let in,
With some few hairs upon her chin:
She'd been a wife, had lost the chain,
And doubly wish'd for one again.
The cat, that never tasted mouse,
Creeps silently about the house;
But once enjoying the repast,
Ardently seeks another taste.

Though *Dorcas'* group of charms were fled,
She burnish'd up what were not dead;
Aided by dress, some few could show,
Though turn'd of forty long ago.
The careful man, of wealth bereft,
Will doubly cherish what he's left;
But people said, perhaps in spite,
Her's blaz'd but with a dimish light.

She had, however, 'tis confess'd,
That which would balance all the rest:
She'd house and land, and cash beside,
Would make the *blind* or *lame* a bride;
So that we're authoriz'd to say
Her beauties in her pocket lay;
Prevailing beauties, we insist,
Such as no class of men resist.
The charms held by another lass
Merely for counterfeits would pass;
But what in *Dorcas* did abound
Will ever be true sterling found.

This trifling diff'rence occurs
'Twixt other females' case and hers.
The girl that's beautiful and smiles
Draws many a lover in her wiles;

If she be rich, and fair, and sweet,
They'll fall by dozens at her feet;
But if she's old, yet wealth discovers,
She may draw men, but never lovers.

Should poverty 'gainst beauty strive,
You'd never keep true love alive.
A union with pure bliss is fraught,
When founded upon prudent thought.
Slipshod would better fortune try—
On *Dorcas* cast a smiling eye.

"O dear!" methinks the ladies say,
"How apt are men to go astray!
Unhappy is a Woman's lot;
We know not when a heart we've got:
And if by chance one is our share,
'Tis difficult to keep it there."

I'm sorry, ladies, but don't cry,
No soul is more your friend than I.
Then let not anxious thoughts be catch'd;
You'll find the sexes nearly match'd.

Could such a youth meet with disdain,
Or ever send a smile in vain?
Dorcas was conscious of the prize,
And sweetly answer'd with her eyes.
None after tedious courtship pants
When each gives what the other wants;
'Tis for a husband *Dorcas* lives;
And 'tis a husband *Slipshod* gives.
He longs a fortune to command;
She puts a fortune in his hand.

Dorcas of such a youth was glad;
She sign'd and seal'd o'er all she had:
Her cash, her houses, and her land,

She gave them all to gain his hand.
With wealth she fill'd his hand alone,
That she might call that hand her own.
Nay, if one anxious thought survive,
It was that she'd no more to give.
The lawyer well his work had wrought;
Slipshod the tempting prize had caught.

Now to that place their feet repairs
Where Priests send folks to bliss by pairs;
Where Happiness, a lovely guest,
Enters, and sooths the *mind* at least.
Serene's the view for one short space,
And not a cloud dares shew its face.

But why, when bliss poor *Dorcas* feels,
Does sorrow tread upon its heels?
This was design'd to humble pride,
Or prosp'rous folks would be o'er-joy'd.
Not many hours were fully gone—
The welkin clouded—storms came on.
Marriage had answer'd every end
Which *Slipshod* could at first intend.
He pick'd a quarrel with his bride,
And swore "he'd ne'er lie by her side:"
Nor should it be display'd to view
That one house ever held the two.
She, lost, in tears, and, what was worse,
He left her with a solemn curse—
Flew to Miss Flora's arms for life;
Cohabits with her as a wife
Hence are a race of beauties bred—
By *Dorcas'* fortune cloth'd and fed.

Our hero now two wives had gain'd;
And two important points obtain'd.
For *wealth* and *beauty*, Flora sings,
Will weigh down half a score good things.

Had gentle *prudence* been the word,
He must have sought out wife the third.
If *sense, wit, learning*, he'd pursu'd,
You would have half a dozen view'd.

Poor *Dorcas* mourn'd week after week
A livelihood she had to seek:
That bliss was fled which should have lasted;
Her marriage prospects all were blasted.
Choice nuptial fruit before her placed,
Like Tantalus, but must not taste.

Her houses, lands, and money fled,
She keeps a pot of ale for bread.
Let romance-writers, to a man,
Match *Slipshod's* conduct if they can.

Sept. 8, 1795

Poems: Chiefly Tales

Mutation

In Nottingham there dwells a lass,
Of three-score-years-and-ten,
With whom I jocund hours did pass;
The loves were with us then.

With more of love than money bless'd,
You'd said, if you had seen us;
For all the capital possess'd
Was half-a-crown between us.

An ample stock of beauty we
Inherited, you'd own;
But then the looker-on might see—
That stock was her's alone.

She was nineteen, and blithe as May,
And I was twenty-one;
Both pleas'd while time pass'd smooth away.
But now the loves are gone.

I had her heart, and she had mine;
We thought the change most clever;
But Fortune said, "a nymph so fine
I must not keep for ever."

Our faces not a wrinkle bore,
Except made by a smile;
But now with lines they're cover'd o'er,
Much like the new-plough'd soil.

Had either of us rivall'd been,
'Twould set that one a weeping;
Now neither of us cares a pin,
For hearts not worth the keeping.

Her taper waist, you'd really think,
Made from a London doll;
But is, by many a cup of drink,
Completely two arms full.

My knee was highly gratified
Whene'er to sit she bent;
But now her pond'rous bulk applied
Would make that knee repent.

The hairs that grew upon our crown,
And numerous as our sins,
Unfortunately tumbled down,
And grow upon our chins.

Mutation waited on those charms
I fancied half divine;
She fell into *Miss Conduct's* arms,
Miss Prudence fell in mine.

That name's disgrac'd in parish-books,
Once lovely to my view,
While mine a little brighter looks,
Varnish'd with E.s.q.

Familiariz'd to poverty,
On charity she stays;
While Fortune has enabled me
To run a pair of grays.

Dec. 10, 1795

The virtues of election ale

OR THE ART OF RAISING VOTES

Of all the ale you drink, my friend,
Election serves the noblest end;
'Twill carry you with ardor through;
You'll vote yourself, and get votes too;
What man of spirit then would fail
Th' indulgence of Election Ale?

Our Constitution, God be thanked,
Is founded on the glass and tankard.
I own my rhyme is rather wrong,
But you may mend it with your tongue.
The remedy does not lie far hence;
You only need remove the *r* hence.

If an Election you would make,
This is the nearest road to take.
We all allow the *higher* class,
Like trout, are tickled with the glass;
Observe then, while your hand is in,
Keep tickling, and you're sure to win.

But when the num'rous fry are took,
Then with the *tankard* bait the hook;
For hungry fish, with joy elate,
Instantly snap the vulgar bait.
Th' appendages are knife and fork;
And *cash* compleats election work.
Whether for wine or ale they call,
The Candidate must pay for all.

My *Lod,* Sir Knight, the 'Squire, we see,
As much in trade as you or me.
Our case exact alike we note,

And he, perhaps, who fighting stands;
Has work enough upon his hands.
For seven long years bids hatred reign,
Till an election comes again;
And then the wounds, barely skin'd o'er,
Break out, and bleed as heretofore.

Shall wisdom this vile trade endure,
And not the state attempt a cure?
Desist from spiggots, knives, and forks;
Draw *lots* instead of drawing corks;
And then each class, quite through the nation,
Must act a part that suits their station.

Thus wonders, far surpassing thought,
Are by the potent barrel wrought.
Strong floods of ale through voters flowing,
Keep our politic wheels agoing;
And great St. Stephen's, much resorted,
Appears by barrel'd ale support'd.

THE SECOND PART

With liquor our first chapter shone;
The art of raising votes comes on.

Who would not drink till he was lost,
When he could drink at others cost?
His relish for the malt and hop
Wont suffer him to miss a drop;
Though like the pail beneath the spout,
Brim-full, whate'er flows in flows out.

John Gretton well could thrive by trade;
For many a leg he stockings made;
Produc'd two hundred pairs a week,
And yet he ne'er had legs to seek.

He from *himself* would not depart;
Emolument lay near his heart.
A few game cocks he made combine
To peck up clean his neighbours coin.
And yet it chanc'd, when ill-luck shone,
That now and then they lost his own.

His keen eye kept a sharp look-out
When profit e'er should float about;
And what the eye had fix'd upon
The hand knew how to make its own.
If neighbours quarrell'd, *John* knew law,
And could a little profit draw.
"The friend of both," his only boast;
But friendly to himself the most.
A widower he was; his bride
One child had left; and stepp'd aside.
Perhaps she found a happier place
Than e'er she found in his embrace;
For *John* was so convinc'd her state
Was better than she held of late,
He ne'er, though she was from him rent,
Express'd a sigh of discontent.

Domestic cares were then convey'd
In total to the servant maid.

He could display, without much fearing,
His talent for electioneering.
Himself a *Burgess,* and he knew
Where ev'ry other Burgess grew.
If opposition started there
Could tell which member'd win the chair.
Such consequence could never fail
To add a weight to either scale;
Could lead up voters for his man;
Himself the Corporal of the clan:

Then muster more; return again;
Become the Serjeant of the train.

In seventeen hundred twenty-two
Baily and *Cavendish* we view,
As candidates of high renown
To represent old *Derby* town.
For *half* John pray'd, and drank, and swore;
Cry'd out *huzza,* and then drank more.

Of *friendship* near as much appears
In drinking as in lugging ears.
Nay, great philosophers decide
These noble arts are near allied.
Howe'er, in either case, we scan,
'Tis liquor constitutes the man;
Knows all things when compleatly mellow,
Except that he's a drunken fellow;
Can regulate the Corporation,
And lead the van in conversation.
His ears may be a little weak;
Can only ear his *own* tongue speak.

Nor can you well his hugs resist;
Or palming of his dirty fist.
Let me, in this case, win the day,
As Hudibras did — run away.

The members chair'd, the happy night
Was spent by moon and candle-light.
Not "Church and King," as now we quote,
But "Church and Chev'rell" was the note.
The Presbyterians, they thought well,
With George the First to send to — .
The joyful voters crown the feast
With twenty thousand oaths at least.

The morn was usher'd by the cock;
The watchman cried "past two o'clock,"
When they reluctantly confess'd
'Twas *almost* time to go to rest;
But there's no *body,* we presume,
Whose parts are scatter'd round a room.
Compleatly vanish'd, head and brain,
Can eas'ly muster them again.
Exactly will our case appear—
The *man* was lost, the *body* there.

In some the drink became unquiet,
And in the stomach bred a riot.
Then with the *man* began to quarrel,
And tried to run back to the barrel;
But after all its efforts o'er,
Could reach no farther than the floor;
But look'd as fine, you'd really think,
As when it first approach'd as drink.

Some famous heroes did not fail
To sink beneath the powers of ale;
While others, us'd to rant and roaring,
Began to change their note for snoring.

Some could not find their own abode,
But took a nap upon the road.
Where man and liquor disagreed
The last determin'd to be freed.
It did not rise, nor did descend,
Yet found a vent at either end.

A happier lot attended *John,*
His burthen he could carry on.
He found his door without disaster,
Gave a loud rap, much like a master.
But who would grudge a rap of pride
To leaders who sit side by side,

Of him for whom they rend the air,
And lift into the statesman's chair?

The maid in bed first heard the din,
And started up to let him in;
So willingly the latch to lift,
She went in nothing but her shift.
A servant-maid, in any state,
Should never let her waster wait.

John's spirits were in elevation;
Perhaps the maid's in expectation.
The mark was tempting, none were near,
And neither *John* nor *she* in fear.
For upstairs not a word was said,
Six 'prentice boys were fast in bed.
The moon herself was no ways rude,
But quite behind a cloud she stood;
Nor did she once, as if by chance,
Even attempt to steel a glance.
His distance *Sol* was sure to keep,
On *Thetis's* lap was fast asleep.
Two tedious hours must also fly,
'Ere he could rise and rub an eye;
Before along the heavens he'd creep,
And into people's windows peep;
Bring all their private acts in view
As our most saucy beggars do.
Old Night was mantled up in shade;
Nor were a goddess call'd to aid.
No green-grass, and no bed was near;
Neither were any wanted there:
For a convenience may be found,
When needful, on the thread-bare ground

Between the two, we must confess,
They muster'd up one only dress;

And as on her no covering shone
He kindly o'er her spread his own.

Now all the histories which I've read,
Declare "each went to their own bed;"
And no more notice pass'd, it seems,
Than if they'd tasted Lethe's streams;
For he no amorous glances cast;
And she ne'er hinted what had pass'd.

Nine months, to consummate his joys,
Brought forth a pair of blooming boys;
Thus *John* by ale a vigil kept,
And rais'd two votes while others slept.

July 17, 1795

To health

Thou lovely Fair, with me abide,
And never after quit my side.
In sickness the most welcome guest;
Yet little notic'd when possess'd.
Treated like *Time*, away thou'rt toss'd,
And not regarded till thou'rt lost;
But then thy worth appears so plain
We'd give the world for thee again.
Dame Fortune's smiles insipid are
When, lovely fair one, thou'rt not there.
For title and estate, we see,
Their value lose when we lose thee.

Thou lov'st an active body best,
And much approv'st a mind at rest;
Art often found rosy and sleek;
Where idle people seldom seek
In mod'rate exercise art seen,
But never in a glass of gin.
Not courting sleep at nine, you lay,
But mushrooms hunt at break of day;
Or, should that tender upstart fail,
Then following the milking-pail.
If thy advice we don't despise,
We'll rise when Sol begins to rise.
A walking shadow thou regards,
Which measures more than twenty yards.

Some knowing people have a notion
Thou'rt seldom found in pill or potion:
Survey this in a proper light;
And ten to one their notion's right.

Thou'rt ne'er attended, as a guest,
At taverns, or a Lord Mayor's feast.

In temperance, while years run round,
And regularity, art thou found.

I have been favour'd with thy cares
For something more than seventy years;
Then ne'er let me perceive thou'rt gone,
While the decays of age creeps on.

Dec. 10, 1795

Poems: Chiefly Tales

Reconciliation

Should wife or husband take delight in
Scolding, or be inclin'd to fighting;
Some good old aunt, to make them cease,
Might drop a word that carries peace.

If you'd enjoy a happy life,
Give all indulgence to your wife;
Allow her, or you'll be absurd,
Always to utter the last word
The sooner then, as'tis her right,
You hear it, you're the gainer by't.
Answer alternate following answer
Will lead you through an irksome dance, Sir.
Retain this as a golden prize—
Great quarrels oft from nothing rise;
Then if, my friend yourself you'd serve,
Such nothings treat as they deserve.

Full often we behold a strife,
Existing between man and wife
Instead of dear, and love, and darling,
Their life consists in petty snarling
Having no quarrels with another
Keep up a jarring with each other:
They've no material ill to mourn,
Therefore make trifles serve their turn.
With words of contradiction teaze,
Much like your back when bit with fleas:
But seldom coo, like dove and dove;
More like two cats when making love;
As if he and his lovely creature
Were the worst enemies in nature.
Should a gay smile *his* features crown,
She can discharge it with a frown—

"'Tis vastly wrong for him to smile,
And she sit silent all the while."

If her request his ears should greet,
He finds denial vastly sweet:
For self-importance would be wanted,
Were her solicitations granted.
For power and beauty, and your shoes,
Are not to lie by, but to use.

And yet, if we attend, we find
A love sincere remains behind;
But, like a maiden in disgrace,
Not very apt to shew its face:
Or, monarchs of the Eastern nations,
Only appear on great occasions:
Or, like a miser meanly dress'd;
For Sunday only saves his best,
But we'll no more a likeness note
'Twixt kindness and a miser's coat;
For if he hacks his coat about,
Perhaps he'll quickly wear it out;
But the reverse good nature knows;
The more 'tis worn the better grows.
Though they, like dog and cat, you'd see,
Who seldom thoroughly agree;
Yet if a stranger dog appears
Both join to pull him by the ears;
As if, of all things, 'twas most pleasing
Each to ingross the art of teazing.

Two faithful *lovers* shall appear;
I'll not tell when, or who, or where.
Yes, I'd as good their dwelling trace,
Why they are found in ev'ry place.
Then only cast your eyes about,
And when and where you'll soon find out.

Their love was of the genuine sort;
Not mix'd, as is our Shrub and Port;
The strictest scrutiny would bear
As any horse who walks the fair;
For if through every part you go
You'd call it sound from top to toe.

"Then, as to marriage altercations,
Often productive of vexations,
They'll shun them; nay, they can't abide them,
There's nothing easier than t' avoid them;
For if a fault *one* speaks a while on't,
The *other* only need be silent;
Then, in an instant, all is well,
Before that one the fault can tell."

Thus things were fix'd, for man and wife
T'insure their happiness through life.
Then who'd delay the joys that please,
When two young people love like these?
For Hymen's lamp, no doubt, will burn well;
They're full of love as nut of kernel.

THE SECOND PART

Spite of resolves, disguise, and care,
Yet human nature will appear.
The Negro's face though you attack
With what you will, it still is black.

Now, gentle Reader, we'll suppose
What you and every body knows—
The happiest part of human life
Is when we venture on a wife.
The prospect's charming to the mind,
For every care is left behind;
Or, if some evils should look sour,
Divide them, and they'll lose their pow'r

Our joys, like two bright flames, of course,
United, double all their force.

How long the nuptial bliss extends,
Before the happy season ends,
We'll not determine.—Yes, we will!
Some end like a short-dated bill;
(Which *need* receives with great delight)
Being only *"three days after sight:"*
Others, a longer season wait,
Reaching to *"one month after date;"*
Demanding still, in many a case,
A farther time of *three days grace.*
Some hold as long, since they begun,
As those which have *"two months to run."*
Thus when eternal love is swore,
It means a month or two—not more.
Our *hero,* and our *heroine,*
Above them all much brighter shine;
Like a *long-winded bill,* Fame says,
Continued during *"seventy days."*

Now novelty its power was losing,
And ardent love was fall'n a dosing;
Civility apace declin'd;
The dregs of temper were behind.
Whether the stream run slow or fast,
The dregs will shew themselves at last.
'Twas needful they should understand
Which of the two should lead the band:
Because in common life we see
A pair of Co's can't long agree.
How can a horse his duty do
Whose bridle guided is by two?

Love dos'd, we said, nay, took a nap,
And yet this sly and random chap
Ne'er left the husband nor the wife,

But lodgings took in both for life:
They'd too much love to cause a riot,
And contradiction to be quiet.

Should dainties on their board appear,
She relish'd nothing—he not there.
Her joy was sweeter than a nut,
When he'd been out, to hear his foot:
But instant, when she launch'd her prate,
He found his joy not quite so great;
And yet whene'er she stroak'd his beard,
She claim'd a kiss as her reward.
Nor was he ever backward yet
To *pay* or to *contract* a debt.
Whether alone, or had a guest,
She slily carv'd for him the best;
Forestall'd his wants, his relish too;
She knew them better than he knew.

If she solicited a gown,
He could deny her with a frown;
Denial was the height of joy,
Because he'd *power* to deny.
For he that's power to act at will
Will seldom let that power stand still:
And yet great pleasure he confess'd
Whene'er his wife was gaily dress'd.

If she was absent, day or night,
His head reclin'd; things were not right;
Full often would escape a sigh;
He knew not when, he knew not why.
Home, at all seasons, he thought dear;
But doubly so if she was there.
What though she carried stings about her,
Home was a wretched home without her:
He'd nothing left him but to mourn,
And count the hours till her return.

Thus jarring, sullen, they appear,
Yet necessary evils were.
The errors which caus'd their contending
Were very seldom worth the mending;
Nor worth a glance of either eye—
A certain cure is—pass them by.
This one remark let me indite—
Who found the fault *was always right.*

THE THIRD PART

The match is lighted, flame runs high;
Our pair fall out—"they know not why."
Under a cloud of smoak is seen,
To end our Tragi-Comic scene.

We think that couple wants decorum,
Who straws collect, and stumbles o'er e'm.
Their prudence ne'er sustains a shock,
Who watch and shun a stumbling block.
The first will bring them plague enough;
The second says, you're rarely off.

Five years roll'd sluggishly along;
Some things went right, but more went wrong;
Which brought forth some few wat'ry eyes,
Answers, rejoinders, and replies;
With contradictions in great store;
Repeated disappointments more.
But, with contentions, came some joys—
One handsome girl; two charming boys.

But how shall we, from hair or pin,
A quarrel of some weight begin?
Or how select one to our mind
When there's a thousand left behind?

"*Tommy*, my dear, has broke his crock;
Has spilt his tea, and daub'd his frock!"

"Well, if he has, what need you brawl?
Procure a remedy for all."

"How!" " At the crock-shop you're well sped—
Send Tommy supperless to bed.
Then at the wash-tub, or the cock,
You'll quickly reinstate the frock."

"So, this is all the care, I see,
You entertain for him or me."

"*I* try to soften all your care;—
But *you*, that I should have my share."

"I wish, by all the power that's true,
I'd never known your care, or you!
My load of grief's already great,
Yet you keep adding to the weight."

"Under a load you need not groan—
A remedy is still your own."

"Then, from this blessed day, we'll part—
Divide the, stock." "With all my heart!"

How often we, like fools at play,
Gamble our happiness away!
'Tis thus a woman and a man
Will not agree, because they can.
One soft'ning word, from him or bride,
Had set the parting scheme aside;
But, as a quarrel they desire,
Like new-made tinder catch the fire.
Though each possess'd the other's heart,

Could not agree except to part.
Their words were now, as were the past
Each side, as usual, claims the last.

But now, through every room they got—
"This shall be yours, and this shall not."
How to divide what each shall feed on,
They soon between themselves agreed on;
Could easily climb a mountain's crown;
But little mole-hills —threw them down.

Each found the art of chattel-clearing
Without another interfering;
But the *live-stock* with all their art,
They could not so exactly part.

"Two children shall my portion be,"
The husband cried, "out of the three.
The largest lot shall be my share,
"Because a *father* has the *care*."

"No; two of them shall be my store,
Because a mother's love is more."

"No, no; first comes a husband's voice;
Therefore he ought to have his choice."

"Indulgence is my sex's due;
I claim priority of you."

From *pro* and *con,* and *con* and *pro,*
Decision *mov'd* on rather slow.
But we must leave their *pro* and *con,*
Or else we sha'n't move one step on.

An *aunt,* with years completely ripe,
Lov'd them as well as she her pipe:
She entertain'd, we're bound to warrant,

Maxims which are not very current:
Old coin, of value and of weight,
Though stagnate, being out of date.

She thought her duty, and her ease,
Consisted in her love of peace;
Nay, farther, she pronounc'd it good
To end a quarrel if she cou'd.
'Twas better too, by far, to *give,*
As well as prudent, than *receive;*
Thought too, the great design of man
Was to do all the good he can.
Right to his dealings should belong;
But never, with intent, do wrong.
She would not, on a slight pretence,
Give or retaliate offence.
Such conduct could not bring, in common,
One enemy to an *old woman.*

Our couple then made no demur
To leave themselves and cause to her;
Fully determin'd to abide
By what the lady should decide.

Now Madam, when the pair had spoke,
Threw out a double puff of smoke—
"Three children are your stock I see,
Pray how can they divided be?
If you'd had four, or even two,
I could have justice done to you.
It cannot be decided yet
You must another child beget;"
Spoke serious, while her pipe was quaffing;
The anxious pair burst out a laughing.

Thus she, for separation loth,
Had dropp'd a word that suited both.

The couple on each other smil'd;
Forgot to part—but not the child.

Jan. 17, 1796

The parish wedding

Too happy is that man, you say,
Who, from his pleasure, runs away;
Pronouncing him a stupid sinner,
Who, hungry, runs away from dinner.

A married life's the hight of bliss;
We'll have it, whether hit or miss.
We're happy when another marries,
Though we suppose the man miscarries.
We've drawn the cork, and tasted gall;
Glad to lead others in the thrawl.
For who would not rejoice to see
His neighbour sink as well as he?

No gloomy thoughts come to perplex us
Upon a union of the sexes.
Of all the trades that England bless,
The wedding trade is wish'd success,

We'll now the envied memoirs write
Of *Jenny Parker—Thomas Knight*;
For never, to the end of life,
While he was husband, she was wife,
One angry word between them pass'd,
After the parson tied them fast;
An even stream, unting'd with mud,
Without an ebb, without a flood.
Would ever loving couple miss
To try a state so full of bliss?
The bacon-flitch, you'd think, was won;
Nay, hold! my friend, I've not yet done.

If you his native place enquire,
He breath'd his first in Devonshire;
By combing wool supported life;

And now and then he took a wife.
Nor did he lose, by death, his flock,
But still kept adding to the stock.
By busy Fame this news was carried,
"That Thomas *seven* wives had married!"
Which number, for aught he could tell,
Were all at once alive and well.
An able stallion oft appears,
Leading a team of breeding mares.

As *combing* he took no delight in,
He chose to change the scene for fighting.
If we allow of freedom still,
A man may change to what he will.

Tom was well-wade, surpass'd most men,
Compleatly measur'd five feet ten;
Enlisted in the Inniskilling;
To fight and swear was always willing.

The regiment now must change its ground,
And in old *Derby* quarters found.
With certainty the date I fix
'Twas seventeen hundred thirty-six.

One silkmill girl I bring to view,
Who'd all the impudence of two;
The softness of her sex forgot,
But all their daring rudeness not.
Nothing the *female* could denote,
But that she wore a petticoat.
Yet *Jane*, it must be owned, had merit;
Held a full share of tongue and spirit;
For, should a *man* a word misplace,
With open hand she'd slap his face.
A *woman* was beneath her slap,
For instantly she'd pull her cap.

Was old enough to be a bride;
Had some accomplishments beside;
Could swear and kick, and scold at will;
Yet entertain a regiment still.

Ah, luckless I! when in minority,
She lugg'd my ears without authority—

"For, in whatever hand is might,"
The proverb says, "will conquer right;"
And though her hand was not divine,
Pain and submission must be mine.
She, after sixty years, ne'er thought
She'd nobly in a song be brought.

Now, whether freeman or a slave,
Who plays at bowls must rubbers have.
To *Tom* of pregnancy she spoke;
For he's the man must find a cloak.
This privilege is hers at least—
Of fifty she can chuse the best.
For a whole troop could throw abuse at:
The modest girl's but *one* to chuse at.

Tom curs'd and swore at her amain;
She curs'd and swore at him again.
Thus we as book-keepers have done,
Balance accounts as we go on.

"The power is mine—I'll not be foil'd."—
Went to the *Mayor* and swore the child.

Now all the racks poor Thomas feels
Of constables about his heels.
A dreadful prison's on his right;
A wife as dreadful comes in sight:
A halter he began to see
Ah! the most dreadful of the three!

An idle girl and child's thought quearish
Lumber upon a little parish—
"They'll give *five pounds,* which is enough,
If *Thomas* will but take her off."
Then who will say, or even think,
That slav'ry is become extinct?
Woman, and *babe* not one day old,
Are brought to market to be sold.

Prosperity will make us naught,
But 'tis distress that brings on thought.
Thomas his life by far priz'd most;
"He could not yet become a ghost.
Nor in a gaol more pleasure have
Than he could find within a grave.
But if a wife he ventures on
She's not the first by many a one.
Her I can manage pretty well;
Besides, *five pounds* will sweetly tell.
This to a sore's a charming plaster;
'Twill heal up many a foul disaster,"

Now, at the church, in wedlock's bands,
The priest began to tie their hands.
Amidst a troop of Dragoon brothers,
St. Michael's overflow'd with others—
"Wilt have this woman?" Parson cries—
"By G— I'm forc'd to't," *Tom* replies.

The solemn Priest disdainful check'd
The *groom,* for want of due respect—
"Sir, 'tis a fact, 'twixt me and you;
And I'll be d—d if 'tis not true."

The congregation, many a score,
Instantly burst into a roar.
Such mirth a church had never reach'd
Though Doctor, Dean, or Bishop, preach'd.

The Priest had half a mind to stand still.
He found his flock above his hand still.
But when he took a second view—
"He'd best make haste, and venture through."
"Wilt comfort, keep her, love, and honour her?"
"By G—I shall away run from her, Sir."
While humble I, a looker-on
Of that great laughing-stock made one.

"*Jane Parker's* married!" Miss Fame tells—
"*Jane Parker's* married!"—Michael's bells.
Now hats thrown up, and shouts rehearse
Just as the joyous crowd disperse.
Tom is attack'd on every side;
He'd turn'd a whore into a bride.
He join'd with laugh the general voice
Rapp'd on his breeches pocket thrice—
"Let the d—d b—h go to the devil;
Here lies a cure for every evil."
While she stood silent in the church;
Nor even ventur'd to the porch;
And a more humble look she bore
Than she was known to look before.

His regiment coat he threw aside;
Put on a drab—ne'er saw his bride:
Thus he, his rising ills to smother,
Resum'd one drab, and left another:
Then off, to seek his fortune, went,
Belov'd; his officers consent.

Thus *Tom* the marriage sprig had planted;
From thence drew all the joys he wanted.
Quite full, you'd represent his store,
Who runs away for fear of more.

Old Time, to disappoint our spite,
Brings many a secret thing to light.

Jenny, like a foot-path appears,
When trodden much it never bears;
For though poor Thomas she beguil'd,
Yet she herself was *not* with child.
She false—he gone—nor will retain her;
The parish bit and Tom a gainer

April 24, 1796

The retort

In native truth be always shewn,
Lest, in disguise, you should be known.

King George the First, as Authors write,
In masquerades took great delight;
For midnight pleasures hither came,
And sent his eye in quest of game.
Beheld a figure 'mongst the rest
With prominence about the breast;
Concluding, though he saw no face,
"A lady must be in the case."

Urg'd by desire his fingers move,
And press the tempting seat of love;
While smiles conceal'd approach his face—
"Dis, I tink, Madam, von soft place."
"I know one softer, Sir," she said.
"Ah vere it is?"—"in the King's head!"

Long breeches

BY A BEAU

Parody

Ladies, I have lost my legs,
Have you seen my breeches;
Pride of all the race of wags,
Which every Beau bewitches?

I for these my legs forsook,
And my belly cram'd in;
Neck and heels they almost took,
And there my legs are jamb'd in.

Never shall you see them more,
For they're past discerning;
All your joys in legs are o'er,
While you their loss are mourning.

Whither can my legs be flown!
Ladies, tell me whither:
Ah, woeful case! perhaps they're gone
For ever and for ever.

May 10, 1796

Poems: Chiefly Tales

The true lover's knot

That man should in a poem move,
Who promises to die for love.

Writers deceive us, when they say
"That Love's too blind to find his way."
Just the reverse, they might have said,
And given him as much eye as head.
Experience marks him for a cheat;
He's full of trick as "egg of meat."
To gain a point, or gain command
He's always some deceit on hand;
And, what's a most unlucky state;
You find him out when 'tis too late.
Is consolation worth a louse
To know the thief who robb'd your house;
When all the goods that were your own
Are irrecoverably gone
All the returns arising there
Are only multiplying care.

Truman of Nottingham, we'll view,
Who lov'd a lass, which liv'd there too.
How far she smil'd upon the swain
We can't at present well explain.

But, as to him, I'd lay a pinch on him,
He was a lover every inch on him;
Not only lov'd, but he declar'd it;
If that won't pass, he even *swear'd* it.
Though this was all man ought to spare,
'Twas not enough to win the fair,
Who look'd but shy, and stood aloof,
And of returns would give no proof.

Then he protested on his life,
"If she refus'd to be his wife,
And still should disappoint his hope,
He'd climb to heaven in a rope."

This declaration, we suspect,
Was coming to the point direct;
For if it pleads a man's excuse,
Who fastens with a Parson's noose,
Which, after all, it may be said,
Is often but a flimzy thread;
What lasting honours may he hope,
Who firmly fastens with a rope?

She ponder'd o'er the great event,
Determin'd *not* to give consent;
For who would venture on the seas
When the rude prospect shall displease?

James Truman, howe'er, did not care
To cast away his life in air
He'd win the girl he had in view;
But lose *himself* would never do.
The knowing mouse, some authors state,
Will gently nibble at the bait;
Yet never stir the trap, they tell ye,
But come away replete in belly.

To take a cord he did not fail;
Tied one end to a pasture rail,
The other end his neck went round,
While half his body press'd the ground.
Close by a foot-path was the scene,
Where people often intervene.

"The first that comes cannot miss spying
A man half-hanging and half-lying.

This plan, no doubt, my life will save;
Of hanging I the credit have."

What springs of joy the mind invade
When we conceive our scheme well laid!

Now watching, with a steady eye,
The first who should be passing by—
The lucky time he quickly found,
Dropp'd on the rope, facing the ground.

A bowl may smoothly be ejected,
Yet meet with rubs we ne'er expected.
The passenger his errand sped,
And, ah! contrary turn'd his head.
'Twill human wisdom much advance
To leave but little room for chance.

Now the tight rope had stopp'd his breath,
And closing were the gates of death;
All sense and motion now were gone—
It chanc'd two other men came on,
Who spied a body on the slope,
The head suspended by a rope.

They cut the string—the head dropp'd down;
More help was needful than their own.
With friction, bleeding, and so forth,
At length James open'd eyes and mouth.

"O, Sally! Sally! thou mayst see
The consequence of loving thee;
The springs of life can never move
Without my dear! my all! my love!"

On him what woman would not dote,
Who tied for her the lover's knot?
She gave consent—who could withstand?

And, at the church, she gave her hand.
What happy scenes appear to view,
Of tender love between the two!

This lasted for three days, not more,
When Jemmy Truman call'd her Whore!
If this beginning you admire,
'Twas but the kindling of the fire.
Though the true lover's knot he'd tied,
In the first week he thrash'd his bride.

Should half our couples, where's the wonder,
Apply the rope to part asunder!
Thus we at matrimony flout,
Yet hang to get in, and get out.

THE SECOND PART

One hanging should you find alone,
Be cautious *not* to cut him down;
Lest in a little time you be
In a more dreadful state than he.

Peruse this second part with care;
Join'd to the last they'll make a pair;
Exactly like gold drop appears,
Which dangles at a lady's ears;
Or sign-board plac'd above the door,
When to the top-part hangs a lower;
Or vastly like what's yearly seen,
Th' Appendix to a Magazine.
An angle-rod is just in point,
When lengthen'd with another joint;
Or bridge convenient, if you'd rather,
That joins two distant banks together;
Or one scale like another scale:
But we'll, dear Sir, begin our tale.

Now Miss Eliza, and young Ned,
Hugg'd, courted, lov'd, agreed to wed;
And, now their joyful bliss begun,
They both were pleas'd with what they'd done.
They'd take their "Bible oath," in fine,
Their happiness was all divine.
The lovely sounds between them were
Prefac'd delightful with "My dear!"
If Edward glanc'd at dearest life,
A smile was answer'd by the wife.

Nature acts perfectly, no doubt,
In what employ she sets about;
When she work'd at the Pairing trade,
Our couple for each other made.

A spring of love, so strong, so high,
You'd really think would ne'er be dry.
But novelty, like cloth, will wear,
And, like your coat, become thread-bare.
Nay, where's the thing, in all the range
Of human life, not apt to change?

Their smiles began to die away;
Instead of *yes,* was answer'd *nay.*
If either had been out awhile,
Might safely come without a smile.
Then sounds discordant, in some cases,
Like wheels before the coachman greases.

"Why do you cut the loaf so ill?"

"Then cut it better if you will."

"You're vastly given, Ned, to tease."

"And you as little, Bess, to please."

"I think you mischief act in spite."

"I wish you'd act a little right."

"The devil take you, rogue, I say."

"I think hell take you first away."

A current's harmless as a lamb
When first the water breaks the dam;
But, gaining ground, no bounds can keep;
Destruction comes with mighty sweep.

From bad to worse our couple stray,
And throw a battle in our way,
With which our placid page is fill'd,
Although in fighting little skill'd.
Like French and English, war begin,
Simply to try which side can win;
And, just like them, they to their cost
Ne'er reckon what by war is lost.

Ladle and *breeches,* in full play,
Exerted each to win the day.
Their looks declar'd, and words and thought,
The combatants in earnest fought.
Whether the gods presided there,
Or whether devils had some share,
To guide the ladle, or the fist,
I neither know, nor will insist;
But this the humble Muse can tell,
Effective blows were pointed well.

Their furious arms brandish'd about,
Till Ned was forc'd to give it out;
Unequal match! boding no good—
Hard timber against flesh and blood!
The active tongue still mov'd; but Ned

In solemn sadness hung his head.
"What man such treatment can endure!"
For this he'll quickly find a cure.
"How can he face the world or day!"
So took his hat, and sneak'd away.
With feelings horrid in extreme,
He sought a rope, and sought a beam.

As *Mr. Sanbrook* by the barn
Was walking on his own concern,
He saw one, which excited care,
Suspended by a rope in air;
His active hands the cord divide
Much sooner than the knot was tied.

The body feeling warm, he knew,
'Twas best to try what art could do.
'Twixt life and death he'd interpose,
So *thump'd* his back, and *tweak'd* his nose.
Small signs of life be saw remain,
So tweak'd and thump'd, and tweak'd again.
These restoratives, that sad hour,
Were all the means within his power.

Observing Edward rather woke,
He boldly follow'd up the stroke.

When Edward could survey things o'er,
Finding his nose a little sore,
Boldly for satisfaction sought;
A writ for "'sault and batt'ry" brought.
Thus he who sav'd a life, ill-sped,
Was now in a worse state than Ned.

No farther then need I indite;
I've prov'd my motto strictly right;
In ten more lines I shall not fail
To prove the moral of my tale.

The Jury pannel'd, box'd, and swore,
Were wiser than some were before—
Declar'd the thumps and tweaks he brought
Were not from "malice aforethought;"
A verdict gave for the defendant;
So they and I shall make an end on't.

One maxim let me state once more;
A maxim stated once before—
"Though marriage we may praise, or flout,
We hang to get in, and get out,"

Dec. 31, 1797

The pen

In joyous strain the verse should move,
Which celebrates the thing we love.

Come, my pale friend, put on a smile,
And we'll in numbers sport awhile.
What though I've made of thee a tool,
Don't thou make me appear a fool.
I own, I could not let thee rest,
But rudely stripp'd thy downy vest;
Ere with impurity wert ting'd,
I scrap'd thee as a pig that's sing'd;
And, as the cook-maid serves a trout,
Have drawn thy tender entrails out;
Often, as folks the magpye tweak,
I've slit thy tongue to make thee speak;
Pursuing still the rude attack,
I've dy'd thy slender limbs in black.

Thou tall and slim grew'st in the water;
But, while with me reducing shorter;
For now and then an eye may see
I cut thy stature one degree:
And when, dear pen, thou'st had thy day,
Like me, worn out, art thrown away.
Our end the same, we're neither free;
A knife cuts thee up — Time cuts me.

When rhyme has started in my head,
At dark midnight I've left my bed;
Grop'd for thee, as for hidden treasure,
Just to secure the thought and measure;
Earnestly wish'd for break of day,
That thy bright work I might survey;
But looking on when Phœbus rose,
Could neither make it verse or prose.

Thy letters I could not distinguish;
They were not Hebrew, Greek, or English;
Nor in a strait line hadst thou got 'em,
Nor rang'd, like *Dyche* from top to bottom;
But marching downward, sinking quite,
From hand the left to foot the right;
In all directions flying glib,
Like sparks when bursting from a squib;
Striving which first should get sway,
As if asham'd at sight of day.

In stupid mood, you've many a time
Stood still because you'd never a rhyme;
Again, you've been in error caught,
Procur'd a rhyme, but had no thought;
Yet if by chance sure nought was sweeter,
You've hit a thought, and hit a metre,
You seem'd as if by joy o'ercome,
Between my fingers and my thumb;
And wish'd, when laid to public view,
'Twould please the world as it pleas'd you.
All the returns you crav'd the while
Were to be treated with a smile;
Not of contempt it must occasion,
No—say the smile of approbation.

Let strictest truth and you agree
Your errors will be charg'd to me;
Nor ever once offend the ear;
No, not the chastest of the fair.

In politics ne'er make a rout;
Let right and wrong-heads deal it out.
An evil grows, you may be sure,
But with that evil grows a cure.

Never with reputations play;
Nor sport a character away;

Much better you had never written;
Nor smite, except you have been smitten.
But, should an evil raise its crown,
You're authoris'd to kick it down.

You'd better be a tooth-pick made
Than follow the poetic trade;
Unless you can, with powers alert,
Instruct the reader, or divert.
But you'll attain a double worth,
If ever you accomplish both.

June 22, 1796

Poems: Chiefly Tales

A receipt to make a Methodist

Take a fat rect'ry—there's one near,
Which brings seven hundred pounds a year;
With such a prize the patron's glad;
Trains to the church his second lad.

Young Master in his gown appears;
Drinks, games, and swears for twenty years;
Makes girls bring now and then a child;
Shoots, bullies, hunts—at length is foil'd.

Then let him sell, when run this round,
Possession for six thousand pound;
To one who cash and head retains,
No need of either to have brains.
Whene'er such teachers hold a prize,
You'll quickly see a meeting rise.

Oct. 4, 1796

A tour to Scotland

If you're a *father*, who retains
A larger store of wealth than brains;
A jewel hold which you prize most,
Are anxious lest it should be lost,
Read but the lines that are behind,
The way to save it you may find.
You'll clearly see, with half an eye,
How matters tend when you're not by.

If you're a fortune-hunter made,
Read, and you'll quickly learn your trade.
Nor think Fate can play you a prank;
She holds a prize without a blank.

If you're a daughter, I'll engage,
Though only fifteen years of age—
Quite charming! you'll become a wife;
And not repent—except for life.

No antique tale shall now be told
My story is but one week old;
Tea-table treasure of the day;
Fresh from the mint it shines away.
A guinea soon as dropp'd is found;
A ball caught at its first rebound.

We'll *Waddle* and his daughter bring
Upon the stage—their travels sing.

The man, 'tis said, who trade commands,
Profit and loss well understands:
But this, we speak without disgrace,
Was only half our hero's case;
And yet it strictly may be said,
"He perfect master was of trade:"

For trade he could whole years pursue,
Yet trading losses never knew;
Was well appriz'd, from day to day,
Where, to a doit, his profits lay;
With one superfluous grain, at least,
Would never let the scale be press'd;
And ev'ry scruple he rejects
More than just what the law directs,
Because 'twould tend, without a doubt,
"To press the measure's bottom out."

The man who strives to get and save
May, in the end, two thousand have.
This bank will make a pretty store,
Yet not destroy the wish for more.
That sum, however, being sent,
"He'd trade decline, and live a gent."

His dusty bags and bins kick'd o'er,
He'll open shop and shut no more;
But, with a *beauty* all admire,
Scarcely fifteen, he will retire,

"Now, since his house was large and fair,
And had a room or two to spare,
They might be to an inmate let
For they'd a little profit get."
And who but misers can tell what
A pleasure's from a penny got?

Olindus, with a longing view,
Survey'd the girl—and fortune too;
Wanted apartments—saw the place—
Agreed—"they suited to an ace."
Thus Waddle, by his saving crown,
Prepar'd a step to throw her down.
Then how to her can blame be let in,
When he was aiding and abetting?

Some said *Olindus* was two score;
Others presum'd a little more.
But this is darker than a riddle,
With which the Muse shall never meddle.
Whether his capital was aught
Above, or was *beneath* a groat,
We'll not determine nor aver;
But guess the last, though we should err.

Now things went well 'twixt him and child;
They whisper'd, glanc'd, and squeez'd, and smil'd.
The little Cupids, and the Graces,
Were there, but durst not shew their faces.
Darts, flames, and tales, her passions move;
At length comes everlasting love.
The new-made dough is pliant still,
For you may mould it to your will.
He eas'ly may his point obtain
Who leads a harmless girl in train.

Waddle began to smell a rat;
Yes, when the thief his meal has got;
And told *Olindus,* with grave face,
"He must provide another place."
Receiv'd this answer on the nail—
"I'll go to-morrow without fail."
The night creeps on—Sol's done his best;
The Muse and *Waddle* go to rest.

THE SECOND PART

Weak talents lead into a snare,
But never aid to get you clear.

Wad. was amaz'd when morn came on,
To find his little daughter gone.
And now black storms and tears were seen—
"O dear, they're gone to *Gretna Green!*

But I'll prevent them in the end;"
So took a chaise, and took a friend.

Now two post-chaises ran apace,
As if they meant to run a race.
Our pair kept foremost all the while
Till they were set down in *Carlisle.*
But shall I tell the tidings sad—
Not one post-chaise could there be had.
Venus, the Graces, Cupid too,
Was not this vile neglect in you?
Like will-o-wisp, lure to the snare,
Then leave unwary lovers there!

If they retreat, they meet the foe;
Debarr'd they could not onward go;
Commanding neither chaise nor coach;
Condemn'd to wait the storm's approach.
Dame Fortune prov'd an arrant jilt,
Destroy'd the fabrick nearly built.

"O la, we're ruin'd, lost, undone!
My father's frowns how shall I shun?"
Not Tommy, when he climb'd up high,
Was caught in gutting a mince-pye;
No Priest, who found himself set fast,
Nor found relief while—hem! could last;
Nor Chloe, when blew up her gown,
Shew'd half a leg with stocking down;
Nor even Madam, when her charms
Were found within the footman's arms;
Were half so shock'd as were our pair
When Waddle and his friend came there.

Our groom withdrew; his suit was cross'd;
The case was broke; the jewel lost;
The child restor'd; the swain bereft;
Like father Adam turn'd adrift;

Nay, worse than Adam, we believe,
Because he went without his Eve.

He saw the chamber-maid come down,
And gently twitch'd her by the gown—
"Will you, dear Molly, by me stand?"
Then slipt two guineas in her hand;
Which Molly thought the highest bliss—
She dropp'd a curtsy, *he* a kiss.
For guineas are, which fortune brings,
The most persuasive earthly things.

Waddle and friend, and daughter sat,
Sometimes in silence, sometimes chat.
He held harangue, and held his tea;
Blam'd naughty girls who disobey.
Whether his views and hers were one,
We'll not determine, but go on.

The chamber-maid, with modest air
And three-inch curtsy, enter'd there—
"Madam, a bed's made up for you;
Be pleas'd to rise and take a view;
For if you any error find
It shall be alter'd to your mind."

'Twixt *Wadd* and friend the glasses run;
A current custom when we've won;
That management they amply bless,
Which had been crown'd with such success.

Some moments praise they both enjoy.
Wadd rang the bell; his pipe laid by;
Molly appear'd, with features mild—
"Where, Mistress Molly, is the child?"
"They're gone, Sir, in your chaise!"—"Oh, oh!
Why then the devil with them go.
They may be hang'd for what I heed;

Another step I'll not proceed.
No fool but I, it's my belief,
Opens his door to admit a thief.
Myself I've gull'd in all that's done;
Nay, brought a chaise to help them on!"

As fresh as mack'rel, might be seen,
Our pair set down at Gretna Green.
They made enquiries, without lack,
"Where was the gentleman in black?
Can you unite us two with ease?"
"I can—ten guineas, if you please."

The swain, 'tis said, look'd rather queer,
But found himself not master there.
"Sir, not a soul beneath the sky
Can tie a faster knot than I."

The blacksmith sought his tools amain,
And quickly forg'd a marriage chain;
Then link'd together, at one stroke,
The rose-bud and the bulky oak.

My tale is done, fair truth you'll find,
But one remark is left behind.
It teaches *when,* if you're *not* poor,
To *open,* when to *shut* your door.

Dec. 26, 1796.

Poems: Chiefly Tales

To a new married man

'Tis easy, when married, to put away strife,
Because a good husband will make a good wife:
Draw gently, be loving, good-humour'd and still;
Then you may be happy as long as you will.

Dear Friend, I'm given to understand
You've ta'en a loving wife in hand;
And probably expect to share,
Like others, pleasure without care;
Serenity and sun-shine too
Are things with ease you bring to view;
But pray what title have you got
For what the major part have not?
For where *one*'s bless'd who takes a wife,
There's *two* repent it during life.

Yet this state is, though ills invade,
The happiest state that e'er was made
For if the evils we're combating
Are evils of our own creating,
We, with some prudence, then may shun them,
Or cut them short if we've begun them.
The traveller should never lack
To strike into the cleanest track.

Full forty years the chain I bore,
And wish'd to bear it forty more;
For when pure love affects the heart,
That couple never wish to part;
Their love will grow through every stage,
In spite of wrinkles, sickness, age.
Large draughts of pleasure I drew then;
Perhaps not known to one in ten;
Nor ever felt one pang of path
Till Fate resolv'd to break the chain.

Poems: Chiefly Tales

Allow then an experienc'd mate,
Long practis'd in the married state,
To tell you where, if you're not blind,
That treasure call'd *Content* may find.

'Tis said, "that state is harmony
When man and wife shall *both* agree;"
But I maintain bliss holds its place
When *half* this only is the case.
Then who would miss a Paradise
When he can buy it at half price?

Use all attention on *your* part,
To *keep* as well as *gain* her heart;
Nor act a child when at its play,
Cry for a toy to throw away.
You'll find this, of all gems found yet,
The richest in your cabinet.
If your address *her* heart procures,
She the same title has to yours.
Dwell on her virtues as divine,
And then she'll make them brighter shine.
Of the minutest take a view,
Which shows none are forgot by you.

If inwardly you feel delight,
Whenever she appears in sight;
If, when with her you're left alone,
You neither tire, nor heave a groan,
You then have fully learn'd your part,
And I'll pronounce she's gain'd *your* heart.

Should common errors be descry'd,
In *anger,* nor in *public,* chide;
Tenderly touch, *without* abuse;
Nay, softly plead her own excuse:
This calls that pride forth in the end,
Which ever shews a wish to mend.

To cherish love and make it thrive,
Attempt to *lead,* but never *drive.*
To persevere be much inclin'd
Then you will mould her to your mind.

Should male, or female friend, but seem
To lesten her in your esteem,
To their suggestions ne'er attend,
They come from a suspicious friend.

Those faults o'er which your eye *must* pass,
View through the small end of the glass.
This my dear Sir, a friend procures,
Who always will diminish yours.

If ever grief attacks her breast,
Take to yourself one half at least.
With *reasons,* gentle *soothings* too,
That cankering enemy subdue.

Contentions in the married state
From *nothings* oft originate;
A candle's end, a thread, a pin,
Are quite sufficient to begin.
Answers, rejoinders, and replies,
Make many a serious quarrel rise,
Which terminate in deep vexation;
Nay, sometimes in a separation.
Whene'er such altercations start,
Let silence end them on *your* part.
Thus the grand point you win with ease;
And you may win whene'er you please.

When you in company shall meet her,
With kind attention always treat her:
Your satire, banter, laugh, or sneer,
On no account must glance at her.
Nor let her e'er be plac'd by you

In a degrading point of view.
If of the two you hold most sense,
Then let it act in her defence.

These maxims I observed—adieu—
If not worn out, will profit you.

Feb. 27, 1797

Poems: Chiefly Tales

The cottager

A cow, a pig, the feather'd brood,
The *cot* which on the common stood,
The scythe and sickle, flail and spade,
Brought *Hodge* and family their bread.

When his kind stars these aids afford,
Hodge is as happy as his Lord.
He felt no want; was blithe as May;
Cattle or wife ne'er went astray.

But now the commons are inclos'd;
His fav'rite stock to sale expos'd;
His cow, his calf, his pig, are gone;
His sheep are "kill'd off" ev'ry one.
His flail, scythe, sickle, and his spade,
Could not supply his cot with bread.

Hunger no fear of law descries;
"No fear of God before his eyes"—
He stole a goose, by famine led,
From that spot where his own had fed,
For where's the man who'd had the use
Of goose, could ever give up goose?

Now, to the Justice brought in haste;
That Justice who'd inclos'd the waste;
His worship in a passion flew
In silence *Hodge* a long face drew—
"A halter, Sirrah, you'll not miss,
For perpetrating crimes like this."

Hodge droop'd his head, and heav'd a sigh;
Then meekly utter'd this reply—
"The crime is small in man or woman,
Should they a goose steal from a common;

But what can plead that man's excuse
Who steals a common from a goose?"

April 13, 1797

Poems: Chiefly Tales

The Valentine

The Senate, College, Hall, and Bar,
Famous for flowr's of rhetoric are;
Yet their persuasive powers are small;
A *child* of *three* surpasses all.

The Minister of State, with ease
Can draw your money when he please;
Although the cash you hold is plenty,
Can quickly leave your pocket empty.
His oily tongue has oft beguil'd;
Yet he must fall beneath the child.

Suet can draw a smile; and *Farren*
A coronet to put her hair in:
The powers of *Erskine* seldom fail
To make his opponent turn pale.
All who in rhetoric strain the throat,
Fade at the infant petticoat.

Near *Derby* liv'd a *Lady Gray;*
At *Risley,* by the turnpike way;
Joining *herself* to *harmony,*
With *hospitality* made three.
She fed the bird; she stroak'd the cat;
Nay, Towser's tail wagg'd with the pat;
Offended none that e'er you knew,
Whether they walk'd on four or two;
Kept wine that rais'd, and drugs that purg'd,
For neighbours when their sickness urg'd.
Whene'er, and what can this transcend,
She saw a soul, she saw *a friend!*
A life like hers was sure to charm;
Often did good, but never harm.

The bunch of keys, a woman's pride,
Was never known to grace her side.
Her doors unlock'd; she ne'er was cheated;
A *confidence* design defeated.
Her face, in converse with a clown,
Was never known to wear a frown.

As by the high-way stood the hall,
'Twas ready for the stranger's call.
A form and table were in view;
A horn of beer, and luncheon too;
So that the wand'rer, by delay,
Was fairly aided in his way.

The Steward watch'd—'twas *Thomas White,*
The tenants, and the lady's right;
Cautious to hold, and never fail,
Between the two an even scale.

His little son began to walk,
And lisp'd as if he meant to talk.
The prattler in the hall at play
Was notic'd by the Lady Gray.
For youth and innocence engage;
They hold a power that's lost in age.

She dandled Tommy on the knee;
They both were equal, both were free;
Held conversation *tete à tete;*
The cake and sugar-plumbs were sweet.
These visits often were repeated;
But not a visit was regretted.

"Tommy shall draw, come dress him fine,
My Lady, for his Valentine;
And you'll observe, when up you're led
By Molly to my Lady's bed,
To make a bow, my dear, that's clever,

And then this pretty paper give her.
If she should ask, without a frown,
What she shall give? reply, a crown!
'Twill put, if Madam should disburse,
Five shillings in thy little purse."

Now *Tom* and Valentine were led
Where *half* was offer'd at her bed.
As innocence came without a guile,
Both were accepted with a smile.

"What shall I give thee?" Madam cries—
"*A town*"—the lisping child replies.
"I will, thy Valentine to crown,
Grant thy request, and give a town.
The town of *Sandiacre*'s mine;
But *Sandiacre* shall be thine."

Time saw, ere two years could expire,
The Lady die—the child a 'Squire;
And, after forty more, observ'd,
The office of High Sheriff [1] serv'd .
His family enjoys it yet.
Who easier could a village get?

Thus if you powerful rhetoric seek,
Apply where folks can scarcely speak;
The most persuasive eloquence
Is found where there's the least pretence.

May 12, 1793

[1] 1729.

N. B. Sandacre; corrupted into St. Iaker, a village one mile East of Risley; divided from Stableford in Nottinghamshire, by the river Erwash. The soil is stiff, bordering upon clay, except an acre, upon the summit of a hill, upon which stands the church, is a bed of sand, hence the name.

Poems: Chiefly Tales

The triumvirate

Now three jolly blades with a sing-song we'll crown,
Who made a gay figure in Birmingham town.
We'll tell how much money they each of them made,
And then, if you please, you may follow their trade.

One of these could engrave without making a noise;
Another succeeded in making of toys;
But toys and engraving appear but a joke;
We'll find out a better, or have our head broke.

At the tavern our heroes dispute o'er the pot,
At which of their trades was the most money got;
For in all our contentions 'tis usually known,
A man speaks his best in support of his own.

The Engraver declar'd it was well in his power
To earn with his fingers three shillings an hour.
"A trifle!" says *Palmer*, "I'll lay you a crown,
I'll pick up more money by *begging* in town."

"And I'll lay a crown," says the toyman, and drew,
"That I get more money than either of you,
By *singing of ballads* in Birmingham Street.
He that wins, like the Pope, shall have three crown "compleat."

They farther agreed, that on Saturday night,
From seven to nine, each should try all his might;
Like a *Courtier*, a *Breslau,* no fear of detection,
Try which of them best could succeed by deception.

His tools the Engraver collected in hand;
The *beggar* perceiv'd there was no time to stand,
So he blufted an eye, and he tuck'd up a leg,
And like other beggars he set out to beg.

Poems: Chiefly Tales

One crutch, and one leg, were expos'd to the view;
Then who can deny that he stood upon two?
But he was appriz'd, though you could not observe,
That, in case of assault, he had one in reserve.

His opponents the laurel must certainly yield,
When he, with three legs, was equipp'd for the field;
For who could be better prepar'd for a fray?
With *one* he could fight, or with *two* run away.

Brown walnut, black eye-brows, the shrewd toyman seeks,
And cover'd his chin with the growth of six weeks;
A few quires of ballads his hand did not lack,
Nor patches nor rags did the coat on his back.

The singer sung sweet, and the beggar bawl'd loud,
As beggars and singers when fleecing the crowd;
And like every beggar, and like every singer;
They laugh at the people whose money they finger.

When our three contenders two hours had gone through,
In graving and begging and Sol-faing too,
'Twas needful to state all their profit amounts,
So retreat to the tavern and settle accounts.

Seven and four-pence th' Engraver before them both spread,
And till some one oppos'd him was that much a-head;
But the Beggar immediately open'd his store,
And with eight and eleven-pence soon did him o'er.

The last gave a smile, and the Engraver a frown,
But the sweet singer instantly brought them both down;
For exclusive of capital, he by fair trade
Ten shillings and sixpence two farthings had made.

From henceforth, good people, the graver throw by,
And if you've ambition to climb pretty high,

You may traverse through begging, resume limbs and eyes,
And probably up to a ballad may rise.

June 4, 1797

Poems: Chiefly Tales

The button

A subject much smaller than this I rehearse
Was never attempted in prose or in verse;
A pitiful button is all I shall own;
You may sing it, or say it, or let it alone.

That button, though polish'd, won't answer quite pat,
With which the recruit first adorns his new hat,
For this I consider no part of my charge,
Though round as a trencher, and nearly as large.

Nor shall in my poem that button be found
By which Mr. Bratt acquir'd ten thousand pound.
Though it pleases the eye while the pocket it fills,
And causes, most sweetly, to run the chaise wheels.

No gingerbread button will suit me compleat,
Nor that often made after eating roast meat;
Nor shall, in my rhyme, any button be seen,
But that finger'd by the loquacious 'Squire Green.

One end of whose tale you may find without pain,
But the other, like fortune, you wish for in vain;
You're restless, you move, but no end's in your pow'r;
Have patience, my friend, you'll not find it this hour.

An ill fated Button on Shipton's right breast
Was held by 'Squire Green, which disturb'd its soft rest;
While one tedious story began to transpire,
Long and sweet as a journey three miles in the mire.

Poor Shipton to ev'ry eye would now appear tied,
And felt but so so with his button and ear tied;
He edg'd and he turn'd every way he could see,
But when he'd tried all there were none to get free.

Most irksome he felt from his foot to his head,
And ere the tale ended his patience was fled;
Then instant the button cut off with his knife—
"Take that and be damn'd, and I'll run for my life."

Then let the tale-teller be sure, without fail,
That button and patience will last out the tale;
But if on this plan he should give you no quarter,
Let his tongue, or his story, be cut rather shorter.

June 9, 1797

A precedent

Bess was, for being a *double* bride,
And *Molly* for *manslaughter,* tri'd;
They both were, by my Lord's command,
Sentenc'd to burning in the hand;
Then these two crimes we *equal* view,
Of *killing* one, and *kissing* two.

The cuckold

The Muse, as property is gone,
She should, by right, put mourning on.
The simple smile shall fly the place;
My tale comes with a serious face.

Why is a man disgrac'd, I pray,
Because his wife shall go astray?
Why sneering language at him sent
For evils which he would prevent?
Good boys will never make their sport
Of people who are bent or short.
If he consents not to her shame,
He merits pity, never blame.
But if he aids her acting ill,
Then call him Cuckold if you will;
But he'll regard no more your cries
Than blust'ring winds a lover's sighs.

We'll now the curtain raise, and there
Three sober people shall appear;
Mr. John Carpenter and bride,
With Mr. Aldworth by their side;
They liv'd in peace, shunn'd all demur,
She lov'd them both—they both lov'd her.
Yet every act, though they agree,
Must not be known to all the three.
She'd charms, though not expos'd to view,
Which Carpenter and Aldworth knew.

How, when, and where, we'll not relate,
Only a real fact we state.
Aldworth held thirty pounds a year
During the life of Carpenter:
He'd every motive to shun strife—
Aldworth should try to *save* his life.

What though the sky be calm and bright
For many a day and many a night,
Yet not expect a change is vain;
'Twill end in thunder, wind, and rain.
This our two heroes did betide,
Who shar'd the favours of the bride.
A quarrel rose while she was by;
The lightning flash'd from either eye;
From Aldworth chief it flew apace,
Who call'd him Cuckold to his face.

O, cruel word! it sorely gall'd;
'Twas gone, and could not be recall'd.
The rage of Carpenter we sing,
As rising to the treble string;
His best revenge is, we suppose,
To kick the bottom; ring the nose.
And was this styptic in his power,
He might apply it half an hour.

But Carpenter, who, lost in thought,
Other retaliation sought
Determin'd he would soon cashier
Aldworth of thirty pounds a-year—
Jump'd in a pond, where he was drown'd;
There full *revenge* on Aldworth found.

Should this be every Cuckold's case,
How much, alas, 'twould thin our race!
The world would suffer to its cost,
For half the husbands would be lost.
She mourn'd because she, to her woe,
Lost one of two strings to her bow.
He curs'd the name, and griev'd for life;
He'd nothing left—except the wife.

Preserve a Cuckold, if you can;
You'll find him a most useful man;

A screen as needful as attire
To guard against a scorching fire:
But if the screen you over-turn,
Your reputation soon will burn.

July 23, 1797

Happiness

Read but these lines, and you'll confess,
They'll point direct to happiness.
Though plain the picture brought to view
You'll find the features strictly true.

Why should the poet ever deign
To coin a fiction in his brain;
Then speciously a tale's unfurl'd
Of falshood, to reform the world;
When, if of life he takes a view,
There's incident enough that's true;
Which fit a case exact, when put,
Just as a shoe will fit your foot.

As no condition man must share,
E'er was, or can be, free from care,
So some small joy will be the lot,
From palaces down to the cot;
Then that's most happy, we must grant,
When prudence gives what we shall want;
For if great wealth brings care and doubt,
He's happiest who can do without.
To think the same you'll be inclin'd
Except "ambition fires your mind;"
But, if you doubt the truth I write,
I'll place it in the clearest light.

Joseph and *Sarah* shall be brought;
They'll ratify the lesson taught;
Young people, who, in days of yore,
Labour'd for what they eat and wore.

Joseph, a farmer's son, was found
To save, by caution, forty pound.

As he a married state would try,
On Sally cast a lover's eye.

When they'd through smiling, pressing gone,
Besought the Priest to make two one.

If prudence springs in single life,
It flourishes in man and wife.
He built a house for forty pound
Upon 'Squire Mundy's cottage ground;
Behav'd as peaceful tenants ought,
And paid the 'Squire a yearly groat.

To this abode he took his wife,
And took *his* station during life.
`Their whole œconomy, I knew,
Sprung from the stock from whence I grew.

Joining the house you might behold
A little yard, high nam'd—"The Fold,"
Stock'd well with chickens; ducks a dabbling;
Besides three geese, most stately gabbling;
Which boldly star'd you in the face
As if joint sovereigns of the place,
And would have said, as you look'd on,
Could they speak English—"Sir, be gone!"
One of the bristly race, not more,
To aid the house with winter-store.

A crazy barn with one small bay,
Not over-stock'd with corn or hay;
Where strolling beggars, through a gap,
Enter'd at night to steal a nap.
And that was all a thief *could* steal
From this nocturnal commonweal.

A shed, whose entrance fac'd the house—
This held a treasure—three sleek cows;

Whose profits, studiously to count,
Would quickly rise to some amount.

A garden, small, but warm snug spot,
Meant chiefly to supply the pot;
Whose produce made friend *Knowles* look big,
When on his plate it met the pig.

Behind the barn an orchard neat,
Grac'd with one tree, whose fruit was sweet.
This will admit of no dispute;
I've scal'd the tree to taste the fruit.

All I've describ'd, an acre near,
Was wholly under Sarah's care.
And not a soul beneath the skies,
Perhaps, could make more profit rise.
This garden snug, and orchard warm,
Compos'd exact our hero's farm.

"Who," says the critic, looking deep,
"On this small patch three cows can keep?"
Why, the waste lands, and open fields,
During nine months, a tribute yields.

Let me just add to what I've said,
Six sheep upon the common fed:
These were friend Joseph's care, no doubt,
Who strove to keep the maggots out.

THE SECOND PART

If peace of mind you wish to see,
Let your concerns contracted be.
The more expanded your affairs,
The more they'll multiply your cares.
What fisherman has cause to fret
If all be well with boat and net?

What shepherd can exert his sway
Over his flock when gone astray?

Joseph in servitude appears;
A lab'rer more than three-score years;
And, with his masters, in such grace,
Was never known to change his place.
In winter eight-pence was his gains;
In summer twelve rewards his pains.

He, strait and thin, near six feet high;
She, short and thick, with but one eye.
Two sons, one daughter, and no more,
Came, at long intervals, as store.

They rose at five; they din'd at noon;
At seven they supp'd—the day was done.
Tea-equipage ne'er made its way;
Milk-porridge smoak'd at break of day.
At nine repose they seek, and find;
Result of labour—peace of mind.
An early hour ne'er threw away,
Nor need they catch one through the day.

In summer-time, you might observe,
His scythe and sickle make a curve.
In winter days, his flail sublime
True as a fidler's foot beat time.
Should you attend, morn, night, and noon,
You'd find his instrument in tune.

They fairly got their little store;
Made both ends meet—and something more.
No penny e'er sustain'd abuse;
Each answer'd to some proper use.
The want of money brought no sorrow;
They rather chose to lend than borrow;
Nor would object, sometimes, to spend

A social hour with pipe and friend:
With none but friends such hour might be—
It could not with an enemy.

If we survey their chimney's nitch,
'Twas honour'd with a bacon flitch
When to their house approach'd a guest,
They cut that part which seem'd the best;
But what was of more value yet,
The visitant a welcome met.
This would sincerity impart,
Which coming from, it reach'd the heart.

Wine, brandy, spirits, or strong beer,
Were rather shy at ent'ring there.
Master and Mistress were as shy;
This happy cot they ne'er came nigh.
Joseph and *Sarah*—modest brace!
The Priest gave these—they kept their place.

Unpolish'd language you might hear;
But then that language was sincere.
Falshood in silk will be dispis'd;
But truth's admir'd, though homely guis'd.
Into disputes none could decoy them;
The lawyer got no profit by them.
Content, food, work, diseases put out,
And these the hungry doctor shut out.

The parish Priest far better sped;
Attentive both to what he said.
From conscience their small tithes they paid,
Although unconscionably laid.

In wedded love so bright they shin'd,
I'd match them against all mankind.
When fifteen years had wing'd full fast,
One angry word had never pass'd:

And I'm convinc'd the same you'll find
In all the fifteens left behind.
Neither commanded nor submitted,
She ne'er was halter'd, nor he bitted.
They harmoniz'd in what was done
Exactly as if two were one;
Just as two bones which form one joint;
Or two feet marching to one point.
In scales let two new guineas chink,
One ne'er will let the other sink.

Their stile of dress, from foot to crown,
Ran many an age of fashions down.
His Sunday suit quite fresh appears—
The Sunday suit of twenty years.
To many a generation known,
Who could declare it was his own.

Their manners simple as their dress;
In all their living no excess.
With innocence and prudence join'd,
What sorrow could attack the mind?

Our couple to each other true,
Punctual in word and action too,
Pass'd four-score years, then cross'd that bourn
From whence no traveller can return;
Leaving behind, in humble station,
A lesson worthy imitation.

Dec 10, 1797

Poems: Chiefly Tales

The lover

Now ponder well, ye fair ones dear,
And eke ye bards also,
"The gallant Lady's fall is here,"
Mark well her overthrow.

Poor *Thomas,* from fair Dolly's view,
So many wounds has got,
His heart was pepper'd through and through,
As if 'twas with small shot.

To all the world he would impart
His love was not a vapour;
Her name being written on his heart
He'd write it too on paper.

Firmly resolv'd, his pen he takes;
Solicits aid sublime:
Then crams himself into a jakes,
To try his hand at rhyme.

Let Dolly and your pen alone,
Or else you'll make a din;
For noisome tallow's ever known
To keep the candle *in.*

Of verse deliver'd, not of love;
Pleas'd with his offspring dear,
Resolv'd it through the world should rove;
A *Poet* he'll appear.

But how could this poor author live,
Counting without his host?
He could not *sell,* nor *lend,* nor *give*—
Then said—"It sha'n't be lost.

Though she's unkind, I'll never drown,
Nor dangle in a rope."
He pinn'd it to the roast meat down,
Converting verse to sop.

Then sorrowful that verse's end is,
Which can't procure a wife;
Though holding what we all contend is
The grand support of life.

The beef digested—Thomas took
What guarded fat and lean
To where you hate to smell or look,
And ev'ry part made clean.

Thus Dolly, who possess'd the heart,
Twelve inches sunk her head,
By dropping in that dreadful part
We never wish to tread.

Ye fair, be warn'd by Dolly's fate,
Who, 'stead of being married,
Was doom'd to a degraded state—
Where she was *born* was buried.

June 14, 1798

Poems: Chiefly Tales

The auctioneer

A period pass'd over I'll bring back to view,
When the sons of the hammer were wont to *tell true*;
When the buyer saw timber, and land, brick, and stone,
Not with Auctioneer's eyes—but he saw with his own.

Now assembled all ranks, from the knight to the clown,
To see an estate of *great value* knock'd down;
All attentive, while round the great table are seated,
Are able to pay—but submit to be *treated.*

"But five thousand pounds! Gem'en, what are you doing?
Five thousand one hundred—a going! a going!
The lands are most fertile; the buildings are good;
The premises grac'd with a *fine hanging wood.*"

"Whereabout, Sir, this beautiful wood can I see?
I've examin'd the whole, but can scarce find a tree."
"What! been over the premises, yet not descry'd it;
If you'd had half an eye, Sir, you must have espy'd it.

Pass close to the orchard, and over the fallows,
Then turn to the left, and you'll come to the gallows."

April 3, 1798

Poems: Chiefly Tales

The way to rule a village

That Village is perfectly under command,
When the Justice and Rector will go hand in hand;
Their power o'er the peasant can ne'er be shut out,
When jointly these two toss the bottle about.

But when it shall happen the two disagree,
Ill-nature, retorts, and returns, you may see.
The Peasants alarm'd will begin to take sides;
The plague becomes pow'rful—the village divides.

Then take this advice—you no farther need seek,
Let the 'Squire and the Parson get drunk once a week;
When into their breast they've transported the barrel,
Let the Priest and the Magistrate then shun a quarrel.

A Rector of Pride, and a Justice of Peace,
(With sentiments high, they could ne'er coalesce)
Met point-blank together, one day, on the road,
Though the ground each detested the other had trod.

"So, Sir," says the Justice, "you ride a fine horse;
Won't follow your master, who rode something worse;
For he, though divine, on a jack-ass we view;
Methinks the same animal might have serv'd you."

"I own," says the Parson, "your judgment is good,
Like our Saviour, I'd ride on an ass, if I cou'd;
But none I can purchase, so riding must cease,
Because every ass is a Justice of Peace."

May 8, 1798

The state of matrimony

Into Love's arms my Lord was carried—
So was my Lady—then they married.
In this state some take no delight,
Nor smile when *in* each other's sight.
But our fond pair ne'er made a rout,
Except their "dearest dear" was out.
Thus when two folks affections mingle,
They're twice as happy as when single.

If 'tis from *Time* our comfort springs,
Time changes quite the face of things;
And nothing, take a Bard's confession,
Will spoil a husband like possession.

Upon his hand reclin'd his head—
"Why do you yawn?" my Lady said.
The Peer reply'd —"As Scriptures spake,
A man and wife but *one* can make;
And I, my dear, feel, I must own,
Quite irksome when I'm left alone."

Sept. 1, 1798

Poems: Chiefly Tales

The profits of the field

It may by chance happen, exciting surprize,
A fool may be wiser than one counted wise.

A lunatic—I could tell where,
Was plac'd beneath a Doctor's care,
Who ply'd the medic art—and, more,
To fit his head up as before.
A tenement should be kept whole,
Whether for body made, or soul;
And he who best can mend the flaws,
Mason or *Doctor*, gains applause.

Our patient's case, we humbly guess,
Attended was with some success;
And he allow'd when better found,
To traverse the adjacent ground.

With horse, with gun, and three dogs nigh,
A sporting gentleman pass'd by—
"I'm glad," while o'er the horse he hover'd,
"To see you, Sir, so well recover'd.
What method is the Doctor taking,
That the complaint is you forsaking?"

"A water-tub he puts me in,
And makes me stand up to the chin.
So you expect to be a winner
By changing powder for a dinner.
But pray what *game,* 'twixt you and I,
In one whole year can you destroy?"

"Why thirty pounds worth, I should guess;
I think not more-perhaps 'tis less."

"Then what expence this profit clogs,
In horses, ammunition, dogs?"

"Why, to support this annual feast,
Three hundred, I suppose, at least."

"Then, Sir, inform me, are not you
The greatest *madman* of thetwo?
I almost tremble for your doom,
Lest my sagacious Doctor come.
Retreat! The moment he appears
He'll duck *you* over head and ears."

Sept. 9, 1798

The Grenadier

The eye that reads this poem learns
How the great *wheel of fortune* turns.

No Muse by me shall e'er be sought;
I think their aid not worth a groat.
They may consent to lend a hand
When Bards can neither go nor stand.

But, as for me, I've blessings got,
Blessings beyond a poet's lot;
No noise of wheel, or brat sublime,
To squeak in prose, and murder rhyme;
A room as silent as the night;
A farthing candle burning bright,
And, if the blaze to dulness tends,
Can snuff it with my fingers ends;
A fire, which I suppose is in,
I think it rather warms my skin;
A pen, but of the bluntish sort;
A stand, although the ink be short;
A list of rhymes before me stuck,
To state in verse, should I have luck,
Th' adventures of a Grenadier,
In perfect truth, in language clear.

Lysander I shall call the name
Of him I've chosen for my theme;
A Gentleman—his birth we'll trace—
Cold Denmark was his native place.
His person, though not quite divine,
The ladies would call vastly fine;
Such as they might, in high degree,
With pleasure, but with danger, see.

"The world," and none to cross his views,
"Being all before him, where to chuse,"
Upon the shining sword he ventur'd;
And in the Polish service enter'd.

A smile descended from the throne;
And regiment, which he call'd his own.

To keep her heart what lady can—
A Col'nel! and a handsome man!

Though beautiful, it is confess'd,
Yet *more*, now in reg'mentals dress'd;
For scarlet is, the ladies own,
The most enchanting colour known.
Perhaps he'd conquer, deck'd in charms,
More with his eyes than with his arms.
Whether a *male* dropp'd, we can't tell,
But, certainly, a lady fell.
Immensely were her riches grown;
And she commanded them alone.

When *two* each other seek to gain,
They very rarely seek in vain.
Loadstone and needle, by fix'd laws,
Each other in its vortex draws.
Her bait was *wealth*—'twas what he sought—
His *beauty*—by which *she* was caught.
And now the marriage rites come on,
Each side was pleas'd, for each had won.
What happiness from wedlock flows
A married couple only knows!
What blessings in their lap were hurl'd!
She brought two sons to tell the world.

"My dear!" they by each other sit—
Says she, "you shall the service quit,
And we'll from Poland turn our face

To Denmark—'tis our native place."
The pliant husband, at one word,
Forsook the military sword.
The art of killing he forgo,
And only wear a sword for show.

When child and gew-gaw first unite,
That union gives supreme delight;
But, when the child is satisfied,
The fav'rite gew-gaw's cast aside.
Union of bodies, 'tis confess'd,
Has never long a couple bless'd,
No marriage can give true delight
Except a pair of souls unite.

This, in our couple's case, we view;
As wedlock now had nothing new:
The novelty had died away,
And love was in a swift decay;
That love which they so much adore
Grew colder than it was before.
The fuel which kept up the fire
Was scarce, and let the flame expire.

When surly disappointments rise,
Ill-nature then each spirit tries.
To *know* is absolutely fit,
Which is to govern—which submit.
The trial made—the Fates befool him—
He must submit, and *she* must rule him.
This would most monstrous seem in woman,
Only the fashion makes it common.
Shew me the female, if you can,
Who power usurps to rule a man,
Who would not try that power to mend,
And rise a tyrant in the end.

Lysander, now turn'd out of door,
Her person must behold no more.
Her treasure great she kept alone,
For not a farthing was his own.
Her power increas'd—she did not fail
To throw her husband into jail;
Where wretchedness, affliction, lies;
Want, damp, and filth, before his eyes.
His life must end in one short day,
So watch'd the hour, and ran away.
Thus evils follow twenty fold,
When love has no substantial hold.

THE SECOND PARTt

The Reader may express some fear,
And cry, "Pray where's the Grenadier?"
Sir, let not disappointment flow;
You've seen him many a line ago.

Perhaps, you'll ask me to reveal
What cogs there are in Fortune's wheel;
Urge me to tell you if, or not,
Our hero's to the bottom got.
Depriv'd of friends! imprison'd! poor!
Pray, is it needful to be lower?

"The world was all before him" twice,
But *where* to chuse he'd now *no* choice;
Like *Cain* must wander; and, what's worse,
Without a shilling in his purse.

When many a dismal scene he'd pass'd,
In London he arriv'd at last:
His clothes in rags—his visage thin;
Stomach and pocket nothing in:
But, that he might be better fed,
Enlisted in the Guards for bread.

Full six feet high—a person clear,
Instantly rank'd a Grenadier;
Was oft in should'ring arms beheld;
Often the centry-boxes fill'd.

His dismal tale, by Fame dispers'd,
Assail'd the ears of George the First—
"I'll see the man!"—Now pity presses
And, to relieve his sore distresses,
Three hundred pounds his case rewards.
Still he did duty in the Guards.

His lady, in her right, was found
Possess'd of forty thousand pound
Of South-Sea Stock—in trust was held;
Which not a doit to him must yield.
Thus *Tantalus* was hungry quite;
Yet food enough was plac'd in sight;
Rich dainties; but, though full in view,
Above his reach an inch or two.

To marriage it portends a curse
When ladies hold a private purse.

Now gracious *Caroline* was seen
To mount the throne a British Queen;
Who the two arts well understood,
Of shunning evil—doing good;
Made her great power, kind acts, and time,
Go hand in hand—I gain a rhyme.

His cruel state her mind depresses;
Was anxious to relieve distresses;
Summon'd the Lawyers of the Crown;
Making *Lysander's* case her own.

A bill was fil'd—the cause was heard—
Against trustees was made award—

"That to the hungry man shall come
The annual int'rest of that sum,
During his natural life; and then
Revert unto the heirs agen."

In Fortune's wheel some elevated;
Some are to deep depression fated;
But our suprizing hero's found
To trace the *Wheel of Fortune* round.

Lysander now, superbly dress'd,
Again the gentleman profess'd
At balls and birth-nights he'd appear
The most conspicuous person there:
Shone bright, and that with variation,
In the St. James's constellation.
Cupid from him threw many a dart;
And now and then there fell a heart.

Thus he who had been Fortune's sport
Figur'd in George the Second's court.
In the gay world he made a show,
And *Caroline* trick'd out a beau.

Oct. 23, 1798.

Poems: Chiefly Tales

The way to bilk a Constable

Read, and practise these verses; and then you, with ease,
May cozen and cheat folks whenever you please.

Mr. Brown was a Gel'man, who willingly shone
With any man's labour excepting his own.
That person, you'd think, much more eminent stands,
Who lives by his *talents,* than one by his hands;
A pocket could fathom; this art he could shine in,
With ease and with secrecy take out the lining.

Our Culprit, at *Hicks's Hall* lately appearing,
In a pocket his hand had been much interfering.
The action was prov'd—to the sentence submitted—
Was immediately back to the prison committed.

Retreating, our hero was close by his guard,
And passing through Clerkenwell spacious Church-yard—
"Sir, I'll speak to the Sexton, if you'll give me leave"
Who stood on the brink of a wide and deep grave.
"You're heartily welcome," the Officer cried;
And while, for a moment, they stood side by side,
The Culprit, before he one sentence could say,
In the grave push'd the Constable—then ran away.

Thus the pris'ner once more quite a freeman was made;
Let loose on the public to follow his trade.
The grave, it is said, puts an end to our living
And yet it can't cure a great rogue of his thieving.
The Officer, ere to the jail could arrive,
Was forc'd to submit to be buried alive.

Oct. 28, 1798

Poems: Chiefly Tales

The Robin-red-breast

An helpless animal, distress'd,
Excites compassion in the breast.

Poor Robin to the garden steer'd;
He'd lost his wife; his children rear'd;
And sought, his family being gone,
Retirement, till the spring came on.
Methinks 'twould vastly suit high life,
Could they but yearly change a wife.
So sure a remedy there's none,
Effectually to cure Crim. Con.

Pride taught him to find out a stand
Like man—a mansion rather grand;
In a large holly soon was seated,
Most beautiful and variegated.

Guarding the window stood the tree,
Where Robin ev'ry act could see.
As morning rose he march'd in view,
Asking the ladies "how they do?"
Till Spring he shunn'd the feather'd race;
Familiar with the human face.

Short, dark, and cold, the day was said;
For surly winter rear'd his head.
The night was dark, and colder far;
The Heav'ns cou'd not produce a star.
What bird can either dine or sup
When snow has lock'd his cupboard up?
He seemingly, though silent, said,
"I'll thank you for a crumb of bread."

Nancy the crumbs of comfort took,
And instantly obey'd his look.

Nancy, whose claim is the last word,
Directly christen'd him "My Bird."
The laundry's open'd, solely, we guess,
To give him daily *e* and *re*-gress;
And where our worthy Robin's fate is,
To find both food and lodging gratis.
He'd liberty to strol all day;
Amuse himself, or seek for prey;
At night he might whene'er he chose,
Retire to thaw his icey toes.

Ne'er bid to go—came at command;
And took the crumbs from Nancy's hand.
Pleas'd with his hopping up and down,
She valued him at half-a-crown.
A rising flame the nymph discovers;
She'd hardly change him for two lovers.
Her wrath might boil up to the brim,
But not a drop was aim'd at him.
Her truest friends may scalded be,
Who ne'er offended more than he.
Take this advice, 'twill bliss afford,
Your husband treat as you the bird.

Now *John* to shut the laundry steals
While *Hamlet* follow'd at his heels;
But neither of them once suspected,
Robin was perch'd and unprotected.
The keen-eyed dog made no delay,
Instantly fastened on his prey;
The suff'rer left, without a pause,
His little life in Hamlet's jaws.

Now Hamlet was, O dreadful doom!
Directly charg'd to quit the room;
And would have felt a basting sore,
Only a fav'rite was before.

From *Ann* a scold began to flow,
For, by long practice, she knew how.
The elements exert their power,
Then terminated in a shower:
Thus, though loud thunders cease to creep,
The dismal clouds in sorrow weep.

Dec. 2, 1798.

Poems: Chiefly Tales

The coachman's fall

Let not deceit excite surprize,
For the whole world is one disguize.

In sober lays, in simple truth,
We'll fill our poem with Miss *Ruth.*
A Poet, if not void of spirit,
Will dip his *pen* in praise of merit;
Disperse the cloud that's in his way,
And give it a meridian day.

Ruth, from the cradle, which is common,
By aid of *time* became a woman.
Brown, strait, and clean, which we all prize,
But rather of a smallish size.
When Love, who knew his usual trade,
On her his soft approaches made;
For *Richard,* if her passion burns,
Richard knew how to make returns.
Her flame burnt bright, and with good-will;
His burnt a little brighter still.

Whatever envious tongues might say,
Their private acts would bear the day;
The strictest honour was her part,
For she lost nothing but her heart.
"A love like this could ne'er be blasted;
They're happy sure"—yes, while it lasted.

No antient maid in Nature's range
But knows that man is apt to change;
And if the rover once should stray,
He seldom after finds his way.

The words and kisses Richard bore
Were not so warm as heretofore.

Though he attends from day to day,
His fire began to die away.
His stay was shorter—cold the while—
He took his leave without a smile;
And, what she rather thought amiss,
Forgot to give the parting kiss.
He visits less—she's less admir'd;
The flame in fifteen months expir'd.

"What tortures rise! My treasure's gone
That which I've set my heart upon.
No equal left—the greatest cross!
The world can ne'er repair the loss!
A shock! My Richard from me torn!
Too great to bear—but must be borne.
From thoughts of love I'll now desist;
In me no more it shall exist.
For no temptation man can see
Shall ever take its rise from me.
No more shall he to love incline;
The female habit I'll resign
The male apparel I'll put on;
From hence assume the name of John;
Exonerate the mind of care;
Despise the sex whose dress I wear."

Now John had left his gown at home,
And, by good luck, became a *groom;*
His duty did with all his power;
In time the bud will rise a flower;
For Johnny was a coachman made,
And drove the horses he had fed.
His love forgot, his fortune good,
Now master of the kitchen stood.

The maids, to Johnny, on their parts,
Were willing to resign their hearts.
But he, who knew his breast alone,

Found no room there but for his own.
What if they frown, and think amiss,
No more could do than toy and kiss.
He both performed to save his credit;
If a smart thing was said, he said it.
By the whole house this truth was known—
He won each heart, and kept his own.

THE SECOND PART

Our second part excites surprize—
A woman comes without disguise!

The 'Squire must now a journey go,
And John was order'd to put to.

Their stage was long—one inn was there,
Which only had one bed to spare.
This put the 'Squire in angry plight—
Says John, "Sir, I'll sit up all night."

"Then you'll take cold—it shall not be;
No, no, John, you shall sleep with me."
Alarm'd—"Sir, I no evil know—
Chair, squab, or floor, for me will do."
But all his rhetoric lost the field;
As servant he was bound to yield.

The Master now to bed was gone;
And, terrified, up stairs crept John.
Then to undress he set about;
But early put the candle out.
He was "requested to lie still."
Between the two there rose a hill;
Which rather dissipated fear—
"Four inches was a nice barrier."
Who rested, snor'd, slept ill, or well,
The little coachman best could tell.

Rising betimes, the Master said,
"Why do you early leave the bed?
No glimpse of day appears to me."
"Its time, Sir, I the horses see."
Thus he came out as free from sin,
And good a maid as he went in.
What other 'Squire a night could pass,
And never touch so sweet a lass!
What lass could with a 'Squire lie still,
And give no items of her will!
The 'Squire was glad his bed to share;
And John that he'd escap'd a snare.

The Master would a hunting ride,
And John attended by his side.
What hedges, ditches, gates, they cover,
We'll wave, for they'll at night tell over.
It happen'd, which the Muse shall moan,
That, from his horse, poor John was thrown.
In this base fall was then descry'd
What he had ever wish'd to hide.

Now all his schemes were blasted quite,
And to success must bid good night.
Coach, whip, and harness, are laid by
The petticoat once more must try.

Thus *Ruth,* by one deceitful swain,
Turn'd future pleasure into pain.
From love her changes came about;
Forc'd into breeches and forc'd out.

Ladies, your hearts expos'd to man,
Perhaps may suffer by trepan.
Protect them with a watchful eye.
My tale is ended—so good bye. [1]

Dec 25, 1798

[1] Ruth afterwards married John Shephard. They lived many years together, and had several children. He died in 1734. She seemed then about 48; and continued to reside with her two daughters, neighbours with whom I was intimate. She was a woman of good-nature and prudent; well esteemed by her connexions. She never wholly relinquished her male dress; but retained the hat, shoes, air, and work of a man to the end of her life—about 1745.

Poems: Chiefly Tales

The way to church

During all the six days farmer John was beheld
In loading his dung from the fold to the field:
On Sunday his wife and his three daughters started;
And John drove to Church with his family carted.
Being met by a friend, ere he'd driven a mile,
Who survey'd the dull march—then remark'd with a smile—
"Your horses would curse you, John, if they could speak,
For dragging out rubbish *seven* days in a week."

Feb. 2, 1799

To Dr. Chevasse

The humble Petition of the Left Foot in Favour of the Right.

The Doctor, which makes my heart ache, has just said—
"That I must, for three days, be confin'd to my bed;
Must rest till 'tis night, and from night till 'tis noon;
Because, from a blister, I'm quite out of tune."

If on me, the left foot, you shall vend forth your spite,
Then pray tell me how it will fare with the right.
We're closely connected in Friendship's strong band;
As your right or left eye—or the spoon in your hand;
Attend on each other, and have such regard,
We are rarely discover'd asunder a yard.
You can't, if this critical case you pursue,
Commit one to prison, but must commit two;
Then justice and honour, and order, must end,
If ever you punish a man for his friend.
Besides, this grand maxim, from Ethics, we offer,
That the innocent ne'er for the guilty should suffer.

Let the right foot, my peaceable brother, go free,
And then you may do what's your pleasure with me.
When that, unmolested, pursues its own way,
Your humble Petitioner shall ever pray.

April 6, 1799

Poems: Chiefly Tales

The Leicestershire parson

Tim and *wife* were harmonious when first they were wed,
As the sun and the moon are, or needle and thread;
But the first month expiring, a too common case,
His thread broke in two, and she wore a dark face.
Then our couple, when walking, or standing, or sitting,
Each other regal'd with their biting and spitting.
Whate'er was transacted or said by one side,
By the other, with malice afore-thought, was tried.
And the worst of constructions were brought forth to view,
When the word or the action would ever bear two.

It happen'd one evening, for wonders ne'er cease,
Our quarrelsome heroes were sitting at peace;
While the dog and the cat on the hearth-stone were lying,
Or amusing each other with innocent toying.

"What reason," says Madam, "my dear, can you see,
Why we, like these animals, may not agree?
For they never quarrel or fight for a feather."
"'Tis because they're quite free, and we're tied fast together."

June 19, 1799

Poems: Chiefly Tales

The spotted coat

This proverb is allow'd by all,
That lofty pride will have a fall.

What dire calamities await
(Proceeding from sly foes)
The man who never shew'd his hate
When dress'd in his new clothes.

William exerted all his care, in
Learning to be a Fop;
As girls of twelve most studious are, in
Learning to twirl a mop.

He tried to deck himself a beau;
This pleasing view ne'er flags;
But Fortune cruelly said "No;"
Then threaten'd him with rags.

Attention, and a smiling trade,
However, came in view;
Frugality unites her aid,
With *Snip* the taylor's too.

A suit of *claret,* fine as ever,
Rose from a taylor's goose;
The lining white, the buttons clever;
What beau could finer use?

The button-holes, we will impart,
Were wrought with silver all;
Design'd to catch a lady's heart:
Whoever sees must fall.

To church, on Sunday morning, he,
Fine as a pink in May,
Or sipping butterfly could be,
Went forth to kill and pray.

Before one street he'd footed quite,
A wicked bird shot flying;
And a warm load of black and white
On his gay suit was lying.

Thus, from the people, sly and vain,
Rich, poor, and young, or older;
William was singl'd out, like Cain,
And mark'd upon the shoulder.

The stain, in wiping, spread abroad,
Which caus'd a new surprize;
William had rather all the load
Had been in *Tobit's* eyes.

A brow contracted, it was said,
And sorrow was his portion;
The colour of his coat was fled,
And with it his devotion.

March 22, 1800

Poems: Chiefly Tales

The birth-day

In nought but your own I'd advise you to deal in;
Your fingers will then be prevented from stealing.

No system of politicks I ever vent,
Lest people find meanings which I never meant,
Nor ever attempt, by resuming debate,
To point out the faults which creep into the state;
But in silence retreat the remainder of life,
Like puss in a corner, and never court strife;
Nor wantonly will I my glass shake about,
But let it be still while the sand shall run out.
That Doctor, we all think, will act his part best,
If he can't cure his patient, will give him some rest.
Nay, should critic-venom against my Muse tend,
I'd not take the field—but had much rather mend.
No illustrious falsehood my pen shall relate;
A truth, though but small,'s worth a lie that is great.

I'll sing of a birth-day, and train the Muse for it;
For why mayn't I sing one as well as the *Laureat.*
Though his Muse up to heroes and gods may aspire,
And mine, like its Master, must wade through the mire,
Yet while that lov'd Muse in full freedom can strut,
I wish him much joy of his *hundred* and *butt.*

A husband, for years, Martha tried to trepan;
But though none she could find, she at length found—a man.
A union succeeded—no knot tied the two—
She found he could do what a husband could do;
But she, if the world were inclin'd to dispute it,
Could shew them Miss Sally, and that would refute it.

A twelvemonth is spent in her railing at John,
For doing precisely what she wanted done.

Thus, when our friend's absent, we can, with great ease
Heap on him whatever abuses we please.

Now Sally's a year old. Little Martha's delighted;
"Her birth-day we'll keep," so her friends are invited,
"A gooseberry-pye we'll accomplish, if able,
So large, that, perhaps, it will break down the table."

But, at length she concluded, so mighty a pye,
She fear'd, would be rather expensive to buy.
A garden she spy'd, full of excellent fruit;
Then onward she ventur'd, and found it would suit;
Three times she survey'd it—the fruit appear'd fine—
"By jingo," she thought, "some of that shall be mine."
Her eyes glanc'd about, as attended by fear,
But could not discover one creature was near.

A body so little might slily creep in,
Which, a thousand to twenty, would never be seen;
While there not an hawk's eye could ever have spy'd her;
She knew any one of the bushes would hide her.
Thus her couzen, *Tom Thumb*, like my tale, rather brief,
Thought himself quite secure while hid under a leaf.

Now heavily laden, she thought it was meet,
Like commanders and thieves, to secure a retreat
Not the road which she enter'd; she thought that unwise;
Because her small bulk had increas'd double size.

But who was more happy! in looking again
She found a snug way o'er a smooth and green plain;
But, attempting this road, she perceiv'd by her feet,
It was false as a lover—and not quite so sweet.
Can a man, when he's loaded, more evils acquire,
Than to find he sticks fast in the worst of all mire?
The whole length of Martha might easily be found;
Two feet were below, and two feet above ground.

A release was effected, and though you might view her,
She retreated in safety—no soul durst pursue her.
Or, were she quite gone, you might easily tell,
As well as friend *Jowler,* the road by the smell.

Learn hence, for a birth-day, let gooseb'rries alone,
Unless you can fairly call gooseb'rries your own.
You'll there pick at ease, like a school-boy that lingers,
Avoid tainted garments, and pricking your fingers.

April 28, 1800

Poems: Chiefly Tales

Receipt to make a priest

The place t'ordain him is an hotel;
The proper season—o'er a bottle.
But, ah! what mischief oft commences,
When men get drunk and lose their senses.

Of *Sedley, Allison,* and *Granby,*
I'll sing, my friend, and you may stand by:
One a Knight's patent held possession;
The next a Marquis by profession;
The third sold wine, when he could sell it,
So excellent—who could repel it?

Close friends this Merchant, Knight, and Lord;
But closest when sat round the board.
In other places pride might boast,
But here were all distinctions lost;
Or, rather, though in Fortune's spite,
Wine rais'd them to an equal height.

These friends, the pleasure to enhance,
At Nottingham were met by chance.
Al. was at home, both safe and sound;
The Knight was then for London bound;
My Lord "could only three hours stay,
Then must for Yorkshire shape his way."

As the kind glass, without much force,
Made a quick circuit round its course,
The joyous spirits became brighter,
Just as the bottle became lighter.

"Dear Allison, I do insist,"
The Marquis cried, and wrung his fist,
"That you give up this wretched trade,
And instantly a priest be made.

I have a living brings in clear
More than two hundred pounds a year.
'Tis in the road I'm now pursuing—
Shall ride with me, and I'll put you in."

"How can I in a pulpit stand
Till my crown feels the Bishop's hand?"
"Leave that to me," the Marquis said,
"There shall be no objection made."

"Alas! what charges must occur!
They're sure to make my purse demur?"

"To cover all expence I'm willing;
It shall not cost my friend a shilling."

"A pasture rich I might grow fat in;
But can't write Sermons, nor speak Latin."

"You now object as if afraid;
These points are answer'd soon as made:
Ne'er let a word of Latin fly
While any Latin scholar's by;
But, when he's absent, 'mong the mopes
Let borrow'd Latin fly in tropes.

"Then, as to making Sermons, you
Must tread the road that others do.
The moderns, grown polite and lazy,
Seldom with studied Sermons teaze ye.
For Atterbury, Clarke, and Blair,
With twenty at their elbow, are:
From these cull flowers; leave weeds behind;
You 'll soon the congregation blind.

Or, if from these you fear to quote,
Take authors of inferior note:
This plan, well-manag'd, snug you lie—

To find you out is vain to try.
No more can they your authors mark
Than find a needle in the dark.

Then, in selecting Sermons, you
Only need muster fifty-two;
Which will, in you, like Sol appear,
And make a circuit round the year.
As for detection—fear it not;
A Sermon! Nought's so soon forgot.
A Priest but one grand point pursues—
To teach his flock to pay their dues."

The bargain made, joy onward hasted;
And Allison the first fruits tasted.

The sky was dark; the hour was late;
The servant bow'd—"The coaches wait."
Their heads were giddy; room turn'd round;
The street, with guides, our heroes found;
Where, by mistake, at Al.'s approach,
He enter'd into Sedley's coach.
My Lord flew North, nor did well know,
Whether he solus was or no.
Al. too thought he was pointing North
After a benefice of worth;
But his gay vision ne'er was undone,
Till he was set down safe in London.

He gone, the living would not stay;
But took, like him, a different way.
The whole to one delusion turn'd,
And Al. in his dull wine-vault mourn'd.

June 19, 1800

Courtship

Let not your expectation rise
To palaces that reach the skies;
For if there's no firm basis found,
Your house may tumble to the ground;
And if you yield the world some fun,
Be worse than when you first begun.

And, gentle Reader, pray don't you
Despise my tale because 'tis true.

The numerous Fletchers race we'll hail,
To form a short and curious tale.
Father and mother rise to view;
We'll bring six handsome daughters too.
But only one bright son you'll see;
"Hope of the family" was he.

No crooked name my pen shall forge;
Then, if you please we'll call him George—
For why should we expunge a name
Which *pure* from his god-fathers came?

Of all the tribe the street contain,
They stood the first in Walker Lane;
By trade were bakers of renown
Chief of the craft in Derby town.

The dough the ladies moulded true;
The pious father *set* and *drew;*
While a choice stall of sweet-meats were
Consign'd alone to George's care.

The sight, the scene, of this repast,
Made the observers long to taste;
Who, though unable were to buy,

Would lick their lips, and gladly try.
George found he'd customers enough;
His stick would barely keep them off.
He gives sufficient cause to teaze,
Who sets his honey before bees.
Nay quickly finds they'll sorrow bring him,
Not only rob him, but they'll sting him.

The mother's darling, this great boy
Was all-accomplish'd in her eye;
For when she look'd within, without,
Not one defect could she find out.
Horse, child, and dog, will bear the test,
Are by each owner counted best.

Back'd by the mother, in our case,
He chose to Hector all the race:
Thus they were govern'd by a boor,
Much like a boat without an oar.

But there were wicked people found,
Who christen'd George "An awkward Hound;"
And said, "if you his dress descry,
You'd think he'd recent left the sty."

His limbs were strong, but far from limber;
One half his head, they thought, was timber;
While others thought, but could not see,
"One half a vacuum might be."
Others precisely calculate,
"His two ends were of equal weight."

The boys surround his stall, and stare
Both on the market-day and fair;
As if they'd eat up what he said;
But really eat his ginger-bread.
And when he drove them three yards off,
They, at his elocution, scoff.

The pickle rogues, so fond to joke too,
Never regarded whom they spoke to.

"George, on your stall what profit's found;
Twice seven ounces make a pound.
Fifteen and fifteen pence (now speak)
Exactly will *three shillings* make—
No, two times eighteen pence, I own,
Will make exactly half-a-crown."

The mother thought her son disgrac'd—
"The saucy brutes are void of taste.
Go, George, and dress you out of hand;
These charms no lady can withstand;
For if at thousands they essay,
Thousands they'll quickly bring away.
You shall set out when you've done dinner—
Address Miss Pole—you're sure to win her.
One hundred thousand pounds in hand!
This fortune you will soon command."

Dinner and George met at the table;
He ate as quick as he was able;
Nay, he could scarcely wait for grace;
Good fortune star'd him in the face.

Black, on his boots, was made appear;
The only black of half a year.
But spurs, when they were brought to view,
Carried exactly the same hue;
And though he rubb'd them with great care,
The rogues would not a polish bear.
However, George no torment feels;
His head must win the fair—not heels.

Madam his stock plac'd in a trice;
Adjusted his fair bosom nice;
Hat, cock-and-pinch, which you'd perceive

Was wip'd quite clean with his coat-sleeve.
Thus harmony bless'd one another;
For here one garment clean'd his brother.
That none might from perfection fall,
The household-brush compleated all.

He took his whip—the lash was gone
George Hickinbottom put one on.

THE SECOND PART

Or right or wrong we peace shall find,
If we can satisfy the mind.

Improv'd at least fifteen *per cent.*
The horse and man a courting went;
For, in this point, we all agree;
The horse could plead as well as he;
Nor can we say, if brought to test,
Which of the two was second-best.

Now George for Radburn shap'd his way—
The boys but thrice cried out—huzza!
A rising stile will reverence draw,
And strike the saucy things with awe.
Perhaps George thought, perhaps did not;
Howe'er, to Radburn Hall he got;
Survey'd himself above, below;
Adjusted all, from top to toe;
Then boldly to the great door trips;
Prim'd well his mouth; moisten'd his lips;
To give admission servants strive all;
Eager announcing his arrival.
They introduce him soon as come,
Into the lady's sitting room.

"Your servant, Ma'am," the lover cries.
"Your servant, Sir," the fair replies.

"I'm not appriz'd, Sir, who you be.
But pray what's your request with me?"

"A loving wife I mean to take you;
And a good husband mean to make you.
I've got three trades—their profit's great;
Exclusive of a good estate.
The baking business I hold fast,
Can do the work from first to last.

A second trade—besides a baker,
Of ginger-bread I am the maker.
I am too, which will crown them all, a
Confectioner—and keep a stall." "Ah!"
"These great advantages you'll see,
My Lady, and accept of me."

George waited for a little while—
The lady then return'd a smile—

"Sir, for the present, you may go,
And take refreshment here below.
You still may follow up your trade—
I'll think upon the offer made;
And if my fortune, which you scan,
Will not procure a gentleman,
No other lover shall pursue,
Depend upon't I'll send for you."

George saw good fortune in her stile—
" She first receiv'd me with a smile
What reason then have I to fear;
A promise too brought up the rear."

The servants thought they smelt an ass,
And ply'd him plenteous with the glass.
As briskly as the liquor move,
They briskly fill his head with love;

Till on the ground was seen to be
Hope of his numerous family.

Depriv'd of action, it was said,
They clubb'd to drag him up to bed;
He snor'd aloud till five o'clock—
Was waken'd by the crowing cock;
Then sneak'd away, no soul could doubt it,
And you'll peruse six lines about it.
He left in bed a curious—hold—
It was not silver, neither gold.
Like garden fruit, a little mellow;
Something between a brown and yellow.
'Twas what a chamber-maid would yell at;
As neither fit to taste nor smell at.

July 22, 1800

Poems: Chiefly Tales

The triple courtship

What reason can there be assign'd,
Why the Fair Sex mayn't speak their mind?
Man pleads his cause in open light;
But female thoughts are hid in night.
His flames before the sun aspire;
Theirs cover'd as a *Curfu* fire.
His by the tongue can find relief;
Theirs hid in secret, like a thief.
Can we of errors them impeach,
Who learn a lesson that *we teach?*

How can a race-horse win the day,
Stuff'd to the throat with corn and hay?
So Poets verses must be dull,
If written when his belly's full.
Then sleepy works would be but few
That meet the eye of me or you.
Hence it is necessary quite
That hungry bards alone should write.

Three sisters, beautiful and neat,
Who stood the first in Castle Street,
Follow'd gay fashions to the height,
But rather were in pocket light.
They long'd for husbands—none apply'd:
How then could each become a bride?
They walk'd the street; they spread the sail;
But by no art could catch the gale.
They ogled, smil'd, but durst not ask;
To speak was a forbidden task.

William sold books, some books he hir'd;
His lounging shop held folks when tir'd.
To read the titles they delight in;
A bachelor was most inviting.

The younger pair, as in a tether,
Came often, and as oft together;
As if the ladies had in view
That William stood in need of two.
They enter'd morning, noon, and eve;
But ne'er express'd a wish to leave;
Open'd and shut books without heed,
As if they were not made to read;
Began a conversation pat,
Which just amounted to all that;
Moulded their words, some right some wrong;
Before they sent them from the tongue;
Caps, handkerchiefs, adjusted right,
With some few matters out of sight.
If red Morocco grac'd the foot,
The shoe was rather forward put;
But if black leather, black betide it!
The petticoat knew how to hide it.

The eldest beauty left behind,
Thought there was something in the wind;
"Her sister's absent!"—Now suspecting
A husband might be worth accepting,
Survey'd the rising scene with joy—
"Her luck she'd in the lott'ry try."
As in her glass she took a view
"Surely the prize can win from two."
For where's the lass, since first created,
Her beauty ever under-rated?
Now view three goddesses again,
Striving the apple to obtain.

But William's heart, like theirs, might move,
Part to'ards int'rest, part to'ards love.
Besides, before a bargain's made,
Some trifles should be nicely weigh'd;
As—will that match delightful prove
When there's no money, and no love?

He who spends two years gets in one,
In the *Gazette* has splendid shone.
Neither do girls make wives quite meet
Who fellows pick up in the street;
Nor that œconomy be lasting
Who've fifteen hundred pounds been wasting.
Who'd take a wife without demur,
Whose mother bullies hen-peck'd Sir?

These reasons weigh'd on William's part;
He kept the steel upon his heart;
Yet smil'd and play'd, drank tea, and talk'd,
Just as before; and jok'd and walk'd.

The eldest, weary of delay,
Resolv'd to open first the way;
Then, part in earnest, part in sport—
"Answer three questions-they're but short."

"I'll answer them with free good-will,
Should they not prove above my skill."

"Then do—for all the three are small—
You'll in a moment answer all."

"Madam, my knowledge you shall share;
"I'm happy to oblige the fair."

"*Do you love me?*"—The swain, 'tis said,
Utter'd a "Yes" but three parts made.
Law, then, the female tongue should tie;
For if they ask, who can deny?

"*Will you have me?*" was the next cry.
Dumb stood the swain, and rather shy.

Another "Yes" poor William said,
Which was at least three parts un-made.

Not quite two seconds more she tarried—
"Then tell me-*"When shall we be married?"*

William was stupid as a post;
You'd really think he saw a ghost;
And look'd as caught in vile Crim. Con.;
The vengeful husband looking on.
His passions were in woeful case;
A Court of Law flash'd in his face.
A better station he'd have found,
Had the grim stocks his ancles bound.

He forc'd a laugh as if he'd burst—
"Madam, my turn to ask comes first."

Feb. 20, 1801

Poems: Chiefly Tales

The art of speaking

Whatever shall rise in a subject debated,
Deliver yourself in a stile elevated.
A Priest lost himself, by my tale it appears;
A lad lost his fee; and a horse lost his ears.

Where nature plain speech to the tongue shall deny,
A language is well understood by the eye;
If you through the race of dumb animals seek,
Truer meanings you'll find than in us who can speak.
The birds of the air understand one another;
Dog comprehends dog; and a monkey his brother:
If your cat is in want, is ill-humour'd, or pleas'd,
Another cat knows, whether well or diseas'd;
Nay, this observation will farther arise,
Their eyes tell the truth, but our tongues can tell lies.
Can it answer the motive a person intended,
To speak in a stile which is not comprehended?

Of *Lingo*, the parson, my Muse shall tell truth;
And join in the tale *Curry Whisp*, a poor youth.
The last was a lad Fortune rais'd to enjoy
The eminent station of hostler's boy,
At Grantham's chief inn, on the stables to wait,
Where Lingo and horse enter'd in for a bait,
As a ruler of slaves in authority figur'd;
Like a nabob commanded, but paid like a niggard.

But inform us what great obligation appears
To excite in the traveller these haughty airs.
A servile behaviour the landlord debases,
While his guest, like a tyrant, insults him with graces.
Perhaps we can bring this affair to a sequel,
And say obligations on both sides are equal;
For if any gentleman offers to flout him,
Then pray tell me how he can travel without him;

Why just, should he offer to lock up his doors,
As the sailor can move on without sail or oars.

The Priest, having baited, without more demur,
Went into the yard, and cried, "Hostler!"—"Sir!"

"When a period my palfrey has put (which you'll see)
To his provender—then you'll produce him to me."

The boy look'd astonish'd, but made no reply—
Then turning to two men who chanc'd to stand by,
And scratching his hair near as smooth as his hay,
Stepp'd forward—"Pray what did the Gentleman say?"

"An Hostler not know! Why, he spoke rather cross.
Every word that he said was concerning his horse.
You ignorant blockhead! this plain sense appears—
When he's ate up his corn you must cut off his ears."

"*Fow Wot?*" says the lad, mouth and eyes open full;
"Because, after eating, he's apt to be dull.
To this operation an hostler is willing,
Because his demand, as a fee, is a shilling."

Now the *will, fist,* and *knife,* are employ'd by the donors,
To rob Ros'nante of his highest honours.
Tied down to the manger, and urg'd by vexation,
Shook his head, indicative of disapprobation.
Then who is secure of his goods or his life,
When Ignorance holds the sword, scissars, or knife?

The Priest was enrag'd when he found out the evil,
And swore he would send the poor lad to the devil;
But the promise he broke, as was afterwards found,
Because, it appears, Curry Whisp kept his ground.

Now Whisp, as the group in a small circle stand—
He fing'ring two thirds of a hat in his hand—

"Sir, as your dark speeches the company ravel,
You ne'er should without an interpreter travel."

March, 1801

Poems: Chiefly Tales

The timid lover

What lad or what lass without love has e'er been?—
Miss Page won my heart when I was but sixteen;
But no prospect appear'd, my fond wishes to crown;
Her ruffles were lac'd and she wore a silk gown.

While I issued forth in a more humble sphere,
With a coat you might see through—my *best* was threadbare;
Then what expectation to win a fair maid,
When the tongue or the dress never come to our aid?

But yet no great difference *ought* to oppose;
Her father made *shoes,* and by trade I made *hose;*
So that, if of true honour we judge not amiss,
My trade was, at least, a peg higher than his.

Besides, the shoe-maker had nothing to give;
Then should we unite, like two nothings must live.
Nay, should *she* attempt to collect all her store,
If she gave me herself, she could give me no more.

If we chanc'd, which was seldom, to pass in the street,
My head made a bow, but my eyes view'd my feet.
At her sight all my powers in confusion were found;
What was left of my heart sunk as low as the ground.

If at church on a Sunday I gave her a glance,
The instant she caught me my eyes turn'd ascance;
She *might* send a look, which by lovers alone
Is well understood; but, alas! mine was gone.

When day-light was over I often crept out,
At the season when lovers and cats prowl about.
Through a hole in the shutter I sometimes could see
The girl that I lov'd—whom I wish'd to love me.

Ten years I was shackled, but never durst speak,
Though I saw my dear charmer at least once a week;
When another succeeded, who spoke as he ought,
While I lost my fair one by courting in thought.

April 14, 1801

Poems: Chiefly Tales

The wedding night

And now, my dear Sally, you're chang'd to a wife,
And I am enlisted a husband for life.
The darts, and the flames, and the killings are o'er,
With all the false ware Cupid keeps in his store.

Ne'er let us look back to the days of our courting,
And say, with a sigh, "they were those we'd most sport in."
The fault is our own if with others we class them,
For we may, if we will, make the future surpass them.

Pure love is the root from which bliss rises free;
Then who'd ever shake down the fruit from the tree?
It will ripen with time, and the taste is divine;
I know I've your heart, and I know you have mine.

Let me tell thee, *Miss Prudence* must not make a stand,
But she must attend us—we'll each take a hand;
For if this chaste damsel should never be driven,
Our faults will be fewer and sooner forgiven.

Should *one* find an error, and scold for a while on 't,
Let the other take *Cranmer's* advice—and be silent;
'Twill lead us directly to sweet peace before us;
Let us not, like the *fife* and the *drum,* bear a chorus.

If in turning the shilling two half-pence we have,
We'll live upon one, and the other we'll save;
And if it shall prove our returns should be more,
We'll rise in our living, and rise in our store.

And then, my dear Girl, it is twenty to one,
This will be our support when old age shall come on.
If imprudent, a workhouse may fall to our share—
The reverse may produce us a chariot and pair.

Besides, 'twill enable us both, in the end,
To live independent, and succour a friend;
For happiness surely from that man is flown,
Who acts as if he for himself liv'd alone.

Domestic concerns are with thee to denote;
While I keep the vessel of commerce afloat.
Of mutual assistance we'll ever be heedful,
With help or with council, whichever is needful.

Time kept marching forward, while thirty years close;
Nor car'd he a farthing who fell or who rose;
Then sprung up (these maxims attended with care)
A snug country-house, with a chariot and pair.

Forty-one years pass'd over—the tide ran one way—
We still liv'd two lovers—it seem'd but one day;
But when they were gone she was torn from my side,
And left me a wound that will ever abide.

If with time love increases, as authors engage,
In spite of diseases, of wrinkles, or age,
Then my daily feelings what mortal can tell;
Except he has lov'd one as *long* and as *well?*

May 6, 1801

Poems: Chiefly Tales

Preferment

Attack the Sovereign's ear;
Delight her;
Reward shall be, ne'er fear,
A mitre.

The man who will a race begin
Must persevere, or he'll not win;
Or, at the door, must fast and quake,
Except he makes the knocker speak.
What miner ever finds a vein,
Except he tries and tries again?
If you'd let fortune through the door,
You must invite her o'er and o'er.

However, I'll no longer comment,
But give the subject up this moment.
Let *Maddox,* who was oft translated,
Advance, and prove the point debated.
Isaac, in training, it was said,
Like me, on scanty commons fed;
Or, with more truth, may be observ'd,
Like me, on barren commons starv'd.

His aunt was poor, his parents gone;
Th' unhappy lot of many a one;
Was plac'd, when he his play forsook,
Apprentice to a pastry-cook.

What tastes he pleas'd is quite unknown;
But, it was thought, he pleas'd his own.
For where's the man, among a host,
Who will not think of self the most?

He, notic'd by a stander-by,
"Could read a book, or make a pye."

This friend perceiv'd the lad had spirit;
Lent authors to improve his merit.

At Glasgow's sacred school, we find
The youth, who'd left the tart behind.
The Presbyterian fund, he'd try,
And fill a pulpit by and by.
The food he made was chang'd—the whole
Then for the body—now the soul.

His patron died; much us'd to bless,
And left the pulpit in distress.
Then poverty, with awful pace,
Advanc'd, and star'd him in the face.
His aunt must give him, in retreat,
That bread which she herself could eat.

Time, in the shape of months, pass'd by,
But nought occurr'd to chear the eye—
"Dissenting int'rest dormant lies—
The *Church*! Ay, that's the place to rise!
A Mr. Roper has some weight
With the First Minister of State;
Request him, aunt, if you think meet,
To lay me at Sir Robert's feet."

Roper attends the hungry bevy
Of leeches at Sir Robert's levee.
"Sir, there's a youth can well support
The Whiggish int'rest of the Court—
He'll prove most faithful; has a spirit;
Then let a smile reward his merit.
To serve the Church his talent lies;
Nor shews a backwardness to rise."

"The Court Retainers, Sir, abound;
Places for not one-third are found.
The vermin hatch, and become pests,

Sooner than we can find them nests.
Then let solicitations end—
No nest is vacant for your friend."

With solemn voice, with lengthen'd visage,
The aunt reported Roper's presage.
Isaac receiv'd this sore denial
Not like a man when brought to trial.

"O, never mind—the case will do,
If Walpole has been spoken to.
Like a philosopher, 'tis clear,
It rests with me to persevere;
Must stedfast hold, be silent still,
Though bullied, kick'd, and cuff'd at will."

Isaac, next day, assum'd his best;
Brush'd well his hat, his shoes, his vest;
Powder'd his wig; the whole to crown,
Put on his gloves, his band, and gown;
Then issued forth in this gay mood—
T' invite Dame Fortune, if he cou'd;

"And 'tis a guinea to.an ace
Sir Robert's levee is the place."

Here Isaac constantly attends;
The only man unpropp'd by friends.
Each levee, for three months the same,
He silent went, and silent came.

The Bishop of old Chichester
Address'd the British Minister—
"Pray, what young Clergyman stands there?
I never come but see him here."

"Pray, Sir, inform me whence you came?
What is your business, and your name?"

"My name is Maddox, Sir,"—and bow'd.
All eyes upon him from the crowd.
"I'm he whom Roper had in view,
Who lately waited upon you."

"I think you've great assurance, Sir,
To follow me with your demur;
After what I to Roper said,
You never ought to shew your head."

Confusion seiz'd the trembling Priest;
The subject of a courtly jest.
He sunk, he blush'd, he eyed the ground—
The ruler of thee kingdoms frown'd!

If Walpole's heart obdurate felt,
The Bishop's heart began to melt.
Modest distress he's hurt to see,
Then whisper'd—" Sir, come dine with me."

Whether they try to cultivate
Points of Religion or of State;
Rehearse the virtues, while they dine,
Of Royal George or Caroline;
Or whether they, in their debate,
Change most their subject, or their plate;
Best in heroics will appear—
How can I tell? I was not there.
But Maddox from restraint was eas'd;
They din'd, they drank, and both were pleas'd.

The Bishop, with a look benign,
Took by the hand the young divine—
"From this day, while I hold the see,
You shall, dear Sir, my Chaplain be."

He now could say—in a defeat,
Out of a bitter comes a sweet.

Sir Robert's heart of flinty stone
Struck up a light which burnt and shone.
The Bishop's heart of soft desire,
Like tinder, caught a milder fire.

This inference will follow clear;
He that would rise must persevere.

THE SECOND PART

The Hunter, with a Fox in view,
Holds the best motive to pursue.

Fix'd to content, he cast about
To find Court Places which fell out.
For deaths, removes, near Queens and Kings,
To rising pride, and charming things;
His watchful eye, to place inclin'd,
Number'd the beating pulse behind;
And, though some distance from the call,
Knew, to an hour, when placemen fall.

Our persevering Isaac said,
"A Clerk of the Queen's closet's dead—
One word, my Lord, to Caroline,
From you, would make the closet mine."

The worthy Prelate smil'd assent,
But ere he on this errand went,
Great London's Bishop, in a trice,
Enter'd the palace for advice—
"A place is fallen—have you a friend,
My Lord, that I can recommend?
For none in my large train are seen,
I apprehend, will suit the Queen."

"Yes, I've a youth, the most acute,
Who will the Queen exactly suit—

My Chaplain. He the *knack* has got
To please my wife's ear to a jot;
And all this with surprizing ease;
Then surely he the Queen's can please."

Now Isaac, at St. James's seen,
Became a favourite of the Queen;
A favour, half the world could tell,
Would add a lustre where it fell.

Our Royal Chaplain, by some means,
Procur'd a list of English Deans;
"Noted their age, their income, wealth,
Who had, but most who wanted, health.
But few were from diseases free;
For all were nurs'd on Lux'ry's knee."
Affliction rais'd his spirits high;
The term of life could prophesy.
"The Dean of Bath and Wells seem'd worst—
He hop'd the Lord would call him first."
Procur'd a spy to wing news fast
The moment he should breathe his last.

Short time elaps'd; death seiz'd the Dean;
Isaac, as quick, flew to the Queen.
But here we must the maxim wave—
"Good fortune will attend the brave."
The Queen in contemplation gone
In *Privy* Garden, and alone,
Where all intrusion was forbidden,
Where every action must be hidden,
But Isaac could not stay awhile;
Open'd the door in suppliant stile;
Told her the case—he wish'd the thing—
"Begg'd she would move it to the King."

"Me don't know dat I sal," she said,
In angry mood—then turn'd her head.

Isaac, with humble powers, was seen
Employ'd to pacify the Queen.
"The pressing case was his excuse;
He hop'd the Queen would not refuse.
Her pardon begg'd agen, agen."
"Vell, me vill tink upon it den."

Another Prelate now appears
Who'd serv'd the Church near thirty years.
He bent his back and upper end,
"To beg the Deanry for a friend."
"'Tis gone an hour, vor Maddox spake;
Good Lord, my verd me cannot break."
"He deals with Belzebub, I'm clear on't—
I wonder how he came to hear on't!"

His copious list of Deans and ills
May light his pipe, or hold his pills,
Be useful in a humbler case,
But to another must give place;
To that of Bishops much diminish'd;
Two dozen names, and then 'tis finish'd.

His Mercury had soon to tell
The Bishop of St. Asaph fell.
The ear of Caroline must know—
An ear he guided long ago,
"Wish'd in a mitre he might sleep,
The Deanry in *commendam* keep."

George would but half his wish fulfil;
Only replied—"take which you will."
The Bishop-hunter lov'd the scent;
Was now a Lord of Parliament;
His catalogue told with great ease,
Whether to Heaven or other Sees
They were translated; in his case
He only wish'd to take their place.

The learned *Hough* of Wor'ster fell;
His mitre fitted Isaac well.
Thus circumstanc'd, could he lament
That death's a sorrowful event?
Neither in this can we agree—
Physicians *only* gain a fee.

His ghostly list was not to seek
'Twas regulated once a week.
Intelligence could never lack;
His was a true Church Almanack;
Could better tell when Bishops die,
Than any star that decks the sky.
But in this point we *must* agree—
Death kept a list as well as he;
And stopp'd him short; or, left alone,
He'd found a way to Becket's throne.

Jan. 21, 1801

Poems: Chiefly Tales

Nancy's courtship

(TUNE—LOTHIAN LASSIE)

A promising Lover sent word from Bridgnorth,
He'd see me the fifth of November;
Lord, surely he's young, and has beauty and worth—
I long'd for the day, I remember.
Remember, I long'd for the day I remember.

What lass would not shew some delight in her eye,
When she this good news should discover?
Who'd seen six-and-twenty long winters pass by,
Yet ne'er had the sight of a lover?
A lover, &c.

We met, and we smil'd, and we toy'd, and all that;
The scene was quite new, I declare it;
My fluttering heart gallop'd on pit-a-pat,
I scarcely could tell how to bear it.
To bear it, &c.

He press'd me with vehemence to give him my hand,
And vow'd that long courtship he hated;
I started, and told him we must make a stand,
Some trifles must first be debated.
Debated, &c.

What mode of subsistence have you pointed out,
That will keep us from starving in future?
What trade, or what cash, or what lands lie about?
I fear all your silver is pewter.
Is pewter, &c.

The swain looked "as although he could not tell how;"
Or like a man caught in horns-making;
A soul in confusion, and unmeaning brow—

The question depriv'd him of speaking.
Of speaking, &c.

When silence was ended, he scratch'd his head twice,
As if from a stupor returning,
I've laid a rare plan—we shall rise in a trice,
And you shall drink tea night and morning.
Morning, &c.

A farm I will take, for the lease must be sold,
My dearest no longer shall mutter;
The purchase is only ten guineas in gold,
And you shall stand market with butter.
With butter, &c.

But pray can a lover be likely to please,
Who no lining has to his pocket,
Who'll melt down my guineas to purchase the lease,
And then take my fortune to stock it?
To stock it, &c.

So make your retreat, ere my cash runs away,
Or you have consum'd all your courting,
Look out for a second without more delay,
And follow your hunt for a fortune.
A fortune, &c.

While I remain single I'm perfectly free,
To say *yes* to the man with a calling;
I'm willing, I own, to be tied to a tree,
But not to a tree that is falling.
Is falling, but not to a tree that is falling.

Nov. 22, 1801.

Hay-making

(TUNE—THE SILKEN SNOOD)

When Master would, and Mistress too,
For pleasure. and sea-bathing,
Of fair Carnarvon take a view,
I must of love be raving.
Then bring the fork, and bring the rake, in making hay I'll serve one.
The lassie of a lover sung, while they were at Carnarvon.

My Sunday shoes, and stockings white,
Were sure to be engaging;
And as they'd every eye invite,
They'd set the swains a raging.
Then bring the fork, and bring the rake, my love I will not starve on.
The lassie of a husband dreamt, while they were at Carnarvon.

I spread a smile upon my face,
In hopes to catch a lover;
The smartest girl in all the place
Might surely fix a rover.
Then bring the fork, and bring the rake, my lover's name I'll carve on.
The lassie most delighted was, while they were at Carnarvon.

I set my cap at Joseph D—,
Expecting store he'd set by't;
He saw I nimbly turn'd his hay.
A husband I would get by't.
Then bring the fork, and bring the rake, at table I will serve none.
The lassie thought her fortune made, while they were at CarNarvon.

Shall I proceed, or let you guess?
You blame him who discovers;
Think what you please, I'll not confess
What pass'd between the lovers.

Then bring the fork, and bring the rake—a husband, I deserve one.
The lassie slipp'd, and tumbl'd down, while they were at Carnarvon.

But what lay hid beneath a veil,
You shall not find me naming;
I'll leave a boy to tell the tale,
Who after nine months came in.
Then take away the fork and rake, in future I deserve none.
The lassie brought a little *Joe,* when they had left Carnarvon.

Nov. 26, 1801.

Poems: Chiefly Tales

The impatient lass

Miss Bell gave a glance as she often pass'd by;
A preface to Courtship depend on 't;
And as she no more could perform by the eye,
She added a smile at the end on 't.

Too well had she sped the connexion to drop,
As one doubtful corner she'd got by,
She saw me alone, and she enter'd the shop,
To buy a book, or else to—not buy.

Now two people might be imagin'd to smile;
For where is the swain who would doubt it?
I gave her one hug, and two kisses the while—
As to love, we said nothing about it.

She departed well pleas'd, as a gamester who'd won,
Or sycophant promis'd a pension.
"A courtship like this, which so sweetly begun,
A union must be his intention."

She sent me a note, when three days had pass'd on,
In the stile of a mistress forsaken,
Requesting to know, in imperious tone,
What I meant by the liberties taken.

"Dear Madam, I wonder you start at a kiss,
Three days, at least, after its ended;
You ne'er, at the time, thought I acted amiss;
But by me you'll no more be offended."

A girl may attempt to strike fire in the dark;
The match, flint, and steel, she may handle;
But who, like Belinda, would put out the spark,
Before she had lighted the candle.

Dec. 2, 1801

Poems: Chiefly Tales

The way of doing penance

When Charles the Second wish'd to climb'd the throne,
Duke Hamilton stepp'd forth to help him on;
But fail'd, and lost his head. Ah, woeful view!
His aiders were proscrib'd, and suffer'd too.

'Squire Gordon, Lord of Feckill, must come forth,
To face the Presbyt'ry, and feel their wrath.
Unhappy case, alas! What man can stand
Against a troop well arm'd—he single-hand?

Sentenc'd to lose his chattels; or appear
At Kirk, in *sack-cloth,* and do penance there—
"The penance I'll submit to—cloth will warm;
But I and goods turn'd out shall meet with harm."

Gown of coarse horse-cloth he procur'd with speed—
His legs put in the sleeves; tail o'er his head.
You'd really think, should you this figure meet,
A Russian bear was strutting on two feet.
Now standing at the porch, gave some sly lears
To all who pass'd—"Sir, Ma'am, I beg your prayers."

The Presbyt'ry appriz'd, pronounc'd him vain;
And, in sheer anger, summon'd him again.
The culprit made appearance in his gown,
And met the Reverend Fathers, and their frown.

"To passengers you practis'd foul grimace;
Shew'd many a face, but not your own true face.
Who can such vile impiety rehearse?
You turn the solemn penance into farce."

"To *wear* the gown your sentence seem'd to be;
But *how* to wear it, that was left to me.
When your turn comes to wear a rug like this,

Wear it yourselves whatever way you please."
The penance o'er, the Sexton came with glee—
"The robe demanded as his ancient fee."

"Nay, hold my friend, it can't belong to you;
My horse was guilty—he shall wear it too."

Dec. 31, 1801.

Thirteen wishes

I wish'd, when young, I had but clear
That lovely sum *ten pounds a year.*
For work or play, I must confess,
Produc'd a sum a *little* less;
Nay, peeling straws is better game
Then working worsted in a frame.
I'd be contented with this store,
And never send a wish for more;
Could eat, and dress a little gay;
Besides, could either work or play.

Before three years were fully come,
Good Fortune gave me thrice that sum.
And when successful flows the tide,
A river soon swells up with pride.
If one wish is not spent in vain,
Who could another wish refrain?

"Dear Fortune, if I've favour found,
Then let my second wish be crown'd;
Enable me, who humbly seek,
To lay by half-a-crown a week.
Sufficiently 'twill swell my store;
And I shall trouble thee no more."

She gave a nod—she smil'd assent.
I found within compleat content.

But what mind in the human range
Won't change as oft as seasons change?
For though to win gives present joy,
"A little more" is all the cry.
The wheels of trade were taught to go,
Which gather'd cash as wheels do snow;

And steady rolling oer the ground,
Rais'd up a wish at every round.

"To walk on foot will hurt my pride;
'Tis needful I a horse should ride.
And who would not, his joy to crown,
Wish for a man to rub him down?"
Dame Fortune listen'd all the while;
Said not a word, but gave a smile.

"Two maids in waiting would be best;
My servant in a livery-dress:
For these I have a strong desire;
Higher my wishes can't aspire.
If both are plac'd to my account,
Not one step more I wish to mount."

But who his bold resolves can trust?
Man's born to wish, and wish he must:
Pride is the itch, sets nails a scratching;
And, like the itch, is just as catching.

"My friend a country-house can see;
I long'd for one as much as he."

A house was in the picture found—
A chariot fill'd up the back ground.
"The first I'll build when I have clear,
In land, one hundred pounds a year.
Chariot and pair I'll sport in view
The moment I can muster two."

He who has wish'd to sixty four
Is seldom known to give it o'er.
As well might beauty *damp* a flame;
Or, the gay winner *leave* his game:
For though engag'd to wish no more,
The past forgot, I look'd before.

A manor will a title bring,
And E S Q's a pretty thing.

Thus having reach'd the ladder's top,
It must be nearly time to stop.
One word of man, it shall be true—
He always holds a future view.
Wish following wish, proceed in train,
Like water-blobs in heavy rain;
Which, with each other, we'll compare;
For both are fill'd with empty air.

Feb. 18, 1802.

Poems: Chiefly Tales

Penmain Mowr

When you proceed down Sych-nant's track,
The wind will try to force you back;
As if asham'd to let you view
A barren sea and mountain too.
No—pent by hills it can't be free;
That freedom lost it held at sea.
The sea looks stern, the tempests lour,
And now you see Great Penmain Mowr;
Then you conclude, being full of dread,
There can't be room for foot to tread.

Ere you this dreadful terrace pass,
Recruit your spirits with a glass.

You venture on, though nothing's still;
And almost wish you'd made your will:
Wish the rocks would, and, with a sigh,
Suspend their fall, while you pass by;
The sea its horrid rage abate,
Just till you reach the turn-pike gate.
Then—"What a simpleton was I!
So frighted! yet no danger nigh."

May 5, 1802

A day

TO DR. WITHERING; WHO ENQUIRED HOW I SPENT MY TIME

So much one day is like another,
It might be taken for its brother.

At six o'clock I raise the head;
Toss the warm covering off the bed;
Dress; and, if thoughts sprung in the night,
Distinguish them in black and white;
Survey the skies with half a scowl,
And prophesy if fair or foul;
Then to my girl I softly creep,
To steel a kiss while she's asleep;
For when the foot but lightly moves,
We stand a chance to win the gloves.

My hat put on, I quit the door;
Attempt to walk two miles, or more:
Animal powers now set a-going,
The mental spirits sets a-flowing;
Which orderly begin to chime,
Ending in measure, tipp'd with rhyme.

At Birmingham I meet my boy;
But never meet him without joy;
For life to melancholy tends
Were we to live without our friends;
Nay, if to solitude we give,
How can we then be said to live?

Thoughts of the pen are now laid by;
On paper only cast an eye—
"'Twill suit you, Sir, to buy this lot;
The best, and cheapest sort we've got."

"Nay, Sir, it will my warehouse fill;"
"Not it; take all; pay when you will."

My glasses, news-papers, and I late,
Enter the parlour to be private—
"Let's see what Statesmen are contriving;
How the politic nags they're driving."
But how can I men's actions view,
Who know so little what they do?

My joyous breakfast comes at last in,
I relish like a ploughman fasting:
Chat with all comers on each head;
But, after all, there's nothing said;
Till Molly finishes, debates,
Opens with, "Sir, the dinner waits."
Who would not enter with all his heart,
To taste plumb-pudding, pye, or dessert.
Let me to these sweet dishes join,
And you, my friend, may take sirloin.

Nought now remains (the floor well trod)
But warm my shins, or take a nod;
Till gloves are on, hat o'er the eye—
"'Tis striking five—and so good by."

The bulky town recedes from view;
I meet with bows, and how-d'ye do.
Miss Rain and I each other chase;
We're often found in close embrace;
Though fair without, and pure within,
"I duna like her tuch ma skin."

When Aston steeple strikes the eye,
It steals for her I lov'd a sigh;
An intercourse now lost I mourn;
How to forget could never learn.

One mile walk'd o'er, the traveller sees
My little cot peep throgh the trees.
Dear cot! for thirty years inclin'd
To furnish me with peace of mind;
Which ne'er gave anxious thought or sigh
Until the fourteenth of July;
Reduc'd to ashes by ill men,
But from her ashes rose agen.

Hid from the world, from care, from din,
I cast a pleasing look within.
There I, with truth it may be said,
Write for the living—wake the dead;
Converse with those who liv'd of yore,
And feed on what they fed before.
Transaction at command appears,
Bring back to view a thousand years.

Now, in heroic verse, we'll state,
At that sound when I pass my gate,
Bounces old Cerb'rus from his bed,
Not grac'd with three, but with one head;
Bullies in thund'ring strains about,
Resolv'd to keep invaders out,
But instant finding who I am,
Converts the monster to the lamb;
Smiles at me with that mouth and eye,
Rais'd the past moment to destroy;
Makes his tremendous jaws expand,
And gently leads me by the hand.
Severity might give him blows;
Humanity the pat bestows.

The birds my little grove retain,
Welcome me with their pleasing strain;
In gratitude they sing their best,
Because they hold a peaceful nest;
For neither nest nor bird, have been

Disturb'd since first my grove was seen,
A place, perhaps, by right divine,
As much their freehold as 'tis mine;
And as we both are now possessors,
May both bequeath it our successors.
Nor shall it in the frost be said
I e'er with-held a crumb of bread.

My pair of greys, the Muse engage,
Who, in my service see old age;
They hear my voice, they make no stand,
But take the bread from Master's hand;
Perceiving an exhausted store,
Lovingly follow me for more;
I turn, which their dull footstep checks—
"So, my poor lads," and pat their necks.
They never knew a treatment harsh;
Strangers to want as to the lash.

I meet my servants, growing old,
But never meet them with a scold.
My equals in an eye Divine—
Why not my equals then in mine?

Puss cocks her tail, begins to crawl,
And rubs her side against the wall.
She ne'er, in all her life, has spoke,
Or she would say, "Give me a stroke."

But what that pleasure can surpass
When my girl sees me through the glass?
Rises to meet me, while the joy
Takes full possession of her eye?
Where is the man that could look glum
Who sees the best of women come?
Whatever comfort age can find,
Lies in the storehouse of her mind.

Now garden, converse, book, or pen,
Tea, supper, music, please till ten;
When the bell rings "to bring a light,"
I rise, and burrow for the night.

Of blessings can I wish for more?
They amply satisfy fourscore.
Thus I enjoy, others partaking,
A little heaven of my making.

Nov. 20, 1802

Poems: Chiefly Tales

Maxims

My Muse, like your weather-cock, turns round its joint;
But she never fixes at any one point.

If hopeless in love, you should torments endure,
Take *absence* and *time*-they'll most certainly cure.

Who strives to *get*, and strives to *save*,
In ten years time will riches have.

We'll allow you to fret at what evils betide,
Except what you *can* and you *cannot* avoid.

If to old age you would he bless'd,
Let peace of mind possess your breast.

Have you a wife who murders peace?
Be silent, and her tongue will cease.

If you no enemy would make,
Against another never speak.

Reeds bend their long back, a *rush* stands the wind's rage;
Thus tall men the soonest bend under old age.

"Trade makes the man," some have debated;
But 'tis when he's that *trade* created.

You talk much of chastity; who *can* abuse it,
When she who's the owner on't *wishes* to lose it?

Our *honour* stands fair till temptations abound;
Then *honour*, like echo, is all empty sound.

To *fear* no man should be a stranger;
This tends to keep us out of danger.

For if a dog-fight you'd be in,
Perhaps may meet a broken shin.

The grand support of life in *hope* is found;
Just as the body's held up by the ground.

Trust your cash with a *rogue* who has riches o'er grown,
Before him, who though honest, has none of his own.

A *rose,* a bright *guinea,* and beautiful *lass,*
Are the finest of pictures—but away soonest pass.

A conscience and a cabbage net
Are by one rule attended;
They'll narrow to an inch, and yet
May widely be extended.

If he who speaks has interest in the case,
Suspect at least *one half* the words he says.

He who of honour boasts away,
And *she* who boasts her virtue,
Give reason to suspect that they
Tell neither *him* nor *her* true.

What can the married state excel,
When both love equal, both love well?

Is Tommy naught? give a frown, word, or nod,
But never, never, treat him with the rod.
Or if he well performs what you intend,
Give him due praises, and he'll strive to mend.

He whose theme is divine, and whose actions are wrong,
Proves religion is *solely* confin'd to his tongue.

Despise no bodily defect,
Favour'd or not with pelf,

Except the owner, by neglect,
Made that defect himself.

Of the two sexes' love, 'tis said,
(Disprove it if you can,)
Woman loves *least before* she's wed,
But, *after* wed, the man.

Some diff'rence a loving wife soon can discover,
Between a man *when* he's wed and when a lover:
While a lover he *smiles,* and will let a yes go;
When a husband he frowns, with the little word—*No.*

Your mild replies, if you but hold in,
Will never *make,* but *cure* a scolding.
After a quarrel, while you live,
Let the next business be—forgive.

From pride bright actions rise, 'tis justly said.—
The tulip rises from a filthy bed.

From human minds important trifles spring,
Like empty bubbles floating on the wing.
The child, at four, is pleas'd with taw and ball;
I, at fourscore, to view a broken wall!

Time changes our passions—dress in youth is the rage;
A mode most compleatly despis'd in old age.

Some proud of humility are found;
Thus the lac'd shoe treads on the dirty ground.

Religions treat kindly whatever the case is;
Men have reason to vary, as much as in faces.

The man inur'd to court soft ease,
Need do no more to court disease.

Ne'er waste your fortune like a careless drone,
Except you'll be *contented* when 'tis gone.

If you would be happy, this truth never doubt ye,
Attempt to *make* happy the people about ye.

For fear in wrath you play the fool,
Take four-and-twenty hours to cool.

If you're charm'd with *Miss Beauty,* be charm'd at a distance,
If you'd lead to the *altar,* give Miss Prudence assistance.

Dec. 20, 1802

Poems: Chiefly Tales

The Septennial stages of life

1723

In seventeen hundred twenty-three
I saw the world—the world saw me.
She frown'd, as having drawn no prize;
Nor was she view'd with cheerful eyes.
Both of us rather look'd askew,
Just as two surly people do.
My mother saw, but not with joy—
"She fear'd she could not love that boy."
The world has since giv'n many a frown;
Like foot-ball kick'd me up and down.
This truth, however, I can say,
My rattle I ne'er threw away;
Because Dame Fortune prov'd my foe,
And never gave me one to throw.

1730

At one time seven, excessive poor,
Must fall to labour—play was o'er.
'Twas then the bitter cup I drank;
My covering rags; my bowels lank.
Destin'd the silk-mill to attend;
Beat to a jelly; without a friend.
To peace of mind what could restore me,
When seven years rudeness lay before me.

1737

At twice seven years one slav'ry's done;
But then another is begun.
And what advantage could I reap,
The strap exchanging for the whip?

No prosp'rous state brought up the rear;
'Twas water chang'd to dead small-beer.

Now the first spark of love appears;
Which blaz'd in vain eleven years.

    1744

If, at three sevens my state you'd have,
'Twas once an infant, twice a slave;
Not master even of a dish;
Poor as an enemy could wish;
My ear quite fill'd with musick's hum;
My belly empty as a drum;
Though fond of sol, fa, let me note,
I sold my fiddle for a coat;
The willing ear display'd no lack;
Depriv'd herself to please the back;
The back, no carpenter by trade,
To please them both a better made.

    1751

At four times seven, with free consent,
I spurn'd the frame, to books I went;
For who'd sleep in a butcher's shed
If he can warm himself in bed?
And, at this period, I confess,
I took a pleasure in gay dress;
Which was exhibited to view
By hiring books, and selling too.
The girls I follow'd with some glee;
A greater number follow'd me.

    1758

At five times seven was pleas'd to see
Three prattling infants on my knee;

A loving wife look'd on, was glad;
One of the best man ever had.
What incident could mend my state?
Was happier than the folks call'd great;
Nay, than harmonious birds, which build
In safety near a barley field.

   1765

Six times seven years we'll bring to view—
I tried for money; got it too:
Nor ever once did I abhor it;
Pleasure came with it; pleasure for it:
Thus Madam Fortune deign'd to bless
My little efforts with success.
Nay, Fortune seldom will refuse it,
But give a blessing if you chuse it;
Which is not show'ring gold amain,
But an *endeavour* to attain.
For land I chaffer'd—who'd be poor?
I bought for one, and sold for four.

   1772

At seven times seven, my wish to crown,
I bought a house, and pull'd it down.
What of this purchase could remain—
Only to build it up again.
Thus an old moon hid from our view
A few days after brings a new:
The former dress'd in dark decay;
The latter in her bright array.
Two thousands, that I might be seated,
In timber, mortar, lime—and cheated.

   1779

Eight times seven years were follow'd close,
With fifteen evils at one dose;
A monst'rous bolus, 'tis confess'd,
Which took a twelvemonth to digest.
Keen memory, with Argus eye,
Lets no material act pass by.
One mighty evil was my lot,
Which can't for one day be forgot—
My dear's last sickness now came on,
And death, when seventeen years were gone.

    1786

At nine times seven, to Buxton move,
And try the waters, for my love;
Travers'd, with joy, the wonders round,
But health, alas! we never found:
Attended trade, but spent the pauses
In writing books, and trying causes;
Which last, for my reward, I found
They burnt my houses to the ground.
Strange! fire and plunder they brought on,
But never told,—What fault I'd done!

    1793

To ten times seven the thread is spun,
The glass of human life is run;
But things uncommon sometimes pass,
Time splic'd the thread, and turn'd the glass.
Such destin'd favours were my lot,
That tens of thousands have them not:
It tends to make the happy man,
When Prudence shuns what ills she can.

    1800

Eleven times seven are now come on,
Yet mourn what rioters have done;
Though happy, in my state, I feel
They left a wound time cannot heal.
Riches are added to my store,
Besides seven years, just gone before
—hundred acres! charming fee!
From debt and mortgage duty-free.
A Poet is but seldom found
To tune his lire on his own ground.
I've brick and mortar in great plenty,
Which pay ONE POUND instead of twenty.
My children I nurs'd on my knee,
Now they attentive are to me.
Time foots it with me, on my way,
For more than thirty miles a day.

Nov. 29, 1802

The way to supply the navy with liquor

A jolly old tar of the true English breed,
Who to money or gunpowder never gave heed,
At the pump hard at labour, sweat ran in full tide;
He'd rather good brandy'd run down his inside.
Then into a bason he wrung his shirt out,
In the stile of a scullion who wrings a dish-clout.

"'Tis pity such liquor as this should be lost;
I'll send it directly the way it went first.
Its part of myself," he exultingly cried,
"And he's a great fool who *himself* throws aside."
Then the rum-bottle seiz'd, with a leap like a frog,
Mix'd, and drank it, and said "it made excellent grog."

March 30, 1803.

Three eyes

In petticoats if two black eyes you meet,
"The owner's charming, and her kisses sweet;"
But in that dress should *one* black eye appear,
Depend upon 't a scolding wife is there.

April 27, 1803

Poems: Chiefly Tales

To the memory of the dear girl, once named Sarah Cock, who died
Jan. 23, 1796

Sally, when thou first came over,
Not a smile upon me came;
I assum'd the faithful lover,
Two hearts united in one flame.

During forty years possessing,
Whene'er thou approach'd my sight,
My heart, as conscious of the blessing,
Felt a ray of pure delight.

Pity was to love united
When came seventeen years of pain;
Thy drooping head my hand invited,
Which my dear could not sustain.

When ill-natur'd Time bereft me
Of thyself, the source of joy,
Two dear treasures thou bequeath'd me,
Dear as sight is to my eye.

O, I mourn the day I lost thee,
As the year winds round its way,
Many a sigh and tear thou cost me,
Sorrow never sleeps a day.

Gentle Spirit! can I find thee,
When the lamp of life shall cease;
To my anxious bosom bind thee
Where thou long possess'd a place.

Jan. 23, 1804

With thanks to the Literary Heritage - West Midlands
http://www.literaryheritage.org.uk

Lightning Source UK Ltd.
Milton Keynes UK
UKHW011828070519
342270UK00001B/68/P